OECD ECONOMIC SURVEYS

1998-1999

United States

ORGANISATION FOR ECONOMIC CO-OPERATION AND DEVELOPMENT

ORGANISATION FOR ECONOMIC CO-OPERATION AND DEVELOPMENT

Pursuant to Article 1 of the Convention signed in Paris on 14th December 1960, and which came into force on 30th September 1961, the Organisation for Economic Co-operation and Development (OECD) shall promote policies designed:

- to achieve the highest sustainable economic growth and employment and a rising standard of living in Member countries, while maintaining financial stability, and thus to contribute to the development of the world economy;
- to contribute to sound economic expansion in Member as well as non-member countries in the process of economic development; and
- to contribute to the expansion of world trade on a multilateral, non-discriminatory basis in accordance with international obligations.

The original Member countries of the OECD are Austria, Belgium, Canada, Denmark, France, Germany, Greece, Iceland, Ireland, Italy, Luxembourg, the Netherlands, Norway, Portugal, Spain, Sweden, Switzerland, Turkey, the United Kingdom and the United States. The following countries became Members subsequently through accession at the dates indicated hereafter: Japan (28th April 1964), Finland (28th January 1969), Australia (7th June 1971), New Zealand (29th May 1973), Mexico (18th May 1994), the Czech Republic (21st December 1995), Hungary (7th May 1996), Poland (22nd November 1996) and Korea (12th December 1996). The Commission of the European Communities takes part in the work of the OECD (Article 13 of the OECD Convention).

Publié également en français.

Table of contents

● ● ● ● ●

Boxes

Tables

Annexes

Figures

BASIC STATISTICS OF THE UNITED STATES

THE LAND

Area (1 000 sq. km)	9 373	Population of major cities, including their metropolitan areas, July 1996:	
		New York	19 938 000
		Los Angeles-Anaheim-Riverside	15 495 000
		Chicago-Gary-Lake County	8 600 000

THE PEOPLE

Population, November 1st 1998	267 901 000	Civilian labour force, 1998	137 661 300
Number of inhabitants per sq. km	28.9	of which:	
Annual net natural increase (average 1993-97)	1 630 400	Health services	9 903 408
		Unemployed	6 203 833
Natural increase rate		Net immigration	
per 1 000 inhabitants (average 1993-97)	6.2	(annual average 1992-96)	863 600

PRODUCTION

Gross domestic product in 1998		Origin of national income in 1998	
(billions of US$)	8 511.0	(per cent of national income[1]):	
GDP per head in 1998 (US$)	31 413.6	Manufacturing	16.9
Gross fixed capital formation:		Finance, insurance and real estate	18.4
Per cent of GDP in 1998	18.2	Services	23.4
Per head in 1998 (US$)	5 701.6	Government and government	
		enterprises	13.1
		Other	28.2

THE GOVERNMENT

Government consumption 1998 (per cent of GDP)	14.7	Composition of the 105th Congress as of December 7, 1998:

	House of Representatives	Senate
Revenue of federal, state and local governments, 1998 (per cent of GDP) — 34.4		
Federal government debt held by the public (per cent of GDP), FY 1998 — 44.3		
Democrats	206	45
Republicans	228	55
Independents	1	–
Total	435	100

FOREIGN TRADE

Exports:		Imports:	
Exports of goods and services		Imports of goods and services	
as per cent of GDP in 1998	10.9	as per cent of GDP in 1998	12.9
Main exports, 1998		Main imports, 1998	
(per cent of merchandise exports):		(per cent of merchandise imports):	
Food, feed, beverages	6.8	Food, feed, beverages	4.5
Industrial supplies	21.7	Industrial supplies	21.9
Capital goods (ex. automotive)	43.8	Capital goods (ex. automotive)	29.6
Automotive vehicles, parts	10.7	Automotive vehicles, parts	16.5
Consumer goods (ex. automotive)	11.6	Consumer goods (ex. automotive)	23.6

1. Without capital consumption adjustment.

Note: An international comparison of certain basic statistics is given in an annex table.

This Survey is based on the Secretariat's study prepared for the annual review of the United States by the Economic and Development Review Committee on 10 March 1999.

•

After revisions in the light of discussions during the review, final approval of the Survey for publication was given by the Committee on 8 April 1999.

•

The previous Survey of the United States was issued in November 1997.

Assessment and recommendations

Strong economic growth has continued...

Economic growth in the United States continued for the seventh consecutive year, with real GDP expanding by 3.9 per cent in 1998. Private consumption and investment have been the principal factors behind this exceptional performance. Households have stopped saving, apparently as the result of the run-up in equity prices and favourable employment prospects. At the same time, spurred by the falling relative price of capital goods and initially favourable financing conditions, companies continued to increase equipment outlays. Such a rapid growth of private domestic demand has offset the slackening in exports provoked both by the Asian crisis and an appreciation of the dollar due to increased capital inflows. With imports surging, the external current account deficit rose to 2¾ per cent of GDP and, given the shift towards surplus of the general government (see below), this has been reflected in an increase in the net borrowing of the private sector. Indeed, for the first time in half a century, the personal sector has moved into financial deficit.

... bringing a tight labour market but still low inflation

The sustained expansion reduced the unemployment rate to 4.3 per cent of the labour force by December 1998, a level not seen since the second half of the 1960s. In some areas, this has led to labour shortages, with a slight acceleration in employment costs. Nevertheless, inflation has declined once again, with consumer price increases dropping by over a percentage point in 1998 to an annual rate of less than 1 per cent. Although mainly driven by falling import and commodity prices, such a slowdown of domestic prices appears to have also resulted from faster productivity growth, lower inflation expectations and increased foreign competition. The interaction of these factors meant that companies were unable to fully pass on increased domestic costs, which has led to a slight fall in their profits.

Only a moderate slowdown seems likely in 1999...

The strength of private sector demand has continued in the first quarter of 1999, but seems likely to slow from the summer onwards, generating 3½ per cent growth for the year. Indeed, barring a further surge in share prices, households' wealth seems set to increase less rapidly, so that consumer spending might decelerate. In addition, the growth in outlays on plant and equipment appears likely to ease in 1999, as corporate profits come under strain and some companies face increased borrowing costs both from banks and capital markets. On the other hand, with some recovery in world markets, exports should rise, thereby stabilising US market shares from the beginning of next year. Nonetheless, the current account deficit is projected to widen further, to almost 3½ per cent of GDP in 1999. Also, with growth slowing, unemployment should edge up during the year, although the labour market is likely to remain tight. There may be some modest increase in consumer price inflation, as energy prices rebound, while other import costs will not provide as much of an offset to increasing unit labour costs as in 1998. Looking further ahead, the slowdown may continue in 2000, as consumers bring the growth of spending more into line with their incomes, lowering growth to 2 per cent.

... provided financial and external setbacks are avoided

Against this favourable outlook, it must be recognised that a significant part of the expansion of aggregate demand in the past two years has been due to the impact of higher equity prices on consumer spending. While the link between consumption and wealth seems fairly well established, the strength and timing of the link seem less certain. There is a possibility that households will spend more of their increased wealth than assumed in the projections, in which case the recent momentum of consumer spending could be maintained for some time, thus prolonging the rapid expansion of the economy. On the other hand, there is a risk also that share prices might fall significantly if, as a result of domestic or external developments, investors' expectations of company profits and, therefore equity dividends, were to be reduced. That could generate a marked slackening in

consumer demand. Moreover, additional turmoil in Latin
America or Asia could have serious implications for growth
prospects, lowering private-sector confidence and
adversely affecting domestic financial markets.

*Monetary policy
has, so far,
successfully
coped with such
problems...*

Over the past six months, the domestic consequences of
external disturbances have significantly influenced the conduct of monetary policy. When the crisis in Russia
destabilised the US capital market in the autumn of 1998,
liquidity in these markets dried up, leading to increased
risk premia and a marked reduction in the volume of transactions. Three 25 basis point cuts in the federal funds rate,
to 4.75 per cent, over a six-week period (from end-
September to mid-November) largely restored financial stability, aided by the ability of the banking sector to substitute for capital markets in providing financing to firms in
search of funds. Such a move was reflected in a temporary
expansion in the growth of bank credit and monetary aggregates, and resulted in a drop in short-term real interest
rates, though the yield curve is still flat.

*... but its stance
should now
reflect the
persistent
strength of the
economy*

The easing of monetary policy and the surprising resilience
of the economy has led to a marked rebound in the stock
market, following its precipitous fall last autumn, with share
prices moving above previous highs. The resulting higher
wealth may imply that growth may ease back relatively
slowly, bringing only a gradual elimination of labour market
pressures. In these circumstances, additional cuts in short-
term rates do not seem appropriate. With output clearly
above potential, the case for a tightening of monetary policy
could even arise in the near future if there is evidence that
continued weak inflation pressures might not be sustained.

*At the same time,
improved
financial
regulation is
needed*

The recent turbulence in domestic financial markets, with
the near failure of Long-Term Capital Management (LTCM),
has highlighted the need for a careful look at the adequacy
of existing financial regulation. In this regard, increased
transparency is required. Organised markets in over-the-
counter derivatives should be allowed, without the same
degree of regulatory oversight that is necessary for
exchanges serving retail investors. Had such markets

existed, the scale of certain hedge fund operations might have been apparent earlier. In addition, the regulatory framework for derivatives needs to be clarified. However, the main lesson to be learnt from the LTCM episode is that banks must be more vigilant about the quality of their borrowers and counterparties. At the same time, the arguments about how diversified financial institutions should be structured are still to be resolved. The alternative frameworks under consideration in this respect – holding companies or subsidiaries with strict firewalls – would seem to be very similar to each other in terms of minimising risks of financial instability. Consequently, a quick resolution of this issue should be sought in order to achieve a more efficient financial services industry. Furthermore, the consequences of such a reform for the scope of different bank regulations should not be allowed to stand in the way of a solution.

While a significant federal budget surplus has been achieved...

Fiscal policy has exerted a stabilising influence on the economy in the past year. The general government balance registered a surplus of 1.7 per cent of GDP, only the second surplus in the past thirty years, which resulted in net public debt falling to 41 per cent of GDP from a peak of 47 per cent in 1995. Policy decisions that checked the growth of spending played a role in this development, together with the higher-than-expected increase in tax revenues. Part of this surge in tax receipts was due to the high level of equity prices which boosted the value of realised capital gains. Rising real incomes have also raised tax yields both for federal and state governments, as the average marginal income tax rate is well above the average tax rate.

... its maintenance will require a tight rein on public spending...

The five-year expenditure-control programme agreed by Congress and the Administration in 1997 has now reached a crucial stage that will help determine the medium-term outlook for the budget position. While overall spending was allowed to rise somewhat at the beginning of the plan, in the next three fiscal years nominal outlays will have to fall in order to comply with legislated spending caps. Already, the use of emergency spending powers in the FY 1999 budget shows that current limits are proving increasingly difficult to enforce. Indeed, compared with FY 1999 appropriations, next year's cap would imply a cut in spending of the order of $13 billion, corresponding to 1½ per cent of the previous year's expenditure. But international experience shows that spending cuts are difficult when the budgets are in surplus, requiring great determination from the authorities. Beyond 2002, the President's Budget proposal allows an increase in discretionary spending in line with inflation, with the result that net general government debt would fall to around 10 per cent of GDP by 2009, down from its current level of 41 per cent, so helping to prepare public finances for the consequences of ageing.

... the more so since the baby boom generation is about to retire

The next forty years will indeed see a major change in the structure of the US population: the number of elderly is expected to increase markedly while the growth of the working population should slacken. By 2035 (when all of the baby boom generation will have retired), there would be almost twice as many people over the age of 65 for each person of working age as at the moment. Such demographic changes, however, are predicted to be much less severe than in many other OECD countries, as the US population continues to benefit from relatively high fertility and immigration. Consequently, current projections, which are of course subject to uncertainties, suggest that, in 2035, 45 per cent of the population might be working in the United States compared with only 35 per cent in Europe. Moreover, the total number of dependants relative to the numbers working should be no higher then than it was in 1985, if the number of children were to stabilise and participation rates to increase.

Ageing could indeed constrain public finances directly and through slower economic growth

Unlike the 1980s, though, the income transfers to those outside the labour force will increasingly be made by the federal government rather than the family. In the next four decades, according to official projections, social security pension payments and health care costs for the elderly seem likely to expand by 2 and 4 per cent of GDP, respectively. As a result, by 2034, the Social Security Trust Fund will be exhausted according to actuarial estimates and, as estimated by the OECD, the federal deficit could reach 1¾ per cent of GDP. Beyond that period, the budget situation would quickly deteriorate. If no action were taken to restrain expenditure, government borrowing would then increase and interest payments might quickly spiral. Potential strains on public finance could also come from a slackening in economic expansion due mainly to a slower growth of the labour force. In such a scenario, with the elderly consuming more than the working population, personal savings might keep declining in the longer term which, despite capital inflows, could result in lower growth of the capital stock and productivity, and in turn, of living standards.

To face such developments, some steps have already been taken...

A number of policy changes have already been introduced over the last two decades or so in anticipation of these potential difficulties. In 1983, the Social Security System was moved onto a partially-funded basis, allowing its Trust Fund to accumulate assets amounting to nearly 10 per cent of GDP to date. At the same time, the retirement age at which full benefits can be drawn is scheduled to be gradually raised and is now planned to reach 67 in 2027. The working population has also expanded as the result of large inflows of foreign workers and, although this was not motivated by demographic considerations, restrictions on immigration were eased somewhat in October 1998, on a selective basis, to facilitate the entry of certain highly-qualified candidates. In addition, recent reform has induced many people that were drawing welfare benefits to join the workforce. Furthermore, better measurement of price increases in the CPI is expected to lessen the extent of future cost of living adjustments, thereby restraining pension expenditure. Finally, the 1993 Omnibus Budget Reconciliation Act and the 1997 Balanced Budget Act have reduced the extent to which the social security surplus was offset by a deficit in the remainder of public finances through restraining government spending and boosting tax receipts.

... and, more recently, new proposals have been made by the Administration

In his State of the Union message in January 1999, the President outlined a new set of proposals to ensure that sufficient resources would be available to fund Social Security benefits until the middle of the next century and improve the income of the elderly. These are essentially threefold. *First*, given the projected favourable long-term position of public finances over the next fifteen years a total of $2¾ trillion, representing 62 per cent of the expected budget surplus in that period, should be placed in reserve to save the Social Security trust Fund. *Second,* part of that Trust Fund, amounting to about one-fifth of this additional reserve, would be invested in the stock market, with a view to improving the return on its assets. These two steps together would extend the solvency of Social Security to 2059. Third, every year, slightly more than $30 billion, representing 11 per cent of the projected budget surpluses, would be paid to newly-created "universal saving accounts". People would be able to invest in these accounts on a voluntary basis, with the government partially matching such investments with transfers at a rate that would fall with their income. On top of these proposals, the Administration envisages abolishing the earnings test for those people who work while drawing pensions, and, at the same time, improving the treatment of widows.

While these latest initiatives would help secure future pension financing...

These new initiatives would help improve the financial position of the Social Security system and provide individuals with increased assets that can be used when they retire. They imply an annual transfer of about 1½ per cent of GDP from general revenues to the Trust Fund over the next fifteen years. This planned reserve should ensure that the unified budget (including Social Security) remains in surplus and adds to national saving. The President's proposals also appear as a step towards introducing some private management of public-sector pension assets. In practice, given that over the very long run, equities have produced a real return 3½ percentage points higher than government bonds, the Administration plan would mean that, with about 15 per cent of the resources of the Trust Fund invested in equities by 2015, the yield of the Fund would be boosted by perhaps 50 basis points. Such a plan would also imply that the period before which the Fund's assets are exhausted would be lengthened by up to an estimated six years.

*... and
supplement
efforts by
individuals to
build assets for
retirement...*

The proposed creation of individual savings accounts represents an innovation that could boost personal saving in the
future, particularly for low-income groups, as part of the
government transfer to these accounts will be in the form of
a matching income-related credit. As such, this initiative
builds on the successful experience with 401(k) defined-
contribution plans, introduced in 1978 to induce people to
accumulate assets in preparation for their retirement. By
1997, more than $1.8 trillion had been invested in 401(k)
and similar plans, almost three times the size of the Social
Security Trust Fund portfolio. Two positive aspects of this
"success story" are worth noting: 401(k) plans have
improved the ease with which retirement saving can be
preserved when changing jobs; and they have also given
individuals more responsibility as to their own investment
decisions for retirement purposes. Nonetheless, such plans
are not without some problems. In particular, with adverse
selection in the annuity market, there are difficulties in
turning these plans into pensions on retirement. In addition, not all individuals join such plans when they are available and, even after joining, not all take advantage of the
maximum employer match. Furthermore, some may not
make appropriate investment decisions and many smaller
firms do not offer their employees this sort of plan. The
introduction of individual savings accounts with strong
incentives for low-income workers could help to fill some of
these gaps.

*... some problems
are still to be
solved...*

This said, there remain areas where the new proposals will
require further clarification and extension in three respects.
First, the purchase of large amounts of equity by the public
sector will raise issues of corporate governance. over the
next 40 years the planned government stake would, on
average, represent close to 4 per cent of total market value,
potentially making the Trust Fund a significant shareholder
in many companies. Therefore, ways would have to be
found to avoid the government using discretion in choosing
its portfolio and influencing company management. One
option would be to use a passive strategy – such as investing in all companies in proportion to their importance in the
market – and for the government to transfer its voting rights
to trustees. While such a strategy would be extremely cheap

to operate, in practice it would imply having to rely on private-sector monitoring to keep returns high. *Second,* whatever the strategy, should the expected returns not materialise, the question arises as to whether taxpayers would have to foot the bill. *Third,* the government would have to persuade existing holders to sell. Presumably, this would involve higher prices for equities and lower prices for bonds, perhaps adversely affecting government finances.

... which might require reshaping parts of the proposals

Given the complexity of these problems, it may be appropriate to build on the proposed *voluntary* individual savings accounts in order to safeguard the well-being of the elderly beyond 2059 when, even with the proposed transfers, the Trust Fund will be exhausted. To this end, the accounts could be redesigned as *mandatory.* As such, they would indeed be much better suited to become an adequate complement for Social Security benefits in the long run, the more so since, at present, these benefits represent the sole retirement income for a significant minority of the population. In this case, some degree of compulsory purchase of annuities would be needed. Otherwise individuals would be faced with uncompetitive prices from the commercial market due to problems of adverse selection.

In addition, tighter control of medical spending will be essential

In many ways the growth of federal medical spending on the elderly represents a more difficult problem than that of pensions. While the President proposes to reserve $40 billion a year ($1/2$ per cent of GDP) of future budget surpluses for future medical spending, official projections suggest this will only cover part of the resources needed, as medical outlays may increase twice as fast as pension expenditure. Moreover, in contrast to pensions, there is no clear link between health policy instruments and spending outcomes. In a fee-for-service system, lowering prices may result in medical practitioners trying to increase their activity in order to maintain their incomes. In addition, there are fewer incentives to limit the consumption of health care by the elderly, in contrast to the working age population whose care is largely now contained by managed care plans, even though such plans appear to be subject to some excesses.

In the future, more reliance on managed care providers for the elderly, together with a higher level of participation by patients in the cost of medical care outside hospitals, may be required. This is particularly the case in the area of long-term home-based care, where more effective gate-keeping to ensure the medical necessity of government-financed care may also be required. More steps will also be needed to encourage the population to save for their long-term care needs; otherwise, a mandatory saving programme may be required. Overall, the growth of government spending on health care for the elderly has to be permanently reduced if the fiscal position of the government is to remain sustainable without raising taxation.

Elsewhere, too, further reform would be beneficial, notably in education...

Less adjustment of social security and health care programmes would be required if more people participated in the labour force. Already, the combination of a far-reaching reform and a strong economy has reduced the numbers on the welfare rolls substantially, with, as noted, many people becoming newly employed. This has been achieved without a fall in wages for the low skilled. Indeed, in 1998, wages at the bottom end of the income distribution grew more quickly than at the top end. Further progress in improving the economic position of the less favoured will depend on boosting their productivity. The key to this would be enhancing their educational opportunities. As indicated in previous *Surveys*, the quality of primary and secondary education needs improvement. In part, this can be achieved by building on progress made over the last decade in establishing rigorous academic standards to reform instruction, curriculum, and assessment methods. A key element of that effort will be a greater investment in professional development for teachers. Continued federal, state and local support for innovative public charter schools would also advance that goal. Furthermore, the extreme variations in spending among different school districts would need to be reduced. In this regard, state governments should take initiatives to help reduce spending inequalities within their areas and these efforts should be supplemented by more federal measures to reduce disparities across states.

... as well as in product markets and trade

The message of the Job Strategy has been that prospects for employment and a sustained rise in living standards depends on reforms across a wide front, not confined just to the labour market or education and welfare policies. In particular, improving the functioning of product markets and international trade would help to boost incomes. In the telecommunication and electricity sectors some reform programmes have been introduced. Consumers should gain from increased competition and lower costs in both of these markets. With respect to trade, several agreements have been negotiated in the past few years that should yield substantial returns, while other talks have started. Additional progress in this area would be aided by "Fast-Track" legislation that would allow the President to conduct such negotiations more effectively. With the current account deficit widening and growth slowing, it will be important to avoid recourse to protectionist measures and to continue to stay within the due process of international trade law in settling disputes.

In sum

In sum, despite a weak international environment, the US economy has continued to enjoy a strong performance. With output growth maintaining a sustained rapid pace, both unemployment and inflation have reached exceptionally low levels. Some domestic and external imbalances are developing, however, which, despite recent interest rate cuts, are expected to slow down economic activity this year and next. Further monetary easing does not seem to be warranted at the moment, given the still resilient private demand and tight labour market; also, a firm rein on public spending appears necessary to maintain the federal budget in surplus. Additional government savings are indeed required to cope with the projected increased pension and health expenditure associated with the ageing of the population. The Administration has made a number of proposals to safeguard future public pensions until the middle of the next century. If some of them, notably equity investment by the government, raise some difficulties, others, in particular the intention to safeguard future surplus and the initiative to create individual saving accounts, represent a concrete way to improve national savings. In addition, significant efforts will have to be made to restrain the growth of medical spending if an increase in taxation is to be avoided. Finally, among other areas where further reform initiatives appear necessary, enhancing the quality of low-performing schools would improve the prospects of less-favoured groups in society.

I.   Recent trends and prospects

Substantial non-inflationary growth continued in 1998

Output continued to grow rapidly in 1998. Real GDP rose 3.9 per cent year-on-year, the same as in 1997 (Figure 1, panel A). Final domestic demand accelerated to offset flat inventory investment and a deterioration in net exports. With GDP growth well above the Secretariat's estimates of trend growth of 2¾ per cent, output moved further above its potential level. Employment expanded at a fast pace, and the unemployment rate edged down to 4.4 per cent in the fourth quarter (Figure 1, panel B). Inflation, however, declined further (Figure 1, panel C).

Strong final domestic demand...

Household spending was an important element in maintaining the rapid expansion in 1998. Supported by solid gains in real income and healthy balance sheets, significant increases were posted in all three categories of personal consumption – durables, non-durables and services. Sales of cars and light trucks rose 3½ per cent after remaining flat in the previous year. A notable characteristic of this expansion had been the modest increase in expenditures on cyclically sensitive items like automobiles and light trucks (Figure 2, Panel A). After a brief dip in the middle of the year from the GM strike, however, sales have taken off. In addition, household investment increased sharply as real residential investment surged almost 10 per cent on the strength of single-family home starts, that, like sales of motor vehicles, have moved up after remaining relatively flat (Figure 2, Panel B).

Business fixed investment also accelerated in 1998, led by substantial increases in spending on producers' durable equipment. A large part of this gain came from real computer investment, which was helped in part by considerable price declines. In the last three years final sales of computers have contributed ½ percentage point of growth annually to GDP.[1] Other equipment categories also registered significant increases, helped in part by a relatively high level of retained earnings. Investment in structures, however, was flat in 1998 after a

Figure 1. **Aggregate economic indicators**

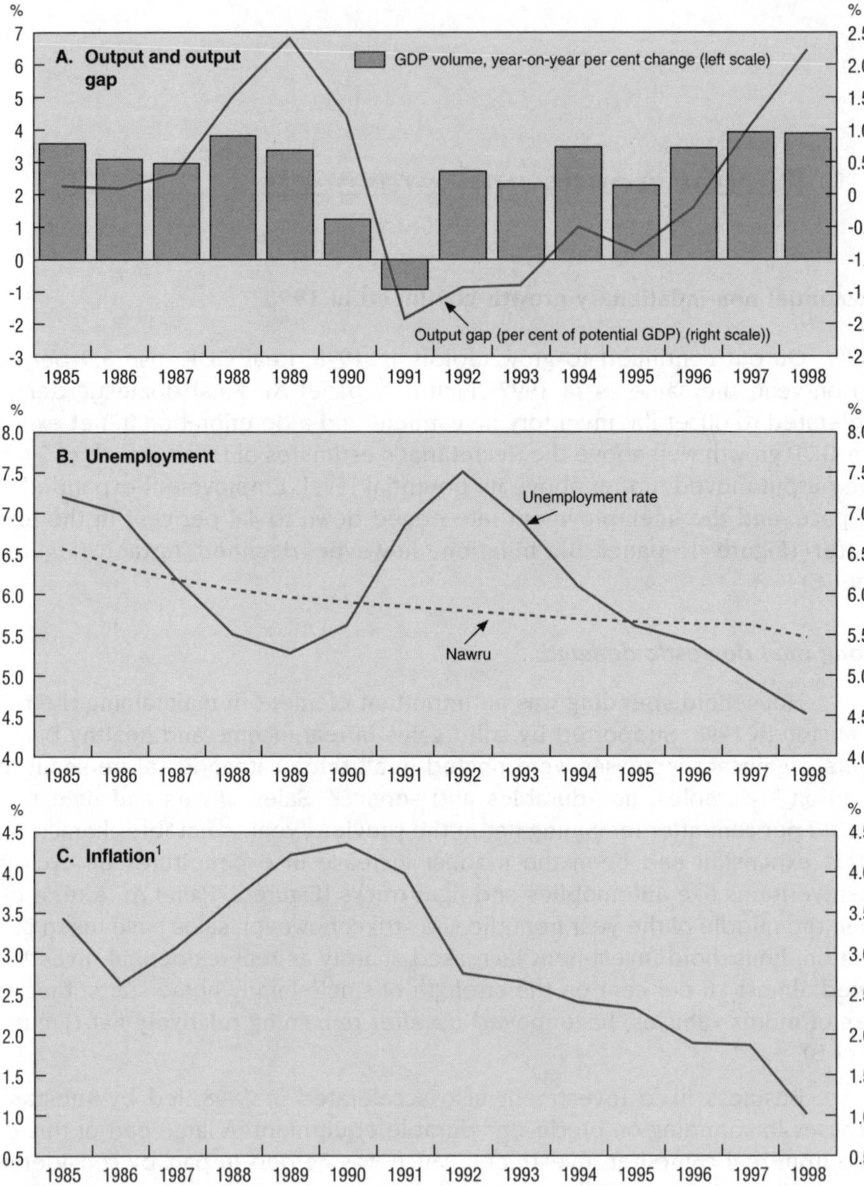
%
A. Output and output gap
GDP volume, year-on-year per cent change (left scale)
Output gap (per cent of potential GDP) (right scale))
B. Unemployment
Unemployment rate
Nawru
C. Inflation[1]
1985 1986 1987 1988 1989 1990 1991 1992 1993 1994 1995 1996 1997 1998

1. GDP deflator measure.
Source: OECD.

Figure 2.   **Cyclically sensitive expenditure items**
Three month moving average

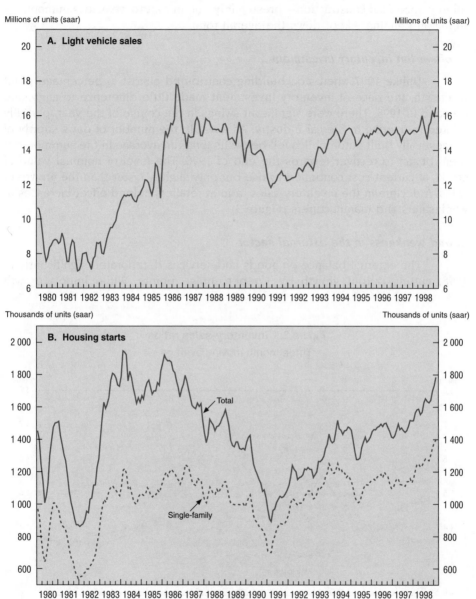

Source: Bureau of Economic Analysis and the Census Bureau.

significant rise the year before. While construction of office buildings remained robust – driven by historically low vacancy rates – sharp declines in industrial and other commercial construction – presumably due in part to weakness in manufacturing and mining – kept down the overall total.

... offset flat inventory investment...

Unlike 1997 when stockbuilding contributed almost ½ percentage point to growth, the pace of inventory investment made little difference to aggregate demand in 1998. There were significant swings in the course of the year, partially related to a strike in the car industry. As a result, the number of day's supply of domestically built automobiles fell below its long-run average in the summer, but then, began to recover towards the end of 1998. The level of nominal value of stocks at current cost continued to rise but only slightly faster than the growth of sales. A decline in the inventory-sales ratio at retailers helped offset increases at wholesalers and manufacturers (Figure 3).

... and weakness in the external sector

The external balance on goods and services deteriorated significantly in 1998, cutting output growth by 1½ percentage points. While import growth

Figure 3. **Inventory-sales ratios**

Three month moving average

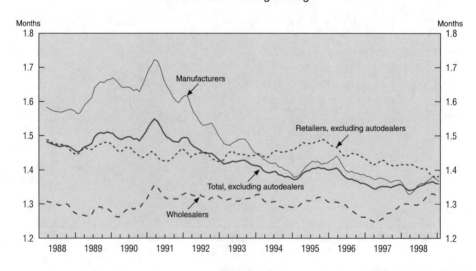

Source: Census Bureau.

Figure 4.   **Real exports to Asia**[1]
Billions of 1992 US$, annual rate

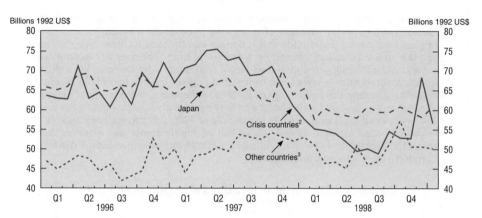

1.   Deflated by monthly export price index from the Bureau of Labor Statistics; nominal data are seasonally adjusted by the OECD.
2.   Hong Kong, China; Indonesia; Korea; Malaysia; The Philippines and Thailand.
3.   China; Chinese Taipei and Singapore.
Source: Census Bureau, the Bureau of Labor Statistics and OECD.

remained firm, due to robust domestic demand, exports decelerated sharply in response to much weaker US external markets and the appreciation of the dollar. After rising 12³/₄ per cent in 1997, real exports of goods and services moved up only 1¹/₂ per cent in 1998, albeit with substantial strength in the fourth quarter. Real exports to the six Asian crisis countries[2] and to Japan plunged, while those to other major developing Asian countries[3] edged down (Figure 4). Overall, diminishing US market growth accounts for about half of the deceleration. Presumably much of the rest of the slowdown was due to the sharp appreciation of the dollar in the past couple of years, which in 1998 led to almost a 2 per cent increase in US manufacturing export prices relative to its competitors.

Despite tighter labour market conditions, inflation remained low

The labour markets tightened noticeably in 1998. The unemployment rate, which had been as high as 4.9 per cent as late as the autumn of 1997, quickly moved down and ended 1998 at 4.3 per cent, a little more than a percentage point below the Secretariat's estimate of the NAWRU (Figure 1, panel B). Non-farm payrolls increased 2.6 per cent in 1998, even though there are some questions about the actual magnitude of employment gains in the economy (Box 1).

Box 1.   How fast is employment growing?

There are two measures of employment growth in the United States, which give different pictures of the strength of hiring: the "household measure", based on a sample of surveys of households and reporting employment for those 16-years and over, the "payroll measure", based on a sample of firms that does not include farm workers, the self-employed and unpaid family workers. In addition, persons with two jobs are counted twice in the payroll figures, but only once in the household measure. Even after adjusting the payroll figures for these differences, the household measure has not grown as fast, and a significant gap in the cumulative employment gains since 1994 has opened up (Figure Box). In the middle of 1998, this gap widened sharply as the payroll-based measure surged. About half of this difference was reversed, however, at the beginning of 1999. Such differences matter for thinking about the dynamics of productivity, wages and profitability.

Cumulative differences in measures of employment growth

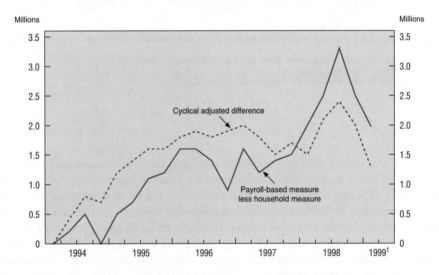

1.   February.
Source: The Bureau of Labor Statistics and OECD.

A couple of explanations may account for part of the remaining discrepancy. First, the payroll-based measure is more cyclical than the household measure. A cyclical adjustment explains some of the differences in 1998, but growth in prior years looks somewhat more puzzling. Some have surmised that the household survey has undercounted employment growth because the population has increased faster through immigration than the Census Bureau assumes. Complete data from the 2000 census, however, will not be available for quite a while.

Employment outcomes improved markedly for the workers on the margin (see Chapter III). Total employment costs in private industry rose 3.5 per cent in the twelve months of 1998, only slightly faster than through 1997, as the result of a pick-up in the growth of benefits. A slightly different picture emerges from the average hourly earnings of production workers, as the growth of these moved down somewhat towards the end of 1998. With inflation decelerating, real compensation costs in the business sector grew $3/4$ percentage point faster in 1998 than the year before. Among other evidence of labour market tightness, the Conference Board's Help-wanted index in January 1999 was 3 per cent above its level a year ago; labour turnover hit an eight-year high in 1997 – the latest year available – and worker absenteeism jumped 25 per cent in the first half of 1998.

In such circumstances, the rate of inflation normally might be expected to pick up. Instead, the GDP deflator decelerated, rising by 1.0 per cent in 1998, compared with a 1.9 per cent the year before (Figure 1, panel C). Consumption prices slowed as measured by both the personal consumption deflator and the consumer price index, but the growth rate of the latter remains somewhat higher (Box 2). Prices of nondurable goods and services slowed substantially. Prices of computer investment equipment dropped 28 per cent in 1998, compared with a 23 per cent decline the year before, while other investment prices showed a more moderate slowdown. The deflator for government consumption and services also decelerated by almost a percentage point.

Part of the reason for this benign inflation performance is that unit costs have not accelerated as quickly as wage hikes would indicate. In the domestic non-financial corporate sector, unit labour costs have been generally well contained, as nominal compensation has barely risen faster than above-average productivity increases (Table 1). Benefit cost increases have remained moderate for two reasons: significant stock market gains reduced required employer contributions to defined-benefit pension funds, and health care costs have not risen as fast as wages and salaries, in part because of the move to managed care providers. Some analysts believe, however, that with many health insurers and service providers losing money recently, the rate of health care cost increases will rise. Indeed, health care costs accelerated in 1998, but to a still modest rate of increase. Unit non-labour costs in the domestic non-financial corporate sector continued their downward trend.

A second factor lowering inflation in the face of robust aggregate demand has been the sharp fall in import prices. The import price deflator plummeted 5.2 per cent in 1998 after declining 3.7 per cent the year before. Oil prices plunged by one-third in 1998, directly shaving $1/4$ percentage point off of consumer prices from lower gasoline and fuel prices. It probably cut another $1/4$ percentage point through lower costs to businesses. Other import prices also fell, as the dollar appreciated and international prices remained weak from poor output

Box 2. What is the rate of inflation?

In the past couple of years, a significant gap between measures of price inflation at the consumer level has emerged that cannot be totally explained (Figure Box). For instance, in 1998 the personal consumption deflator increased 0.8 per cent, while the consumer price index rose 1.6 per cent. Such a difference is important when thinking of the rate of disinflation, the level of real interest rates and modelling the likely course of wages. In addition, it affects long-term budget forecasts because projections of the tax base and discretionary spending are based on chain-weighted price indexes, while by law, cost-of-living adjustments for Social Security and tax brackets are determined by the CPI.

Measures of consumer price inflation
Four quarter per cent change

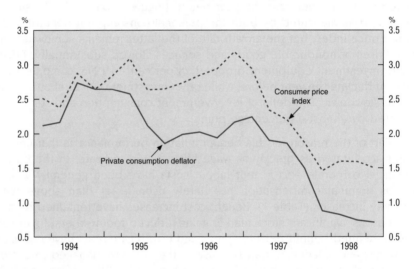

Source: OECD.

Obvious differences in methodology can only explain part of the gap.* As a chain-weighted index, NIPA deflators and price indices do capture the fact that consumers substitute away from broad categories of products whose prices have increased. However, this substitution bias is not measured by a Laspeyres index, like the CPI. It can become marked when the index is far away from its base year. In 1998, the base year of the CPI was updated when the Bureau of Labor Statistics (BLS) replaced the 1982-84 weights with 1993-95 weights, but even the latter are somewhat out of date and remain fixed. A further source of difference is that when the Bureau of Economic

(continued on next page)

(continued)

Analysis issued the 1998 annual revision of GDP, it incorporated some of the geometric averaging techniques that alleviate substitution bias within broad categories of products, and it revised the NIPA back to 1995. The BLS cannot legally revise the CPI and so was only able to incorporate such techniques as from January 1999 onwards. Together these differences only account for 0.3 percentage point of the gap annually. Excluding price imputations for some consumption goods in the national accounts for which no source data exist cannot explain much of the cumulative differences from 1994 onwards, thought it does affect the path. Only a small portion is explained by the larger weight housing costs have in the CPI. Housing costs have been increasing faster than the average.

* See the 1997 *Survey of the United States* and references therein, as well as Council of Economic Advisers (1999) for a discussion of biases in the CPI. The latter also includes some analysis on the differences between the CPI and the national accounts deflator.

growth elsewhere in the world. Prices of commodities have been hit particularly hard; the producers price index of crude materials excluding food and energy dove 9¼ per cent in 1998. Such declines have probably spread to domestic prices through lower inflation expectations and increased competition. For instance, heightened competition from overseas steel producers has led to the closure of some plants and to calls for protection (see Chapter III). Increased competition may also explain the dip in unit profits in the domestic non-financial corporate sector in 1998 (Table 1).

In addition, inflationary pressures have been alleviated somewhat from the recent improvement in potential output growth, mostly as a result of the rapid rise in the capital stock. Strong growth over the past few years has pushed up

Table 1. **Non-financial corporate cost and profit growth**

	1973-97	1992-97	1995	1996	1997	1998[1]
Output	3.5	4.9	4.5	4.5	6.1	5.7
Hours	1.8	2.9	3.2	1.7	3.4	2.7
Hourly productivity	1.7	2.0	1.2	2.8	2.6	2.9
Hourly compensation	5.6	2.5	2.0	3.1	3.5	4.1
Unit labour costs	3.9	0.5	0.8	0.3	1.0	1.2
Unit non-labour costs	4.0	−0.7	−0.7	−1.1	−1.3	−1.6
Total unit costs	3.9	0.2	0.5	−0.1	0.4	0.5
Unit profits	4.7	9.6	6.8	7.7	2.1	−4.2
Price deflator	4.0	1.2	1.3	0.9	0.7	−0.1

1. Average of 1998: Q1-Q3 over same period in 1997.
Source: Bureau of Labor Statistics.

investment to a relatively high level as a share of the net real capital stock of the business sector. At almost 12 per cent, this ratio in 1998 is estimated by the Secretariat to be 2½ percentage points above its peak in any previous cycle since 1945. To be sure, a higher amount of replacement capital is needed than in the past. The implicit depreciation rate has been rising because of greater expenditures on shorter-lived equipment such as computers and because of relatively weaker growth in non-residential construction. Nonetheless, the growth rate of the real net capital stock has picked up in the last few years, reaching rates not seen since 1979 (Figure 5). Indeed, with the relatively high level of investment, little additional growth in investment is needed to continue this rate of expansion. Even if gross investment were to remain flat in 1999, the real net capital stock would still grow 3¼ per cent, the same rate as in 1997. Rapid capital stock growth is also evident in manufacturing where increases in capacity – while slowing – are still high compared to the recent past and faster than current production. The factory operating rate at the beginning of 1999 was more than a percentage point below its average over the past 30 years. This is roughly true even if one excludes the high-tech sector where real capacity and production growth are driven, in part, by falling prices. The low rate of capacity utilisation in manufacturing has helped keep inflation lower than one would expect by merely examining the unemployment rate.

Figure 5. **Real capital stock growth**

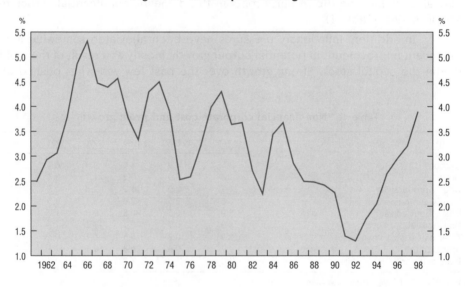

Source: Bureau of Economic Analysis and OECD.

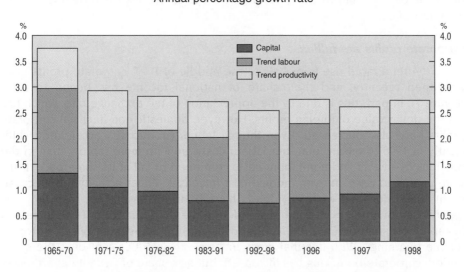

Figure 6.   **Components of potential GDP growth**
Annual percentage growth rate

Source: OECD.

Overall, other inputs, have not led to an important increase in potential growth. In spite of a pick up in total factor productivity growth in 1998 above that which can be explained by cyclical developments, there is little evidence that trend productivity has accelerated (Figure 6). The significant gains in previous years can be explained by the cyclical upswing in the economy that has also boosted the labour force participation rate. Nevertheless, the policy-induced decline in caseloads has drawn on the order of ¼ to ½ million persons into the labour force in the past three years (about 0.1 per cent of the labour force per year) (see Chapter III).

However, imbalances have started to emerge

With the rapid growth in final demand, some saving imbalances have appeared. With increased competition and moderate labour cost increases, corporate profits have come under pressure. Because retained earnings are falling, supporting even the existing level of investment will require additional borrowing by businesses. In the personal sector rapid growth in consumption has come at the expense of a plunging saving rate, which, combined with the fact that households also have invested heavily in residential buildings, has led to increased personal borrowing. The counterpart of this growing private saving deficit has been, in part, an improved government surplus, but also a widening current account deficit.

Corporate profits are falling...

After a rapid rise from 1992 to the middle of 1997, corporate profits have weakened recently, and their share of national income has begun to drop (Figure 7). In part, this is due to the appreciation of the exchange rate, which has cut the dollar value of foreign profits. However, domestic non-financial corporate profits have also decreased. Even though labour productivity accelerated sufficiently in 1998 to ensure that unit labour costs grew no more rapidly than in the previous five years and non-labour costs continued to fall at its same pace, firms were unable to pass on even modest cost increases. Prices actually fell. Because profits have declined while dividends have been increased, net cash flow has barely risen over the twelve months ended in the third quarter of 1998. Increases in capital consumption and the capital consumption adjustment offset a drop in retained earnings. With nominal gross investment up 5 per cent over the same period, corporate borrowing has increased, but as a share of GDP, it nevertheless remains only a little above its average since the 1960s.

Figure 7. **Corporate profits**
Share of national income

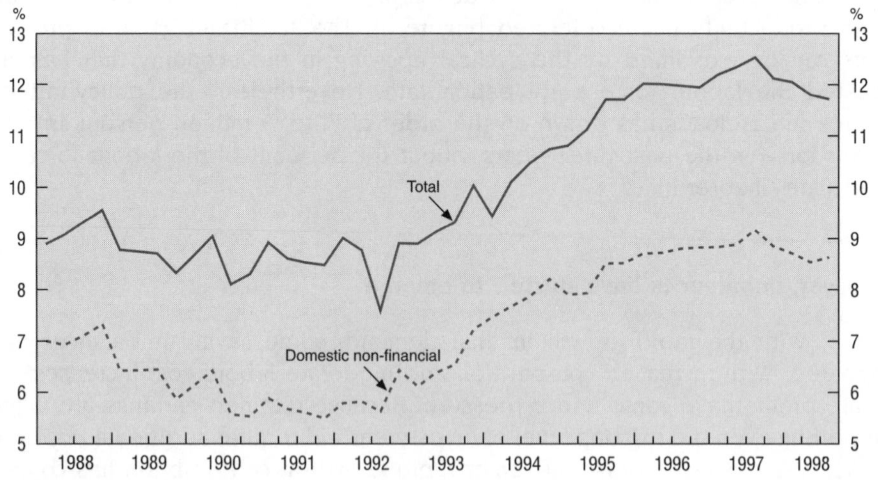

Source: Bureau of Economic Analysis.

... and household savings are plummeting...

Net lending in the personal sector has been dropping rapidly, to −2 per cent of GDP in 1998 versus 0.3 per cent in 1995.[4] This reflects the fact that consumers are saving significantly less of their disposable income; the personal saving rate has fallen from 3½ per cent in 1995 to 0.2 per cent in the second half of 1998. Meanwhile, as noted, households are investing heavily in residential buildings; home-building is booming with the level of starts hitting a cyclical high at the

Table 2.   **Household balance sheets**[1]

End of period, $ billion

	1993	1994	1995	1996	1997	1998	1991–1995	1995–1998
Net tangible assets	9 213	9 508	9 948	10 437	11 113	11 845	3.6	6.0
Real estate	7 105	7 282	7 631	8 031	8 620	9 216	3.2	6.5
Consumer durables	2 108	2 226	2 317	2 406	2 492	2 630	4.6	4.3
Financial assets	17 871	18 439	20 834	22 906	25 954	28 958	6.9	11.6
Deposits	3 109	3 085	3 289	3 458	3 701	3 985	0.8	6.6
Credit market instruments	1 352	1 636	1 524	1 535	1 399	1 362	2.6	−3.7
Corporate equities	2 972	2 747	3 700	4 194	4 939	5 816	11.9	16.3
Mutual funds	965	1 025	1 231	1 540	1994	2 419	21.5	25.2
Non-corporate equity	3 138	3 321	3 519	3 713	4 029	4 095	2.9	5.2
Life and pension reserves	5 313	5 578	6 387	7 178	8 346	9 477	9.6	14.1
Other	1 023	1 048	1 184	1 287	1 545	1 804	6.3	15.1
Financial liabilities	4 014	4 326	4 681	5 018	5 369	5 848	6.5	7.7
Mortgages	2 923	3 097	3 275	3 498	3 737	4 106	5.4	7.8
Consumer credit	859	984	1 123	1 212	1 264	1 334	9.0	5.9
Other	232	245	283	309	368	408	11.0	13.0
Net worth	23 070	23 622	26 101	28 325	31 697	34 956	5.6	10.2
Net financial assets	13 857	14 113	16 153	17 887	20 585	23 110	6.9	12.7
Memorandum:								
Indirect equities held	1 116	1 387	1 510	2 027	2 647	3 607	19.3	37.2
Share of corporate equities in financial								
assets	22.9	22.4	25.0	27.2	29.2	32.5		
Ratios to disposable income:								
Assets	552.3	541.8	573.6	592.2	630.4	665.7		
Liabilities	81.9	83.9	87.2	89.1	91.3	95.4		
Net worth	470.4	457.9	486.3	503.1	539.1	570.3		
Net financial assets	282.6	273.6	301.0	317.7	350.1	377.0		
Adjusted net financial assets in								
personal sector[2]	171.9	164.5	190.1	204.6	229.0	255.0		

1.   Calculated as the difference of the balance sheets of households and non-profit organisations less the balance sheets of non-profit organisations. As the financial data of the latter are available only through 1995, 1996-98 were estimated using 1995 shares. Note, as indicated in the memorandum item, they differ from those of the personal sector.
2.   Excludes government pensions and accumulated net savings by farm corporations from 1952.
Source: Board of Governors of the Federal Reserve System, Flow-of-Funds accounts of the United States.

end of 1998. The low level of net lending is also reflected in the Flow-of-Funds accounts where net financial flows have been negative for quite a while.[5]

Consumers are not inclined to maintain high saving rates because their balance sheets are in good shape (Table 2).[6] Although debt has risen rapidly, financial assets have grown faster, while tangible assets have accelerated too. The net worth of households has increased over 10 per cent at an annual rate in the last three years. Households now hold almost one-third of their financial assets either directly or indirectly in corporate equities – up from one-quarter three years earlier. With stock prices having grown 23 per cent on average for the last three years, as measured by the Wilshire 5000, the capital gain on all financial assets net of debt in the personal sector has averaged 16½ per cent at an annual rate. As a result, even though this sector has pulled money out of financial markets in the last three years, net financial worth has continued to climb because capital gains have been more than sufficient to cover net investment in tangible assets.

Indeed, the increase in the ratio of net financial assets to disposable income in the personal sector can be used to explain the drop in the saving rate (Figure 8). There appears to be a reasonable econometric relationship between the two, at least over a relatively short time horizon. According to OECD estimates, the marginal propensity to consume out of a shock to the level of net

Figure 8. **Personal saving and net financial assets**

Per cent of disposable income

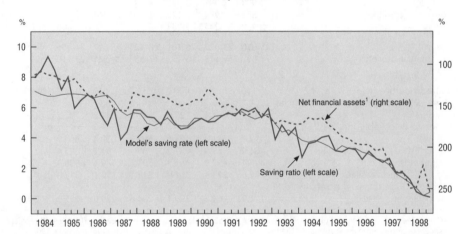

1. Some net financial assets are excluded to conform to the National Income and Product Accounts as described in the text.
Source: Bureau of Economic Analysis, Board of Governors of the Federal Reserve System and OECD.

personal sector financial assets is in the range of 5³/₄ to 6¹/₂ per cent in the long run,[7] which is towards the high end of the range of estimates found elsewhere.[8] Low and falling unemployment rates have also shaved about 0.3 percentage point off the saving rate in 1998, according to these estimates. As suggested in the figure, this model can fully explain the sharp decline in the saving rate, which has accelerated recently.

leading to a wider external deficit

The counterpart to the significant private-sector deficit has been a mixture of a substantial current account deficit and a considerable government surplus. The government sector did offset much of this financing gap (Figure 9) as net lending rose by over 1¹/₄ per cent of GDP (see Chapter II). A precise accounting is not possible, however, due to an unusually large, negative discrepancy between the product-side and income-side measures of output[9] (Box 3).

The remainder of the shortfall in national saving was funded by an increase in capital inflows from abroad. The current account deficit widened significantly in 1998, moving from 1.9 per cent of GDP in 1997 to 2.7 per cent in 1998 – 3 per cent in the second half of the year (Table 3). About two-thirds of the decline was due to a worsening of the trade balance in goods, even though

Figure 9.   **Sectoral net lending**
Per cent of GDP

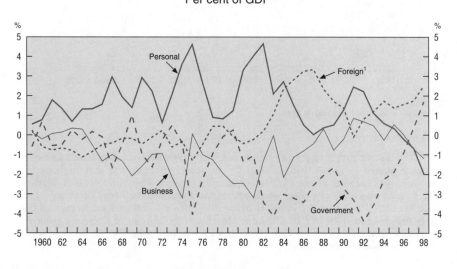

1.   Negative of the current account plus capital transfers, which are zero.
Source: Bureau of Economic Analysis and the Board of Governors of the Federal Reserve Bank.

Box 3.   How fast is output growing?

There are two measures of output: the expenditure measure, GDP, and an income-based measure, GDI, which equals national income plus capital consumption less net factor income and a few other adjustments. The difference between these two measures is called the "statistical discrepancy", and as a percentage of GDP, its absolute value has become increasingly large in recent years (Figure Box). Indeed, the income-based measure has grown on average 0.4 percentage point faster than the expenditure-based measure of GDP since 1993. However, in the last cyclical expansion, from 1983 to 1988, a similar differential emerged. These similarities suggest that the statistical discrepancy depends, in part, on the state of the business cycle, with the income measure being more cyclical.

The statistical discrepancy

Per cent of GDP

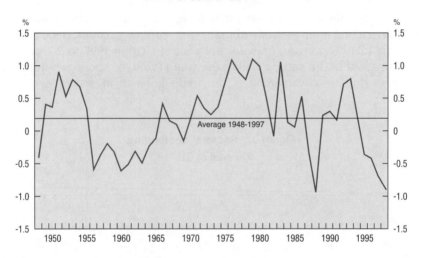

Source: Bureau of Economic Analysis.

The discrepancy matters for two reasons. *First*, some analysts have used the higher income figures to argue that productivity growth is stronger and that perhaps the economy has entered a "new era". *Second*, the discrepancy is also important in forecasting various measures of saving, which mix product and income series, such as corporate net cash flow. Given the volatility of the discrepancy – and perhaps its cyclicality – it is too early to draw any conclusions. Moreover, the Bureau of Economic Analysis maintains that GDP is a more robust measure of output, especially for recent years as its source data are more timely.

Table 3. **Current account, capital account and net asset position**

$ billion, seasonally adjusted, annual rate

	1994	1995	1996	1997	1998	1998 S1	1998 S2
Current account balance	−124	−115	−135	−155	−233	−208	−259
of which:							
Exports of goods, services and income	862	999	1 064	1 179	1 174	1 182	1 166
Imports of goods, services and income	946	1 080	1 158	1 295	1 366	1 352	1 379
Net unilateral transfers abroad	39	35	41	40	42	38	46
Balances:							
Goods	−166	−174	−191	−198	−248	−242	−254
Non-factor services	65	74	83	88	79	82	75
Investment income	16	19	14	−5	−22	−11	−34
Private transfers	−20	−15	−19	−16	−17	−13	−21
Official transfers	−19	−20	−21	−23	−25	−25	−25
Capital account balance (+ inflows)	133	138	195	255	237	209	265
of which:							
US investment abroad	−171	−327	−369	−479	−305	−312	−298
Foreign investment in the United States	304	465	563	733	542	521	564
Balances:							
Official	45	100	134	15	−29	−3	−55
Other	88	38	61	240	266	212	320
Direct investment	−31	−39	−3	−28	64	−61	189
Statistical discrepancy	−10	−23	−60	−100	−4	−1	−6
Net asset position as per cent of GDP[1]	−3.4	−7.4	−9.7	−16.3			
of which:							
US assets abroad	46.3	51.6	56.7	61.7			
Foreign assets in the United States	49.7	59.0	66.4	78.0			
Balances:							
Official	−5.4	−6.8	−8.4	−8.6			
Other	2.0	−0.6	−1.3	−7.7			
Direct investment	4.5	4.1	3.8	2.1			
Memorandum:							
Current account balance as a percentage of GDP	−1.8	−1.6	−1.8	−1.9	−2.7	−2.5	−3.0
Return on assets[2]							
US assets abroad	5.2	6.3	5.7	5.6	4.8	5.0	4.7
Foreign assets in the United States	4.4	5.3	4.6	4.9	4.2	4.1	4.3

1. Assets are valued at market rates, year-end figures.
2. Investment income as a percentage of the market value of assets at the end of the previous year. Returns do not include valuation adjustments to assets.

Source: Bureau of Economic Analysis.

nominal oil imports dropped with the sharp fall in prices. The rest of the decrease was split between non-factor services and investment income. The contraction in net investment income was due to the more rapid increase in assets held in the United States by foreigners than of assets held abroad by US citizens. Returns on US assets held abroad were higher in 1998 than those held by foreigners in the United States, although both declined.[10] The current account deficit led to a drop in the net foreign asset position that was accentuated by an unusually large discrepancy between the current and capital accounts and valuation adjustments not reflected in investment income. Asset prices rose more for those held by foreigners in the United States, and the appreciation of the dollar cut the value of net foreign assets by almost $200 billion.

Which constrain the outlook

Projections for 1999 and 2000

The imbalances that developed in 1998 are expected to slow output growth to 3½ per cent this year and 2 per cent in 2000 (Table 4). The slowdown in final domestic demand growth should be even more marked. In the business sector, tight labour markets and accelerating real wages could push down corporate profits, while at the same time smaller increases in investment are needed to sustain the rapid growth in the capital stock. As a result, business investment is expected to decelerate in 1999 and grow slowly in 2000. As for the personal sector, with a reduced prospect for continued significant stock market gains over the projection horizon, balance sheets should stop strengthening. Although the past effects of the run up in the market could result in additional declines in the saving rate into 2000, continued net borrowing should eventually lower net financial assets relative to disposable income, so pushing up the saving rate. For the same reasons, demand for new housing should ebb, bringing construction more in line with long-term prospects. With final demand slowing, inventory investment could decrease and be subject to fluctuations towards the beginning of 2000 (Box 4). The external sector, however, should mitigate some of this domestic deceleration. While net exports are expected to continue to be a drag on activity, their contribution to growth should not be nearly as negative as it was in 1998. Imports are projected to slow along with final demand, and exports are expected to pick up as prospects in the rest of the world improve.

Despite the slowdown in output growth, some imbalances may still remain by the end of the projection period. Although it is projected to rise to 4½ per cent at the end of 2000, reflecting weaker employment growth, the unemployment rate would still be almost one percentage point below the OECD estimate of the NAWRU. Moreover, high wage growth, the waning effects of the

Table 4. **Near-term outlook**

Per cent change in volume terms (chain 1992 prices, seasonally adjusted at annual rates)

	1998	1999	2000	1998		1999		2000	
				I	II	I	II	I	II
Private consumption	4.9	4.5	2.6	5.3	4.8	5.2	3.0	2.8	1.6
Government consumption	1.1	1.8	0.3	0.4	2.4	1.9	1.1	−0.3	0.8
Gross fixed investment	9.7	6.1	1.0	11.7	6.8	8.5	0.9	0.9	1.5
of which:									
Private residential	10.4	5.3	−5.3	13.5	11.2	8.7	−6.4	−5.4	−3.9
Private non-residential	11.8	6.8	3.0	14.5	6.3	8.7	3.9	2.5	3.0
Government	0.1	4.3	1.6	−2.2	3.2	7.8	−1.4	2.6	2.6
Final domestic demand	5.2	4.5	2.0	5.7	4.9	5.4	2.3	2.0	1.5
Stockbuilding[1]	−0.1	−0.3	−0.1	0.2	−0.4	−0.2	−0.3	−0.1	0.2
Total domestic demand	5.1	4.2	1.9	5.8	4.4	5.1	2.0	1.9	1.7
Exports of goods and services	1.5	2.7	5.7	−2.3	1.1	2.0	5.7	5.6	6.0
Imports of goods and services	10.6	7.6	4.3	11.7	6.4	9.2	5.4	4.2	3.6
Foreign balance[1]	−1.4	−0.9	0.0	−2.1	−0.9	−1.2	−0.2	0	0.2
GDP at constant prices	3.9	3.6	2.0	4.0	3.8	4.2	2.0	2.0	1.9
Memorandum items									
GDP price deflator	1.0	1.1	1.5	0.9	0.9	1.2	1.1	1.5	1.7
Private consumption deflator	0.8	1.3	1.8	0.5	1.0	1.2	1.8	1.7	1.8
Unemployment rate	4.5	4.2	4.4	4.5	4.5	4.2	4.2	4.4	4.5
Three-month Treasury bill rate	4.8	4.5	4.5	5.0	4.5	4.4	4.5	4.5	4.5
Ten-year Treasury note rate	5.3	5.2	5.2	5.6	4.9	5.1	5.3	5.2	5.1
Net lending of general government									
$billion	140.7	172.5	170.0	126.9	154.5	170.2	174.8	175.4	164.5
Per cent of GDP	1.7	1.9	1.8	1.5	1.8	1.9	1.9	1.9	1.8
Current account balance									
$billion	−233.4	−303.5	−320.4	−208.0	−258.9	−292.4	−314.5	−322.3	−318.5
Per cent of GDP	−2.7	−3.4	−3.5	−2.5	−3.0	−3.3	−3.5	−3.5	−3.4
Personal saving rate[2]	0.5	−0.8	−1.0	0.9	0.2	−0.5	−1.0	−1.0	−0.9

1.   Changes as expressed as a percentage of GDP in previous period.
2.   OECD definition.
Source: OECD.

past dollar appreciation and the rebound in oil prices are expected to lead to an increase in inflation over the projection horizon, but could also put added pressure on corporate profits. At the same time, high household wealth is expected to keep the personal saving rate low. Finally, the current account deficit is projected to widen to 3.5 per cent of GDP in 1999 and 2000. Such imbalances will continue to weigh upon the medium growth prospects for the economy.

Box 4. Y2K

On 1 January 2000, many computer programmes will stop working properly because they will have trouble interpreting the correct year, perhaps reading "00" as 1900 instead of 2000. Millions of computer chips that are embedded in equipment and appliances also suffer from this same Year 2000 or Y2K "bug". As computers are ubiquitous in the economy, network disruptions in the finance, communications and power sectors could cause significant losses. Failures in billing and payments systems among federal agencies, state and local governments and private firms, could lead to substantial funding pressures and bankruptcies. Delivery delays in just-in-time inventory systems would reduce output; as an example, the automakers typically have some 15 000 different suppliers. Some economists put the chance of a global recession induced by the problem at 70 per cent.[1] In part, their pessimism stems from its sheer size, with estimates of the total cost of fixing the problem in the United States ranging from $95 to $520 billion. Corporations have been revising up their Y2K budgets.

However, some are confident that the computer-date problem will have only a minor effect on aggregate output in the United States. The President's Year 2000 adviser likens the consequences of the bug to "a severe winter storm",[2] and Governor Kelley of the Federal Reserve System estimates that it will shave GDP by only 0.1 percentage point. In part their optimism stems from efforts made to date. Due to early prodding by regulators, significant progress has been made; bank regulators rate only a few, mostly small institutions, as having made unsatisfactory improvements. By March 1999, the Federal Reserve's payments system will be ready. It has developed contingency plans to provide adequate liquidity and ordered an additional $50 billion in currency to meet an upsurge in demand leading up to the new year. Tests conducted in early March by securities firms went better than had been expected. Utility regulators now expect the communications and power industries to be mostly in compliance with only small, localised outages likely. Large corporations have also redoubled their efforts, and repairs are going faster than had been expected. It now appears that the problems with embedded chips are smaller than previously thought. Some government agencies have also made excellent progress; the Social Security Administration is 100 per cent compliant.

Significant additional work, however, remains, and some disruptions are likely. Many other government agencies will not have all of their repair work completed in time. For instance, the Government Accounting Office expects that some Medicare systems will not be fully compliant, and state welfare agencies are behind in their conversions.[3] The readiness of small and medium-sized companies is less well known, but it is thought that, for the most part, they have made insufficient progress. One survey found that only two-thirds of small and mid-size businesses have begun working on the problem.[4] The Congress passed a bill that would require the Small Business Administration to guarantee loans to help finance the work. According to a Senate report, other countries are lagging far behind the United States, and problems originating elsewhere could spill over to the United States.

---

1. OECD (1998).
2. Chandrasekaran and Barr, (1999).
3. GAO (1998); and GAO (1999).
4. The survey was conducted by Arthur Andersen Enterprise Group and National Business United and was quoted in Pope (1999).

Underlying assumptions

The principal assumption underlying these projections is that monetary policy would stay on hold for some time after the 75-basis point cut in the last half of 1998. Short-term rates on government securities are assumed to remain unchanged at a more usual level, after a narrowing in the gap between the federal funds rate and the three-month Treasury bill rate at the beginning of the year. Long-term rates are expected to remain stable, as the impact of increasing inflation is balanced by weak demand.

Fiscal policy is assumed to follow announced policy changes. Real government expenditures are expected to grow slightly in 1999 and slow further in 2000, in line with the discretionary spending caps. In spite of cuts in income taxes flowing from earlier budgets, the effective tax rate could increase with continued high capital gains realisations and real base drift (see Chapter II). State and local government spending, however, may accelerate somewhat, while tax rates are trimmed in light of large surpluses. Overall government net lending is expected to edge up to 2 per cent of GDP in 1999 before moving back down to 1¾ per cent in 2000 as the economy slows.

As for the international environment, it is notably expected that output will recover in Asia. As a result, import demand there could offset an expected weakness in the Western Hemisphere, so that overall US market growth could accelerate to around 6 per cent for manufactured products by 2000. In addition, both the US dollar effective exchange rate and oil prices are assumed not to change significantly from their level in March 1999, their average level for the year as a whole being about the same and 15 per cent higher respectively compared with 1998.

Risks and uncertainties

The risks to the projection are now evenly spread. Households are now considerably more exposed to the stock market than in the past, making consumption more dependent on equity prices. Indeed, the most likely risk to the projection remains a drop in the stock market triggered by unexpected factors, such as negative international developments leading to weaker export growth and financial instability, or stronger domestic demand leading to a rebound in domestic inflation inducing higher interest rates. A more optimistic scenario would be that the good supply-side performance of the economy, that appears to have occurred in 1998, could continue. In that case, domestic profit margins might improve once again, bringing another boost to stock prices. This would lift personal consumption, raise output and prolong the period of stable inflation, so obviating the need for higher interest rates.

Over the medium term, a further risk might emerge concerning the sustainability of the wider current account deficit. Indeed the net foreign liabilities position of the United States has moved up to 16 per cent of GDP, and, more recently, net investment income turned negative. Continued declines seem likely. So far, foreign investors have been willing to buy US assets and have supported a stronger dollar because they have valued the liquidity of US securities and their relative safety. With improvements in the outlook for developing countries and continued expansion in financial markets outside the United States, their attitude could change as, at given interest rates, they may be induced to diversify their portfolios.

It does not seem realistic to expect a rapid increase in the personal saving rate that might help reduce the current account deficit, as long as asset prices continue to grow at close to past long-term averages. Assuming that the stock market rises on average 5¾ per cent and that net household physical investment drops to around 5 per cent of disposable income, consumers would have to raise their saving rate to 3 per cent in order to achieve a stable ratio of net financial assets to their income (see Annex I for details of the mechanisms at work). Absent a fall in the stock market, however, this mechanism would be slow and only increase the saving rate by 1½ percentage points in the next ten years.

Some of the required saving may, of course, be generated by the restrictive stance of fiscal policy generating fiscal surpluses. The expenditure caps in the 1997 Balanced Budget Act call for flat spending on discretionary items in 2001 and nominal reductions in 2002 (see Chapter II). These translate into real declines in federal government spending of about 2 per cent and 2¾ per cent respectively. Medicare reform, which has not progressed as far, could lead to additional restraints that would reduce transfers. Without changes to the tax code, real income gains will continue to push more households into higher tax brackets, raising the effective tax rate.

Increased public saving by itself may not be sufficient to reduce the current account to a manageable level. By boosting the potential of the economy and so lowering the need for imports, supply side factors would also help in this respect. The recent upswing has enabled the economy to adjust to important structural reforms, including welfare reform that has drawn more people into the labour force (Chapter III). The resulting job experience and human capital development should be long lasting, so boosting labour and, hence potential output, even if a downturn temporarily were to push some of these people into unemployment. Market-opening agreements signed in the past couple of years should increase specialisation, thus also raising supply in the medium term.[11] Meanwhile, once implemented, reforms in the telecommunications and electricity markets may yield gains in productivity (see Chapter III). If, in addition to higher government surpluses, such additional sources of supply prove to be not sufficient to reduce the current account deficit as a share of GDP, long-term interest rates may have to rise to contain demand pressure thereby lowering imports.

II.   Economic policies

The conduct of monetary and fiscal policies during the past eighteen months has been influenced by a combination of sustained growth in domestic demand, strong labour market conditions and particularly low inflation – a situation not seen in the past 35 years. A timely easing of monetary policy in the fall of 1998 has ensured that a period of illiquidity and falling prices in some parts of the capital market ended before its deflationary consequences spread to the rest of the economy. At the same time, fiscal policy remained tight, generating the first budget surplus since 1969. For this to continue, difficult decisions will have to be made concerning which expenditure programmes to reduce. The remainder of the chapter deals with these issues in more detail.

Monetary management

Interest rates fell

After a period when the strength of demand was a concern...

After a short period at the end of 1997, when it appeared that the crisis in Asia might result in marked slowing of the American economy, the concern of the Federal Open Market Committee (FOMC) during the first half of 1998 switched once again to the strength of domestic demand and the tightness of labour markets. This stance was in line with the conclusions of the EDR Committee in September 1997 that some further monetary tightening might be necessary given that current rates of resource utilisation appeared too high to sustain the medium-term disinflation process. In the event, however, the authorities were not faced with any evidence of a pickup in inflation. Rather, inflation has progressively edged downwards. By the end of 1997, the rate of increase of the CPI was almost 1¼ percentage points below the authorities' central projection for 1997 (Figure 10). Although this was lowered for 1998, the actual inflation rate has remained below the projection by a similar amount – with little evidence to suggest that an acceleration in prices was likely in the near term. Moreover, other indicators suggested that the inflation rate was even lower. As a result, short-term

Figure 10. **Actual and expected inflation**[1]

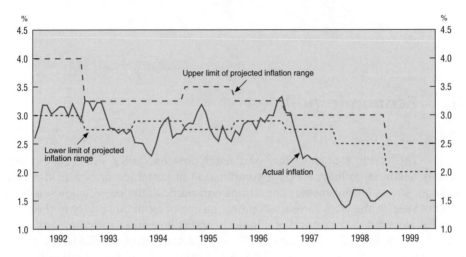

1. The projections refer to the central inflation tendency for a given year identified by the Federal Reserve six months prior to the start of the year.
Source: Federal Reserve and OECD.

interest rates were kept unchanged, though the FOMC still felt that unexpected upside information might call for a tightening of policy.

... interest rates were cut following market turbulence

This period of stability ended when another external development – the effective default in the domestic market for Russian government debt in August 1998 – introduced a degree of turbulence into financial markets that had not been seen for some time. This incident immediately led to a marked re-assessment of risk in capital markets: interest rate margins widened (Figure 11) as investors tried to improve the quality of their investment portfolios. Such developments left market participants that had taken on large credit risks in the first half of 1998 particularly exposed, especially as many were operating with highly leveraged positions. The near-failure of several of these institutions, including Long Term Capital Management (see Chapter III), was an additional factor leading to greater illiquidity in the market. Indeed, the premium that banks had to pay for their funds, as measured by the three-month Eurodollar deposits, over US Treasury bills spiked in similar fashion to the crises that occurred in 1984, 1987 and 1991. Other short-term markets, such as commercial paper, were adversely affected. Liquidity also dried up in government bond markets with the spreads

Figure 11.   **Spreads on various financial instruments**

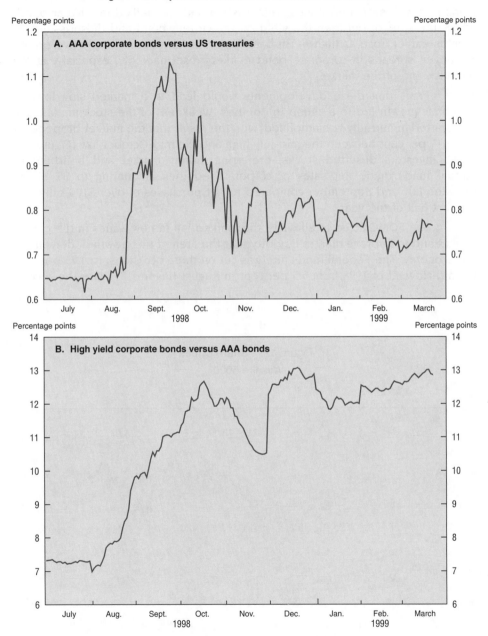

Source: Federal Reserve, Bloomberg and Merril Lynch.

between the current issue of most notes and bonds falling to unusually low levels compared with seasoned issues. This was particularly marked in 30-year bonds where the spread, between the yield on the current bond and those issued six months earlier, rose as high as 30 basis points from a norm of only five points. Moreover, spreads in corporate bond markets rose markedly, especially at the high-risk end of the market.

Fears that these developments would lead to a marked slowdown in economic growth led to a slump in equities. Weakness of the stock market that had started in mid-July was amplified, with the result that the market dropped by some 17 per cent between the mid-July high and the mid-October low (Figure 12). Retail investors deserted stocks, preferring money market and bond funds. Mutual funds made net sales of corporate equities amounting to $5 billion between July and September compared to net purchases of over $100 billion in the first half of the year.

The FOMC acted to alleviate the marked fall in new issues in the capital market and to improve market liquidity that threatened the growth of demand in the economy. The Federal funds rate was cut on three occasions, to 4.75 per cent by mid-November 1998 from 5.5 per cent in August (Figure 13). After the second

Figure 12. **Share prices**
Wilshire 5000[1]

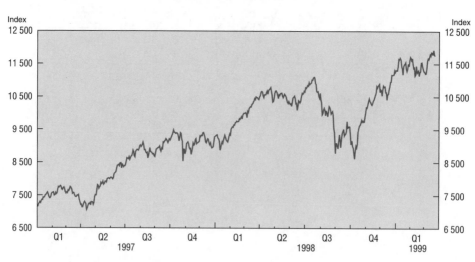

1. Base: December 31, 1980 = 1 404.6.
Source: Bloomberg.

Figure 13.   **Short-term interest rates**

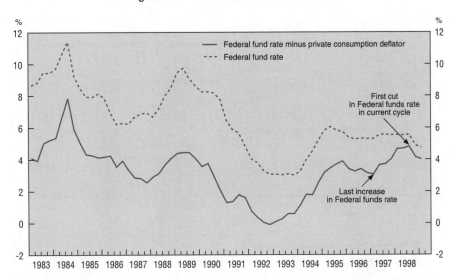

Source: Federal Reserve and OECD.

cut, which came in between regular FOMC meetings, markets rallied. At the short-term end of the market, the premium that banks paid for funding was largely eliminated. For non-financial borrowers, the market segmented. Better quality risks were accepted back into the market with spreads falling to only slightly above the levels of the first half of 1998, leaving rates on investment grade paper unchanged, while those on good quality mortgage paper fell. For poorer quality risks, spreads – while falling – remained much higher than earlier in the year. This was also the case for many asset-backed securities, where borrowing costs for credit card, home equity and commercial mortgage paper hardly fell at all. The equity market rebounded, regaining all of its lost ground, ending the year some 15 per cent higher than a year previously. Indeed, the FOMC indicated that the last cut of the federal funds rate in November completed the process of adjustment to the new market environment and took out some insurance against any unexpected weakness of the economy in future months.

Bond yields also declined...

During 1998, government bonds staged a major rally. The nominal yield on ten-year government bonds fell by about 110 basis points between the

Figure 14. **Government bond yields**

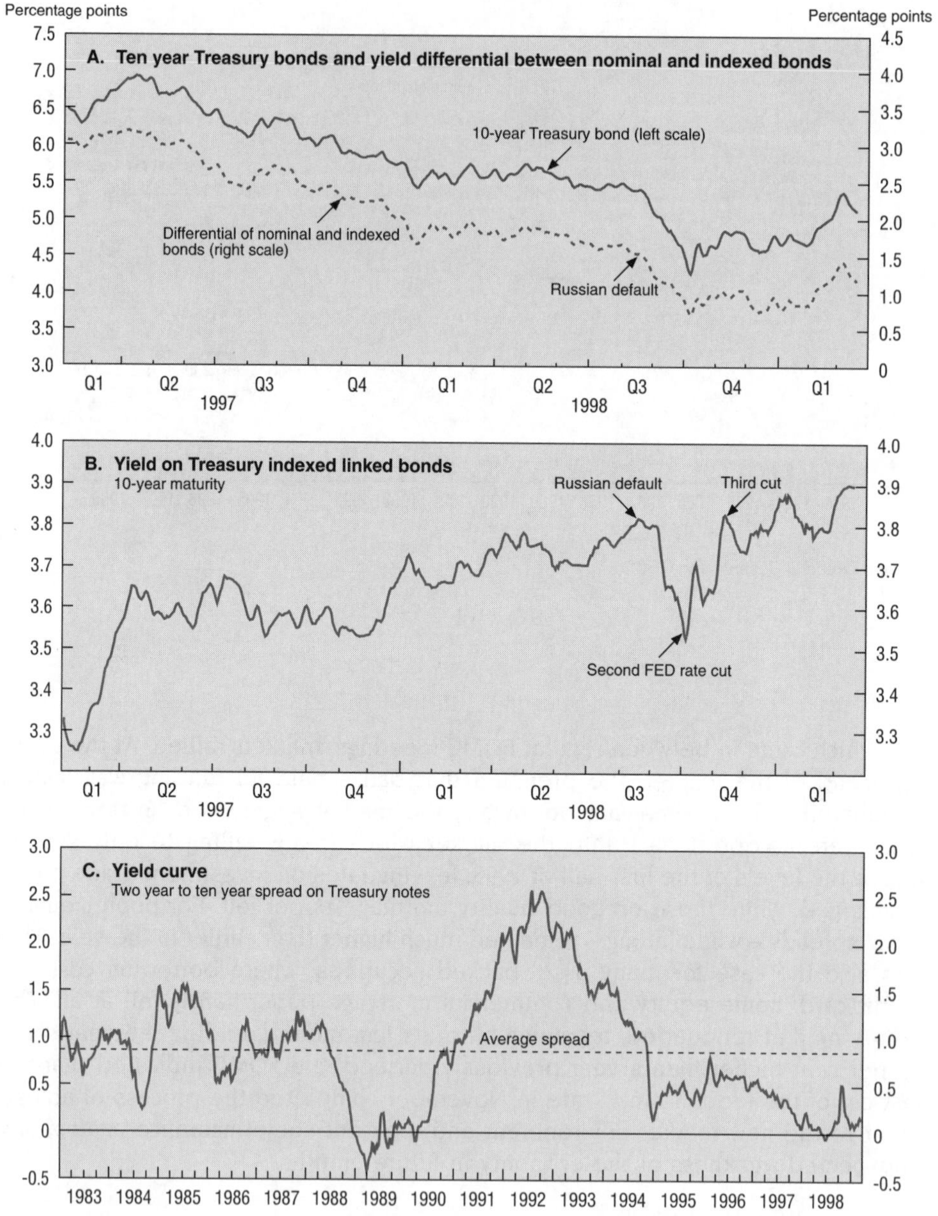

Percentage points   Percentage points

A. Ten year Treasury bonds and yield differential between nominal and indexed bonds

10-year Treasury bond (left scale)

Differential of nominal and indexed
bonds (right scale)

Russian default

Q1   Q2   Q3   Q4   Q1   Q2   Q3   Q4   Q1
      1997   1998

B. Yield on Treasury indexed linked bonds
10-year maturity

Russian default   Third cut

Second FED rate cut

Q1   Q2   Q3   Q4   Q1   Q2   Q3   Q4   Q1
      1997   1998

C. Yield curve
Two year to ten year spread on Treasury notes

Average spread

1983 1984 1985 1986 1987 1988 1989 1990 1991 1992 1993 1994 1995 1996 1997 1998

Source: Federal Reserve and Bloomberg.

beginning and end of 1998. A large part of the fall occurred during the period of capital market tensions and was, at the time, associated with flight to quality. By the Spring of 1999 most of this liquidity premium had disappeared, leaving bond yields only some 50 basis points lower than at the beginning of 1998. One of the factors behind the buoyancy of bonds would appear to be the persistent reduction in inflation. Indeed, during 1998, the fall in nominal yields was accompanied by a similar drop in the differential between the yield on nominal and indexed Treasury bonds (Figure 14, panel A). The fall in bond yields led to the yield curve becoming flatter during 1998, even becoming negative in the middle of 1998, a position that had not been seen since the beginning of 1990 (Figure 14, panel B). Some slight steepening of the curve was evident following the three federal funds rate cuts.

... but short and long-term real interest rates remained stable

The decline in inflation, though, means that, despite the reduction in the federal funds rates, real short-term interest rates, at around 4 per cent, are still somewhat above their level in the second quarter of 1997 ($3\frac{1}{2}$ per cent)[12] when rates were last increased and slightly higher than the average of the past fifteen years. But they have dropped back somewhat from their peak of close to 5 per cent in the summer – a level similar to that seen at around the top of the late 1980s economic cycle. In contrast to developments at the short end of the market, long-term real rates, as evidenced by the yield on Treasury indexed securities, were on a slight upward trend throughout the period under review, with the exception of the financial crisis from September to October when yields fell temporarily.

The exchange rate remained firm

Although the US dollar exchange rate has fluctuated considerably since the beginning of 1998, it has remain at a high level. It started to ease during the summer and continued to fall as short-term interest rates were cut. This depreciation in the dollar, of 7 per cent in both the real and nominal effective rate by end-December 1998, came after an appreciation in these rates of 25 and 33 per cent respectively, in just over three years (Figure 15). The fall against the Deutsche-mark was similar to the overall average, while the fall against the yen was much more pronounced (19 per cent between August and December 1998). This latter movement appears to have been linked to the significant increase in Japanese long-term rates and the de-leveraging in yen of many foreign investors. By mid-March, much of this overall weakness of the dollar had been reversed, with its bilateral rates against the euro and the yen strengthening, thus leaving its effective exchange rate slightly above its 1998 average.

Figure 15. **Exchange rate developments**
Index 1995 = 100

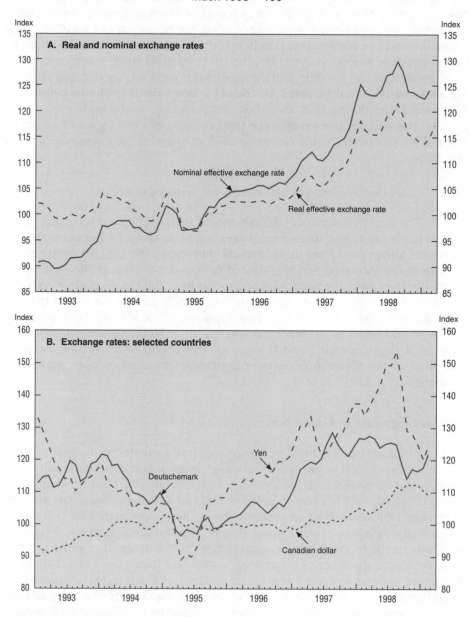

Source: OECD.

Credit markets reacted adversely to financial turmoil

After a strong credit expansion in the first half of 1998...

Overall credit growth both from capital markets and deposit-taking institutions was buoyant during 1998. The growth of total credit picked up towards the end of 1997, after several years when it had expanded as fast as national income (Table 5) and continued to accelerate during 1998. Within this total, credit to the private non-financial sector accelerated to an even more marked extent while federal government reduced its outstanding debt. This pickup in private borrowing was mainly led by corporate sector demand, though parts of household demand (such as mortgages) were also buoyant.

During the first half of 1998, capital markets took an increasing share of overall credit activity. Credit markets were dominated by the two groups of non-bank intermediaries: government sponsored financial enterprises and investment funds such as bond and money market mutual funds (Table 5). The former relies extensively on the issuance of asset-backed securities[13] which rose by 75 per cent in the first half of 1998, taking advantage of various types of government guarantees. Net issuance of private asset-backed securities also grew in importance, mainly financing consumer credit, either through pooled credit card receivables or home-equity second mortgages (Table 6). Direct issuance of bonds by the non-financial sector was also very strong. Most of this capital market activity was undertaken at spreads that were well below historical norms, though in the first

Table 5. **Credit market debt outstanding by class of borrower**

Annual per cent change
End period

| | 1995 | 1996 | 1997 | 1998 | 1998 | | | |
| | | | | | Q1 | Q2 | Q3 | Q4 |
					Seasonnaly adjust annual rate			
All borrowers	7.2	7.4	7.2	9.9	9.3	9.6	6.8	11.8
Domestic non-financial	5.4	5.3	5.1	6.3	6.1	6.1	5.6	7.2
Federal	4.1	4.0	0.6	−1.4	−0.8	−1.9	−3.6	0.7
State local	−4.5	−0.7	5.3	7.2	8.7	7.1	6.4	6.6
Private non-financial	7.3	6.5	6.8	9.0	8.5	9.1	8.9	9.6
Households	7.9	6.9	6.5	9.1	8.2	8.4	8.2	10.6
Non-financial corporate	8.4	6.8	8.2	10.2	9.9	10.8	11.0	9.1
Non-financial non-corporate	2.7	4.1	5.0	7.0	..	..	..	..
Farm	2.0	3.3	4.1	4.2	..	..	..	..

Source: Federal Reserve.

Table 6. **Flows of credit market lending**

	1995	1996	1997	1998	1998			
					Q1	Q2	Q3	Q4
				Per cent of GDP				
Flows of lending by issuer								
GSE's[1]	2.5	2.9	2.6	5.1	3.0	4.6	6.1	6.6
Investment funds	2.1	1.9	2.0	4.3	3.7	4.2	4.0	5.2
Retirement funds[2]	2.9	2.5	2.8	3.4	3.3	3.0	2.7	4.5
Deposit institutions	3.7	3.0	4.2	4.3	3.8	1.9	3.5	7.9
Asset backed securities	1.6	1.6	2.0	3.2	2.7	4.0	2.9	3.4
Finance companies	0.7	0.2	0.3	0.7	0.3	0.3	0.9	1.4
Other institutions	1.0	0.3	1.1	0.0	5.2	−3.0	0.6	−2.1
Total	14.3	12.3	14.0	21.0	22.0	15.0	20.6	26.8
Memorandum:								
Share of deposit institutions	25.6	23.9	30.2	20.5	17.4	12.6	17.0	29.5

1. Government-sponsored financial enterprises, such as GNMAE, and federally-insured asset-backed mortgage pools.
2. Includes all insurance companies.
Source: Federal Reserve.

half of 1998 margins on certain forms of borrowing such as private asset-backed securities and higher yielding corporate bonds did rise somewhat. During the same period, banks and savings institutions saw their share of the overall credit drop to around 15 per cent from 28 per cent in 1997.

... issuance in bond markets slowed abruptly

The increased financial turbulence in the autumn led to a marked fall in bond market activity. The private sector bond market slumped (Table 7), with net issuance by the non-financial sector being halved, the high risk junk bond sector being particularly hit. Borrowing by the financial sector fell to an even greater extent, with finance companies being unable to tap the market in sufficient quantities to refund maturing debt. Only pension funds, insurance companies and banks continued to buy corporate bonds at the same pace as in the first half of the year. Purchases by foreigners fell markedly while households became net sellers. Government sponsored enterprises were largely unaffected by this development and even proved able to increase their issuance.

While banks regained market share...

Total borrowing, however was little affected by the turbulence. Non-financial debt continued to rise at an unchanged annual rate of around 6½ per cent during the crisis period. Banks were able to make good the drop in activity of capital markets. As a result, the share of deposit institutions in credit issuance

Table 7. **The corporate bond market**

Net flows

	1995	1996	1997	1998	1998			
					Q1	Q2	Q3	Q4
				$ billion				
Issuers								
Financial sector	197	196	208	299	342	376	179	262
Commercial banks	19	8	24	28	49	17	21	23
Asset backed	104	108	115	191	162	248	160	−196
Finance companies	53	33	20	30	38	42	−45	8
REITS	2	0	10	19	23	25	16	12
Brokers	−5	−2	8	7	−1	20	−3	12
Funding corporations	24	29	31	34	72	25	29	11
Non-financial sector	73	73	91	132	157	161	87	124
Total corporate bonds	270	248	299	434	499	537	266	386
Purchasers								
Retirement and insurance funds	105	135	140	141	176	126	121	185
Rest of world	58	84	87	122	108	163	95	95
Investment funds	36	39	55	120	122	164	73	73
Household sector	89	3	32	29	100	101	−114	−31
Deposit institutions	−2	−10	22	40	41	43	36	130
Other domestic	34	54	9	1	−35	48	−10	−52
				Per cent increase over one year				
Memorandum:								
Outstanding bonds	13	11	10	13	13	15	14	13

Source: Federal Reserve.

rose sharply in the third quarter and climbed even further in the fourth quarter (Table 5). The growth in bank lending peaked in October with loans expanding at an annual rate of close to 16 per cent in the previous three months. However by February, with new issues on capital markets recovering, bank credit stabilised. The change in capital market conditions also offered banks the opportunity to widen spreads on lending to commercial and industrial clients. In autumn 1998, more banks raised than lowered margins for the first time since mid-1992. Moreover, the difference between the proportion increasing or decreasing spreads was the greatest since the Gulf War period, at end 1990 and beginning 1991, but there were indications that this process was moderating by the beginning of 1999.

In addition, there has been a marked tightening of credit standards involving greater collateralisation and reduced maturities. However, no deterioration in the performance of business loans has taken place. Indeed, aggregate statistics for the banking industry show problem loans to be at a historically low level, averaging only slightly over 2 per cent of banks portfolios, down from just under 5 per cent at the peak of the last business cycle in 1989. Bank profitability also remains good, helped by a low level of charge-offs, and was not greatly affected by the financial turbulence of the autumn, except for a limited number of major institutions. The return on equity of FDIC insured banks is still around 15 per cent, while capital adequacy ratios remain at high levels.

The widening in bank margins came after banking supervisors had issued warnings about the need for banks to have sound lending policies and to avoid the competitive pressure to take excessive risks during the upswing of the cycle. A Federal Reserve study of bank lending practices found that, between the second halves of 1995 and 1997, there had been a noticeable and measurable easing in bank lending terms. In June 1998, federal supervisors called for banks to maintain their lending discipline. The month after, the supervisor of nationally chartered banks was even more outspoken. While banks had tightened credit card lending standards in response to charge-off rates that had reached nearly 6 per cent, the study noted that lending standards had eased in the related home-equity loan market especially in the area of sub-prime loans and high loan-to-value products. More worryingly, in the commercial lending area more syndicated loans were becoming leveraged products, spreads were narrowing and guarantees were falling indicating that the potential for downside risk was rising at a time when loan provision reserves were steadily falling. Bank supervisors also identified commercial real estate lending as an area that deserved special attention from bank credit risk managers.

... leading to an acceleration in monetary aggregates

The buoyancy of bank lending in the second half of 1998 was reflected in a further increase in the growth of the money stock. Most measures of the money stock started to accelerate from the autumn of 1997 onwards. After several years when it appeared that the velocity of circulation had stabilised, monetary growth moved well above the growth of nominal incomes (Table 8). The growth of M3

Table 8.   **Growth in monetary aggregates**

Per cent change over one year

	1993	1994	1995	1996	1997	1998
M1	10.2	1.8	−1.9	−4.1	−0.6	1.7
M2	1.5	0.4	4.2	4.8	5.8	8.8
M3	1.6	1.8	6.0	7.3	9.0	11.2
GDP	5.0	5.8	4.2	5.8	5.6	5.2

1.   December data for monetary aggregates and fourth quarter data for GDP.
Source: Federal Reserve, BEA.

picked up to 10½ per cent by mid-1998 and, continued to grow at rapid pace at the beginning of 1999 expanding at an annual rate of 9½ per cent in the three months to February 1999. The growth of M2 was somewhat lower, with money market funds benefiting from deposits by investors when they exited stock and bond markets. The narrower concept of M1 grew more slowly, after falling in recent years, due to more efficient cash management procedures.

Summary

The stance of monetary policy eased markedly at the end of 1998, in response to severe stress in domestic capital markets precipitated by the Russian government defaulting on its debt. After the federal funds rate was lowered three times, to 4.75 per cent, capital markets became liquid once again. Private sector bond markets partially recovered, though the gains were less for the most risky asset classes and risk premia remain higher than before the crisis. On the other hand, equity markets rose to well above pre-crisis levels, staging a surprisingly strong rally. Overall, the easing appears to have restored more normal conditions in most parts of the capital markets and appears to have ensured the continuation of the economic expansion. Given that continued rapid growth has resulted in continued falls in unemployment, the case for a tightening of monetary policy could arise in the near future, if there is evidence that continuing weak inflation pressures might not be sustained.

Fiscal policy

Favourable outcome of the 1998 federal budget

Repeating the experience of 1997, the 1998 unified budget has recorded out-turns markedly better than expected by the Administration. Indeed, the improvement in the budget balance position was over $90 billion (Table 9) against an initial projection of only $2 billion when the budget proposal was submitted to Congress. In fact, while the Administration still envisaged a deficit when the FY 1998 budget was published in February 1997, when the mid-session review was published, the revised official estimates suggested that there would be a small surplus. In the event, the surplus finally reached $70 billion, almost ½ per cent of GDP higher than expected.

Explanatory factors

Part of the reason for such a favourable out-turn was the *low growth of federal government expenditure*. Congress did not increase individual appropriations in line with its own global caps on discretionary spending. The 1997 Balanced Budget Act (BBA) gave a one year boost to the cap on discretionary spending of $11 billion in

Table 9. **Federal budgets**

$ billion

	FY 1997	FY 1998			FY 1999		FY 2000
	Actual	Current services	Estimate	Outcome	Current services	Projected outcome	Current services
	October 1997	February 1997	February 1997	February 1999	February 1998	October 1998	February 1998
Total revenue	1 579	1 574	1 658	1 722	1 730	1 806	1 872
Individual income taxes	738	708	768	829	793	869	902
Corporate income taxes	182	187	191	189	194	182	187
Social insurance taxes	539	558	571	572	596	609	636
Excise taxes	57	53	56	58	71	68	65
Other	63	67	72	75	76	78	82
Total expenditure	1 601	1 693	1 668	1 653	1 732	1 727	1 774
Discretionary[1]	548	553	553	555	569	577	596
Defence	272	265	265	270	271	277	279
Other discretionary	277	288	288	285	298	300	317
Mandatory	809	890	873	855	921	918	962
Social security[2]	365	381	378	376	396	389	405
Medicare	190	209	195	190	208	202	215
Medicaid	96	105	101	101	108	109	115
Deposit insurance	−14	−4	−5	−4	−4	−4	−4
Other mandatory	223	253	249	245	256	266	274
Offsetting receipts	−50	−53	−46	−53	−43	−43	−43
Total primary	1 357	1 443	1 425	1 407	1 490	1 499	1 558
Net interest	244	250	243	243	242	227	215
Surplus	−22	−119	−10	69	−3	79	98

1. To meet the discretionary spending caps in FY 2000, spending would have to be $ 574 billion.
2. Includes government employee retirement benefits.
Source: Analytical perspectives, Mid-Session Review OMB; CBO; OECD estimates.

1998. In practice, the appropriation bills passed by Congress did not take advantage of this higher cap and limited expenditure to just slightly above the inflation adjusted appropriations for 1997. With some apparent under-spending in the defence budget, the increase in discretionary expenditure was muted (Figure 16). The growth in mandatory spending was also reined back. Most notably Medicare expenditures slowed, to a much greater extent than can be explained by initial estimates of the cost savings envisaged under the 1997 Balanced Budget Act (BBA). Part of this unexpected slowdown may have come from lower spending on home health services where new reimbursement rules have proved to be particularly tight. This development also affected outlays under the Medicaid programme. Finally, states proved slower than expected in drawing down grants for the new children's health insurance programme. Overall, these factors led to total

Figure 16. **Discretionary federal spending**[1]
Per cent of potential GDP

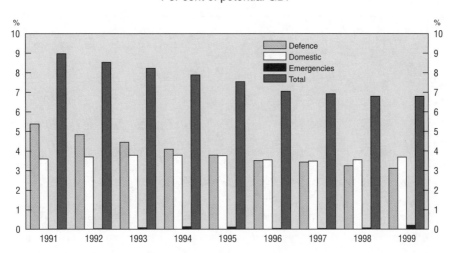

1. Emergency spending is voted annualy by Congress and is outside the limit on other spending.
Source: CBO, The Economic and Budget Outlook, August 1998 and OECD.

primary expenditure (i.e. excluding payments on government debt) rising by just under 4 per cent, in line with the growth of nominal potential output.

But the greater part of the better performance of federal finances was due to a very *buoyant yield from income tax.* This occurred despite the Tax Reform Act (TRA) that included provisions for tax cuts of $9 billion ($^{1}/_{2}$ per cent of 1997 receipts). A large part of the increase in revenues was due to the economy being stronger than envisaged in the budget. In addition, receipts from capital gains were particularly strong. In 1996, taxes on capital gains rose by $20 billion, 45 per cent more than in FY 1995, bringing capital gains taxes to over 1 per cent of GDP (Figure 17). Although 1998 official estimates of the tax revenue derived from capital gains are not yet available,[14] simple calculations based on the rise in the value of the equities suggest that this increase could have been repeated in FY 1997 and FY 1998. Indeed realisations of capital gains through mutual funds jumped by over 40 per cent in calendar 1997.

Income tax receipts, other than on capital gains, would also appear to have also been robust.[15] This is more due to the progressive nature of the income tax system than to any unexpected income gains registered by certain categories of taxpayers. Indeed, the average marginal tax rate appears to be well above the average tax rate. As a result, the tax elasticity when measured relative to total personal incomes now approaches 1.5 (Figure 18). Part of the explanation for this

Figure 17. **Taxes on capital gains**[1]

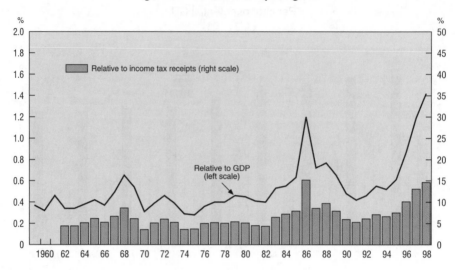

1. Taxes on capital gains have been estimated in 1997 and 1998.
Source: CBO and OECD estimates.

Figure 18. **Average federal income tax rate and the tax elasticity**[1]

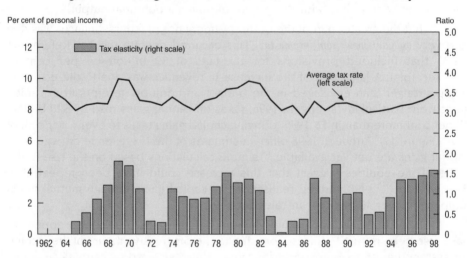

1. The average income tax rate excludes receipts from capital gains. The taxe elasticity is a three year moving average of the ratio of the percentage increase in income taxation to the increase in household income.
Source: OECD.

is that the tax base appears to be rising faster than personal incomes, due to growing withdrawals (relative to contributions) from both defined benefit and defined contribution retirement saving schemes. These withdrawals are taxed as part of personal income. The peak in contributions to Individual Retirement Accounts (IRAs) was in the early 1980s. The holders of these accounts are now progressively reaching the age when withdrawals can be made from the accounts without penalties. Some special factors, such as high incomes rising somewhat faster than average incomes, have also boosted tax yields. A large part of this gain has come from the high value of exercised stock options and the rapid growth of partnership income. Together, the CBO puts the extra revenues from these sources as over $5 billion in FY 1996. However, even without these latter factors, the average marginal tax rate would still appear to be over 12 per cent against an average total tax rate of under 8 per cent (excluding capital gains).

Some of the factors that have led to an increased level of tax revenues over the past three years appear to be relatively permanent. The increase in income tax yields due to higher capital gains is the product of three elements: the rise in the market, the extent of realisations and the tax rate. Since 1993, realisations have been markedly lower in relation to the value of equity portfolios than prior years. In part this may have been due to expectations that the high capital gains tax rate set in that year would be cut. Now that capital gains tax rates have been reduced to the level of the first half of the 1980s, it is possible that turnover will increase. If, in addition, equity prices remain at their values of end-1998, then receipts from capital gains should stay at the level of almost 1½ per cent of GDP seen in 1998, about 1 percentage point above their historical norms. Furthermore, a fall in equity prices would not necessarily be associated with a reduction in capital gain tax receipts. Indeed, share values would still likely be above historic acquisition costs. Moreover a fall in the market is often associated with increased turnover that results in higher realised capital gains and hence tax payments. However, there is a possibility that the share of the income of high earners (those earning over $200 000 per year) in the total tax base may not be permanent, posing a risk to government revenues since the recent gains in tax revenues have come from people with high incomes.

Federal Budget target for 1999

Expenditure

The 1999 budget allows for more rapid increase in spending than occurred the previous year. The first change to already-established expenditure limits for 1999 came with the new Transportation Equity Act. This act allows the outlays for interstate highways and mass transit systems[16] to be increased, on average, by $21 billion in the next five years. Spending will be controlled by two new caps that would be raised if the yield of the gasoline tax rises faster than expected. Effectively, this means that these expenditure caps limit the financial balance of the Highways Fund out of which transportation expenditures are paid and federal gasoline taxes collected. In order to comply with existing legislation, the amount of the increased spending on transport was taken off the 1999 discretionary limits for the remaining spending categories. As a result, these limits fell by $25 billion (almost 9 per cent), adding to the pressure on spending in these areas.

The impact of the cuts in discretionary limits, imposed by the Transportation Act, was cushioned by the decision to allow significant emergency expenditure that is not counted against the spending limit. Outlays under this heading are designed to meet contingencies such as catastrophes, natural disasters or other unexpected occurrences. In the event, it seems that most of the voted expenditure was not of this type, about half being related to defence programmes, such as improving intelligence and military readiness. The authorised civilian programmes were closer in nature to emergency spending and included outlays on natural disasters, farm relief, responses to terrorist attacks and security violations, but also comprised increased spending for year 2000 computer problems. Total authorisations under the emergency heading amounted to around $21 billion, with outlays likely to rise somewhat less. Overall, discretionary and emergency spending outlays seem likely to increase by about 5¼ per cent against less than 1 per cent the preceding year.

After a particularly modest increase in 1998, mandatory spending is projected to rise significantly once again in 1999. In part, this reflects decisions taken in the 1997 BBA or TRA that only take effect gradually or affect expenditure for the first time in 1999. Thus, spending in the areas of child health care, child tax credit benefits[17] and welfare to work grants is expected to surge. Medicare expenses are also projected to accelerate again, as the 1999 budget law partially reverses the rules on home health care reimbursements introduced by the 1997 BBA. Overall, these developments seem likely to ensure that the growth of total primary spending will be over 6 per cent, against just under 4 per cent in 1998.

Revenue

The growth of tax revenue should slow in 1999, mainly reflecting slightly slower economic activity and reduced corporate profits. In addition, it seems likely that the increase in revenues from capital gains will stabilise. There were few changes to tax legislation contained in the budget reconciliation act. Most of the provisions that were enacted in the 1998 OBRA prolonged existing tax exemptions. The most important of these were the "welfare to work" and the "work opportunity" tax credits that pay subsidies to employers hiring underqualified employees or people removed from the welfare rolls. Consequently, they have little impact on the year-to-year change in tax revenues. However, the gradual phasing in of changes in the 1997 TRA will act as a drag on the growth of income tax receipts, lowering them by almost 3 percentage points, as the first refunds are made for child and education tax credits. Most of this loss in income tax revenue will be made up by timing changes that have switched revenue from 1998 to 1999; without these, the 1998 budget surplus would have been $14 billion higher. As a result, the first effect of the 1997 TRA on the surplus will not be felt until 2000.

The above revenue and expenditure estimates suggest that the budget improvement seen at the federal level in the past two years will be sustained in 1999, leaving a surplus of around ¾ per cent of GDP. The OECD estimates that less than half of the current federal surplus is cyclical. The low share of federal spending and taxation means that cyclical variation in the balance is relatively small. According to both OECD and CBO estimates, a 1 percentage point change in the level of GDP changes the level of the surplus by 0.2 per cent of GDP.

The Administration budget proposal for FY 2000

For FY 2000, the Administration envisages a further increase in the budget surplus to $117 billion (1.3 per cent of GDP) from a projected $79 billion for the current fiscal year, based on economic growth of 2 per cent. This projection is based on successful compliance with the discretionary spending caps, a task that may prove difficult as the estimates of outlays, based on a continuation of the current level of government services, are some $13 to 20 billion higher than the caps (Table 9). The Administration proposes a number of new spending initiatives to improve the functioning of the labour market, such as supporting education by recruiting new teachers, rewarding high-performing schools that serve low-income students, making child-care more affordable through tax credits and finally improving the incentives for the disabled to find jobs. In the area of health care, there are proposals to allow some people aged 55 to 65 to be insured by Medicare and to encourage long-term care in the home. Overall, these measures are projected to cost some $23 billion. Increased spending will be balanced by cuts in other forms of discretionary expenditure, a proposed new tobacco tax and various increases and extensions of user fees and taxes.

Developments in the state and local governments

The finances of the state and local sector also improved slightly, as the strength of the economy benefited local tax revenues while, at the same time expenditure growth was restrained due to weak investment and low growth in medical spending. Nearly all states reported a surplus in their general account budget for fiscal 1998, as a result of revenues being some 3 per cent higher than budgeted. Their experience of the 1980s and early 1990s has made them cautious about the use of these surpluses. About half decided to increase stabilisation funds, while others created reserves funds to help maintain welfare spending in the event of a downturn, now that the federal support for this type of spending no longer depends on the numbers on the welfare rolls (see Chapter III). Nonetheless, about 32 states plan modest tax cuts in FY 1999 amounting to $7 billion (almost 0.1 per cent of GDP), somewhat greater than the cuts made in the last three years. In addition, budgets indicate that spending will accelerate slightly, registering 6.3 per cent growth in 1999 against 5.7 per cent in 1998. Overall, these movements are projected to lower the small surplus of state and local governments in FY 1999.

General government finances

Overall, given the continued buoyancy in the economy the general government surplus seems likely to increase this year before easing back slightly in 2000 (Table 10). This slight growth is associated with both an expansion in the state and local government surplus and in the federal government surplus that is likely, once again, to show a surplus well above initial official estimates. Most of the improvement of the general government balance in recent years is not related to the cyclical improvement in incomes. Since the turnround in US public finances started in 1992, the cyclical improvement in the general government balance is estimated to be only 1.3 per cent of GDP. By contrast, the structural financial balance has improved by 4 per cent of GDP, in line with the average swing that has been seen in this balance in other OECD countries in a similar period[18] – with the exception of Japan.

Table 10. **General government financial balances and debt**

Per cent of GDP

	1995	1996	1997	1998	1999	2000
Budget basis						
Federal surplus (FY)*	−2.3	−1.4	−0.3	0.8	0.7	0.7
National accounts basis						
Federal government	−2.3	−1.4	−0.1	1.0	1.2	1.3
State and local governments	0.5	0.5	0.5	0.7	0.7	0.6
General government	−1.9	−0.9	0.4	1.7	1.9	1.8
Cyclically adjusted	−1.6	−0.8	0.0	0.9	1.0	1.1
Debt						
Gross general government	62.2	61.3	59.1	56.7	54.2	51.7
Net general government	46.7	46.0	44.1	41.2	38.7	36.5
Federal debt in hands of public (FY)*	50.1	49.6	47.3	44.3	41.7	39.3

Source: OECD, except for * CBO.

In 1998, net general government debt declined, and this movement is projected to continue in the next two years, with net debt falling to 37 per cent of GDP by 2000, down from around 47 per cent in 1995 (Figure 19). Nearly all of this drop reflects the projected fall in federal debt in the hands of the public. State and local net debt is very low, amounting to only 1 per cent of GDP in 1998 and fluctuates very little, as most states have clauses in their constitution that keep budgets close to balance. Gross debt of general government follows a similar downward movement to net debt at a somewhat higher level. It should be noted, though, that the assets of the social security system are netted from the gross debt figures – in contrast to some other countries where such a consolidation does not take place.

The medium-term outlook

Budgetary plans based on existing laws suggest that the growth of federal public spending on discretionary programmes in the next decade will be modest. The BBA legislated caps that allow only ¾ per cent annual growth in nominal expenditure for the five-year period 1997-2002. Nearly all of the increase is scheduled for the first two years of that period. Thus, from 1999 to 2002, nominal expenditure is expected to remain constant in nominal terms – on the assumption that the legislation is not changed and that the emergency expenditure of 1999 is not repeated. If this target is adhered to, then discretionary expenditure will have to fall by 1 per cent of GDP in the next three years. As yet, there are no legislated caps for individual programmes; rather the cap is a global one. Beyond 2002, there are no legal limits on spending. The CBO and the OMB have assumed that expenditure remains constant in real terms until 2009, so reducing discretionary spending by a further percentage point of GDP in the following five years. Over the whole projection period from 1999 to 2009, discretionary spending is projected to fall by about ¼ per cent annually in real terms.

In the next decade, federal outlays on mandatory spending suffer just the initial, relatively modest, impact of ageing. Social security spending is projected to grow by only 2½ per cent annually in real terms. Medical expenditure, though, is expected to rise at about twice this rate, despite the impact of previous legislation which should reduce the level of spending by 11 per cent by 2002, relative to its previous trend. With other spending increasing somewhat less rapidly than GDP, the CBO puts the growth of total real mandatory spending at around 3½ per cent annually in the next ten years. Given the restraint that is assumed for discretionary spending, total real primary expenditure is projected to grow by just 2¼ per cent.

With respect to revenue, as outline above, the gains in taxation seen in recent years appear to be mostly permanent, provided that there is no significant fall in stock market prices. However, the 1998 reduction in the tax rate on capital

Figure 19. **Government debt**
Per cent of GDP

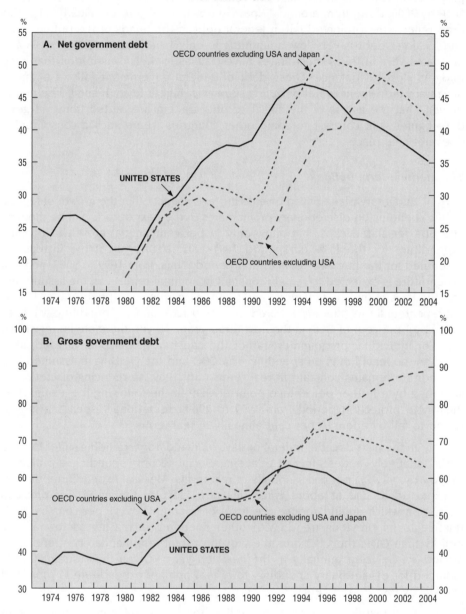

Source: OECD.

gains may have brought forward some revenue from later years. Moreover, as the rate is scheduled to fall once again in 2000, revenue from this source is likely to drop back somewhat in out years. The prospects for remaining tax revenues will be determined by the growth of output. Potential output is projected to grow on average by 2¹/₂ per cent in the next decade, though actual output growth may be somewhat less, at about 2¹/₄ per cent, as unemployment gradually rises back towards its equilibrium rate. With slightly lower capital gains taxes largely offset by fiscal drag, the fall in the yield from income taxes may be limited to about ¹/₂ per cent of GDP by 2002. Thereafter, aggregate tax revenue should start to increase once again as the capital gains tax stabilises.

If expenditure is controlled to the extent that is currently envisaged, then the prospect is for the current substantial federal budget surpluses to increase in the next decade according to CBO estimates, even if GDP growth were to average only 2¹/₄ per cent annually. The current federal surplus of around ³/₄ per cent of GDP should rise to almost 2 per cent of GDP by 2002 and to around 3 per cent by 2009. In this scenario, the nominal value of federal debt would shrink by four-fifths, dropping back to just 9 per cent of GDP (Figure 19). Such an improvement though is driven by the assumption that discretionary spending will fall by 1 per-centage point of GDP between 2002 and 2008. In the 1990s, it has been the fall of defence spending that has checked discretionary outlays. If domestic non-military spending were to remain stable as a share of GDP, as it did in the 1990s, real defence spending would have to start falling significantly once again in order to meet such spending targets. The budgetary projection is also sensitive to growth. The CBO assessment of budgetary plans implies a federal surplus of over $350 billion by 2009. If economic growth were to be ¹/₄ percentage point lower, on average, over the whole of the period, around $100 billion of the surplus would be eliminated by 2009.

An integral part of the Administrations budget proposal for next year is a plan to ensure that the recent budget surpluses continue to increase over the medium term, the main objective being that the bulk of these surpluses lead to an increase in national savings. To this end, the Administration proposes to transfer to social security from general revenues $2.8 billion over the next 15 years (equivalent to 62 per cent of the *ex ante* budget surplus – (Table 11 panel A). About one fifth of this transfer would be invested in equities. Part of the projected surpluses will also be used both to aid the development of "Universal Saving Accounts", in which individuals will be encouraged to invest in preparation for retirement (see Chapter IV), and for transfers to the trust funds that finance Medicare. Finally, resources amounting to 0.3 per cent of GDP (Table 11, panel B) are earmarked for extra spending to meet critical national needs. As a result, the unified budget surplus is projected to be of the order of 2 per cent of GDP by 2010.

Table 11. **The proposed medium-term fiscal plan FY 2000 – FY 2014**

	1999	2000-2004	2005-2009	2010-2014	Total
		\$ billion Annual average			
Panel A					
Sources of the unified budget surplus					
Social security	121	143	189	213	2 724
On-budget surplus	–42	23	127	276	2 130
Unified surplus	79	166	316	489	4 855
Proposed uses of the surplus					
Reserve for social security	79	89	177	287	2 764
Universal saving accounts	..	19	35	53	536
Medicare	..	25	45	67	686
Spending on critical national needs	..	28	36	33	482
Interest	..	5	23	50	386
Total	79	165	316	489	4 854
Memorandum:					
Additional transfer to social security to finance share purchases	..	19	37	60	580
		Per cent of GDP			
Panel B					
The impact of the proposals on the budget surplus					
Baseline unified budget surplus	0.9	1.6	2.5	3.1	2.4
Extra spending[1]	..	0.5	0.7	0.9	0.7
of which:					
Universal saving accounts	..	0.2	0.3	0.3	0.3
Defence	..	0.3	0.3	0.2	0.3
Interest	..	0.0	0.2	0.3	0.2
Proposed unified budget surplus	0.9	1.1	1.8	2.3	1.7
of which:					
Social security surplus	1.4	2.4	3.4	4.5	3.3
On-budget surplus	–0.5	–1.3	–1.6	–2.2	–1.7
Panel C					
The impact of the proposals on the social security surplus					
Baseline surplus	1.4	1.4	1.5	1.4	1.4
Transfer from general revenue	..	0.9	1.4	1.9	1.4
Increased property income	..	0.1	0.5	1.1	0.5
Final surplus	1.4	2.4	3.4	4.5	3.3

1.   Transfers to government funds, such as Medicare, do not increase consolidated spending. Purchases of shares are not counted as expenditure in this presentation, as the outlay on shares is balanced by the acquisition of an asset and so does not giver rise to a net liability.
Source: The FY 2000 Budget, OMB; OECD estimates.

This plan should safeguard Social Security until 2055. Its impact on the overall budget surplus and national savings is, obviously, very dependent on the medium-term economic assumptions. For instance, if economic growth were to be only $1/4$ per cent lower, on average, the budget surplus would be over $100 billion lower at the end of the period. Another source of uncertainty is the growth of the tax base that has fluctuated considerably over past ten-year periods. About three-quarters of the changes over the past fifteen years are grouped within with a range of 1 to 4 percentage points. Such a range in the growth of the tax base would generate, in the two cases, a difference in budget surpluses of over $500 billion by 2009. With such a risk of different outcomes, the administration's willingness not to engage on major new spending programmes appears prudent.

III. Structural policy developments

With rapid technological progress, new businesses are emerging in the United States, leading to continued restructuring of the private sector and blurring traditional market distinctions. The pace of change is all the more apparent with the high rates of investment and job creation in the context of a booming economy. In some areas, rapid growth has made easier the implementation of structural policy initiatives, such as welfare reform. Elsewhere, it has forced regulators to adapt to the rapidly evolving environment. Since 1996, however, the Administration and the Congress have come to few agreements on important measures to address persistent deficiencies in the health, education and financial sectors. In contrast, some progress is occurring in the telecommunications sector and the electricity market, although in the latter area reforms have been mainly initiated by state governments. Recent accords also have served to open up the possibilities for further development in the trade sector, but a growing current account imbalance from faster growth in the United States than abroad has raised the spectre of more intense trade disputes.

Income assistance and labour markets

The 1996 welfare reform has proceeded fairly well. The number of beneficiaries has fallen markedly with many people finding work. At the same time, reduced welfare expenditures has freed state resources for new programmes to help more people move off of public assistance. With improved job security from a low unemployment rate, the focus of the health-care debate has switched to the regulation of managed care providers, rather than the expansion of coverage. Federal programmes have increased access for children, but the working poor continue to be inadequately served. While robust economic growth has brought an improvement in the incomes of the less favoured, permanently reducing income inequality still requires tackling the problems in education that were identified in the OECD *Job Study*. This would imply greater efforts at both the state and federal levels.

Income assistance

In 1996, the Personal Responsibility and Work Opportunity Reconciliation Act came into effect, replacing the old open-ended federal entitlement to welfare assistance with a block grant to states to provide time-limited benefits. Under the new programme, welfare recipients can be paid out of federal monies for at most five years. The law also requires the states to help beneficiaries move into jobs; 25 per cent of families had to be in work programmes in 1997, with that requirement rising to 50 per cent in 2002. In addition, the states must maintain at least 80 per cent of their previous spending levels. In exchange they have wide latitude in the nature of their spending decisions, as well as in determining time limits for welfare payments (Figure 20). Eight have limits shorter than 36 months, while two states, Michigan and Vermont, will extend benefits indefinitely after the five-year limits are used up. States also vary in the sanctions imposed on welfare recipients who do not comply with the conditions for obtaining benefits. In particular, seven states apply a lifetime ban on further payments for continued non-compliance, while fifteen only apply partial benefits sanctions over a limited time period. Nonetheless, it is clear that states have not "raced to the bottom". Monthly benefits have been maintained, with as many states raising as lowering them. States have also generally increased allowable earnings outside of the programme to encourage work effort.

Overall, welfare caseloads have fallen dramatically, plummeting 27 per cent since enactment of reform. Research by the Administration suggests that about half of this decline is due to the strength of economic activity; another 30 per cent is from policy changes, with the rest unexplained. The economy has been generating more job opportunities for low-skilled workers. People are moving into jobs at a slightly faster pace than before, but most are still leaving welfare because of changes in family status or employment of other household members. There has not been a noticeable change in the characteristics of people exiting welfare, although more welfare cases now concern children only. Sanctions for non-compliance explain much of the policy-induced decline.[19] Time limits have not been an important explanation to date overall, but their impact is expected to grow. A few states are seeing some families reach their limits, but many of them are continuing to receive benefits. In Connecticut, which has the shortest time limit at 21 months, by October 1998, 25 200 cases already used up their benefits. Of these, 9100 received extensions, and 400 were granted exemptions. Of the rest, 80 per cent were working three months after leaving welfare. In eight other states, 4 per cent of their caseloads reached their limits by October, with almost 40 per cent of these still receiving some benefits.

The fall in the number of welfare cases has also provided states with widened financial choices. Because the programme is a fixed block grant based on spending levels in 1994 and 1995 when caseloads were high, the states have

Figure 20.   **State time limits for welfare recipients**

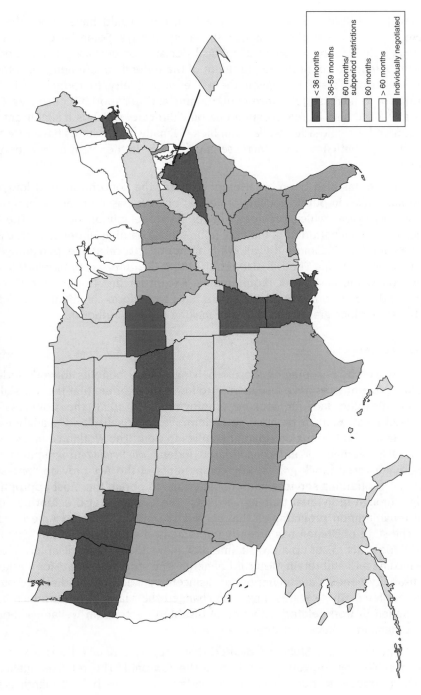

Source: Urban Institute, "One Year After Welfare Reform".

received $4.7 billion (22 per cent) more than they would have under the old system.[20] They have applied this gain in variety of ways. Some have been more generous either as the result of a political decision or because of the need to meet the minimum spending requirement of the federal government. For others, the extra federal grant has given them the opportunity to reduce their own spending or to increase job placement, training and transportation services. Several states have also increased spending on child care, which is a significant job impediment for single-adult welfare families.[21] Finally, many states have reserved money to cope with any future increase in caseloads, in the event of an economic downturn.

There has also been an attempt to lower the concentration of low-paid and welfare cases in public housing projects. Congress passed major reform of *the public housing system*, which provides shelter for three million persons. The law breaks up the concentration of the very poor – those earning 30 per cent or less of an area's median income – by allowing authorities to raise the percentage of higher-income tenants. The bill also requires that the 20 per cent of residents on welfare follow the law's work requirements. Except for the 40 per cent who are elderly or disabled, other residents would have to perform community service. It also transfers block grants and decision making to local authorities.

Labour markets

As well as encouraging those receiving welfare benefits to work, federal and state governments have also started to lower the barriers that the low-skilled and the disabled face in seeking employment. In 1998, the Congress re-authorised Head Start, a programme to improve the quality and availability of *child-care services*, so helping one-parent families to work. The Workforce Investment Act of 1998 overhauled and consolidated federal *job training* programmes into state-administered block grants. Key components of the Act provide "one-stop shopping" for training services and enable adults to obtain the most appropriate training through individual training accounts. The Congress also extended vocational rehabilitation programmes that served 1¼ million disabled Americans in 1995. The state of Oregon has recently implemented a provision in the 1997 Balanced Budget Act to set up a programme that allows the working disabled to earn more income and still retain Medicaid benefits. The strict phaseouts for Medicaid and disability benefits are an important disincentive, keeping the disabled out of the labour force. Thirty states have also changed their laws to require increased participation in work-related activities of disabled persons on welfare, although these programmes have just begun.

The OECD *Jobs Strategy* indicated that improving *education* was a key element in enhancing the future earnings of the low-paid. The relative quality of education appears to decline in the secondary system as by the eighth grade math scores are below the OECD average. Moreover, the dispersion of scores at both grade levels is higher than the OECD average.[22] This may be linked to the significant differences in educational spending between school districts, outlays per-child ranging from $1 500 to $15 000[23] across the country. State supreme courts have declared funding systems unconstitutional in eighteen states,[24] while progress towards a more equitable system has been slow. A recent study shows that court-ordered finance reform substantially reduces within-state inequality through higher spending in poorer districts.[25]

Some initiatives have been taken to improve the quality of education. In October, the President signed legislation that aims to triple the number of public charter schools by 2002. Fifteen state governors called for their introduction or expansion in their "State-of-the-State" addresses. Federal funding for such schools increased from $6 million in 1995 to $80 million in FY 1998. At the same time, two laws re-authorised the programme for federal aid to college students and overhauled and extended federal aid for vocational education. As part of the FY 1999 omnibus appropriations legislation, the Congress inserted language banning federal funds for national testing of primary students, although it did agree to most of the Administration's request for the Goals 2000 programme to promote standards. Some evidence indicates that standards-based reform helps raise academic achievement, particularly for disadvantaged students. The same act also authorises spending of $1.2 billion as part of a plan to hire 100 000 new teachers. Because of a swelling student population and teacher retirement, more than two million teachers need to be hired in the next ten years, thereby requiring additional funds for support and professional development. The President vetoed legislation granting vouchers for private school students in the District of Columbia, but a couple legal decisions confirmed that a Wisconsin project to distribute vouchers that can be used to pay fees in religious schools was legal.[26]

Over the past year there was some modification of *immigration* legislation. Assertions of labour shortages in certain high-tech areas led to passage of an act that raised by 75 per cent for a few years the number of visas for temporary immigrants sponsored by high technology and other companies. Legislative developments in other areas included delaying until 30 March 2001 implementation of an automated system tracking arrivals and departures at the Canadian and Mexican borders. Congress also appropriated $171 million for the Immigration and Naturalization Service to clear the backlog of naturalisation applications. In addition, the 1997 Balanced Budget Act restored Supplementary Security Income and Medicaid benefits to legal immigrants in the country before the 1996 enactment of welfare reform, as well as extending aid for anyone whose status was in doubt until just FY 1998. Now these benefits have been granted to the latter category on an indefinite basis.

The *Jobs Strategy* identified the decline in the number of adults with medical coverage as an important problem. Federal medical programmes cover adults benefiting from public income assistance programmes, the elderly and the disabled. However, basic coverage for poor and working-poor adults is limited and declining. Businesses are cutting back on their coverage for those with short tenure or who work part time.[27] Fewer low-income workers are participating in schemes for which they are qualified, probably due to the high employee contribution.[28] According to one poll, 43 million persons lacked coverage in 1997.[29] The only recent initiative is this area has been the expansion of the federal health programme for children. States are now beginning to draw money from the federal government to implement this project to which $24 billion have been allocated over five years.

More generally, even though health care costs have decelerated recently, employer-provided health plans are still an important fraction of labour costs, and out-of-pocket spending remains high for employees.[30] Part of the slowdown in costs has occurred as businesses have turned to managed care providers such as health maintenance organisations (HMOs). The share of workers covered by such plans has risen from about one-quarter in the late 1980s to about three-quarters in 1996.[31] Because HMOs receive a fixed fee per customer, they have strong incentives to minimise costs; indeed there is evidence that managed care providers do generate savings.[32] Surveys show that employers view them as an effective means to control costs.

There has, however, been some public reaction against these cost reductions. Whereas in a fee-for-service scheme, beneficiaries may have too much say in how much health service they receive, in a managed care system, they may have too little say. HMOs closely monitor the services provided and deny services they deem are inappropriate. In theory, *ex-ante* competition among plans for enrolees can limit the extent of denials, but, in practice, the information available for consumers to make comparisons is limited. There are only a few examples, such as the state of Maryland, of the publication of "report cards" on managed care providers.[33]

In an attempt to deal with this issue of denial of treatment, a Presidential Advisory Commission produced a "patient's bill of rights" that would:

- Guarantee access to a broad range of specialists;
- Grant the right of patients to appeal to a board when providersvdeny treatments;
- Allow access to emergency room care if a prudent layperson would judge it to be necessary;
- Prohibit discrimination in care, enrolment and marketing; and
- Mandate that consumers receive accurate information.

Under existing legislation the federal government only has limited authority to implement these proposals.[34] Congress did consider bills that would have enacted parts of the Commission's recommendations. Other bills envisaged allowing second opinions and longer hospital stays for some cases, prohibiting operators from preventing their doctors from discussing alternative treatments and requiring the provision of services by doctors outside the managed care network. One controversial proposal, the Norwood-D'Amato bill, would have modified the law that currently prohibits many employees with private insurance from suing their managed care providers under state malpractice laws.[35] While the Congressional term ended before it passed any significant legislation, it will reconsider such issues in the new session. Some state legislatures implemented similar legislation regulating health insurance under their purview. Estimates of the costs of such regulation range from 1 to 8 per cent of current costs, depending on the specifics.

Finally, in the area of health, state Attorneys General reached an agreement with *tobacco companies* to end various lawsuits in November 1998. The states negotiated a settlement with the tobacco companies that did not require any changes to federal law.[36] The deal provides $206 billion over 27 years to 46 states to settle outstanding claims, additional funds for anti-smoking programmes and advertising restrictions.[37] To help finance the settlement, manufacturers announced a wholesale price hike that would raise the retail price of cigarettes by 29 per cent. The deal does not preclude federal action including additional cigarette taxes and new regulatory authority over nicotine by the Food and Drug Administration. Currently, a case is before the US courts to judge whether the agency can indeed regulate nicotine under existing laws. The Administration recently announced its intention to sue the tobacco companies.

OECD Jobs Strategy follow-up

The 1996 review of US implementation of the OECD *Jobs Strategy* noted that "input and product markets function well, resulting in high and effective use of labour resources".[38] In some respects, the situation has improved since then. In the context of a booming economy and rising employment growth (see Chapter I) job opportunities for marginal workers have improved. Participation and employment rates for this class of workers have indeed increased faster than for the economy as a whole (Table 12). Some of this may be structural as it appears that there has been more job creation for low-skilled workers in the 1990s than in the 1980s. Wages at the bottom end of the distribution grew more quickly than at the top end in 1998. The poverty rate fell 1/2 percentage point to 13.3 per cent in 1997, the lowest level since 1989.[39] Home ownership rates hit a record high in 1998 with those among African Americans and Hispanics rising particularly quickly.

Table 12. **Employment outcomes in the secondary labour market**

Per cent

	Participation rates			Unemployment rates			Employment growth Q4/Q4		
	1996	1997	1998	1996	1997	1998	1996	1997	1998
Black men	72.3	72.1	72.5	9.4	8.5	7.4	2.2	2.5	3.5
Black women	62.6	64.0	64.8	8.7	8.8	7.9	1.7	3.7	4.8
Hispanic	66.5	67.9	68.0	8.9	7.7	7.2	7.6	6.9	3.4
Women who maintain families	n.a.	n.a.	n.a.	8.2	8.1	7.2	3.3	4.3	2.6
Aged 16-19	52.3	51.6	52.8	16.7	16.0	14.6	3.1	2.9	4.6
Aged 55 and over	30.3	30.9	31.3	3.4	3.0	2.7	2.2	5.0	2.8
Total population	66.8	67.1	67.1	5.4	4.9	4.5	2.1	2.1	1.3

Memorandum:

							Q4/Q4 growth[1]		
Usual weekly earnings of wage and salary workers									
10th percentile							n.a.	3.8	10.9
Median							n.a.	2.4	11.9
90th percentile							n.a.	5.2	4.7

	Average over period		
Share of unemployed over 26 weeks	17.4	15.8	14.1
Average duration of unemployment (weeks)	16.7	15.8	14.5
Share of employed part time for economic reasons	3.4	3.1	2.8

1. Q4/Q4 figures for 1998 may be misleading. Comparable figures from 1997:Q3 to 1998:Q3 were 5.8, 4.2 and 4.8 per cent respectively for the 10th, 50th and 90th percentiles, still showing a relative improvement at the bottom end of the distribution.
Source: Bureau of Labor Statistics.

In accordance with one of the major recommendations of the *Jobs Strategy*, the federal and state governments have implemented numerous reforms to reduce work disincentives for the poor, as noted above. A range of initiatives are underway in training, child care and health that should boost work incentives (Table 13). Important problems, however, remain in two key areas – health and education – that were identified by the *Jobs Strategy*. With respect to health, the 1994 *Survey* noted that a comprehensive overhaul of the sector was needed, predicting that otherwise, the inequality in access to care would worsen. Since then, only small measures have been implemented. As a result, working poor adults continue to be inadequately served, and there is evidence that access is worsening. As noted in the 1992 *Survey*, some additional regulation of private insurance markets may be needed. In particular, rules to ensure that consumers have more information when they choose health plans are required to make this market work better, and a timely mechanism to resolve disputes between

Table 13. **Implementing the OECD *Jobs Strategy* – an overview of recent progress**

Proposal	Action	Assessment/recommendation
I. Reform unemployment and related benefits system		
Reduce work disincentives for the poor	States have increased earnings disregards for TANF recipients. Welfare programme has work requirements, time limits and sanctions for non-compliance.	States should take advantage of the variation across states to find out which programmes and rules work the best and rework programmes accordingly.
Increase access to training for the poor	The federal government has overhauled its training programmes. States have increased money to move people off of welfare.	As above, states need to learn from the various programmes of other states. There is a question of whether states can maintain spending levels in lean times.
Increase access to child care for the poor	The federal budget adds money for child care. States have also boosted programmes.	As above, there is a question of whether the states will be able to keep up their support for child care if the economy turns down.
Increase access to health insurance for the poor	The CHIPS programme boosts health care for children significantly.	New programmes for children have strengthened services to them, but health care access is still inadequate for adults.
Reduce work disincentives for the disabled	1997 Balanced Budget Act creates state Medicaid waiver programme to allow the disabled to earn more while keeping benefits. Oregon has recieved a waiver to start to a programme.	Restrictions and phaseouts for programmes for the disabled create significant work disincentives. Various federal programmes need to be made consistent. Further reform may be needed.
Expand the Earned Income Tax Credit, rather than raise the minimum wage	None.	The EITC could be extended to families without children, and the phaseouts broadened a bit to lower marginal tax rates. The 1996 increase in the minimum wage probably did not have a big impact on employment, but further increases should not be contemplated at this time.
Increase eligibility for unemployment benefits	None.	The work experience requirement is too restrictive; all those with significant labour force attachment should have access to such benefits.

Table 13. **Implementing the OECD *Jobs Strategy* – an overview of recent progress** *(cont.)*

Proposal	Action	Assessment/recommendation
II. Improve labour force skills and competencies		
Promote curriculum or output standards for primary and secondary schools	The Goals 2000 programme has been authorised for another year, and state governments are developing their own programmes.	Improved performance by students, especially in secondary schools is needed.
Provide more equitable financing of school districts	Some states have reformulated their funding systems, but eighteen state courts have found their systems unconstitutional. The Administration's programme for 100 000 new teachers has begun.	State governments need to take an active role to make financing more equitable instead of fighting lawsuits. Federal initiatives need to be broadened to make financing across states more equitable.
Improve urban school systems	There is additional federal funding for public charter schools to increase their growth, along with significant state interest. There are also small experiments with school vouchers and other alternatives. School vouchers for religious schools appear to be legal to the courts.	The expansion of public charter schools is an important step. The other limited programmes need to be evaluated and expanded.
Increase information about the quality of programmes provided by community colleges and technical institutes	The federal aid programme for vocational schools has been overhauled and extended.	Performance and quality of community colleges and technical schools need to be made more widely known.

Source: OECD.

managed care providers and beneficiaries would be useful. Lawmakers, however, need to recognise that limiting services often yields efficiency gains. For instance, even though they may be unpopular, requiring a referral from a general practitioner before a patient can see a specialist lowers costs.[40] As for education, progress so far has been limited. Federal efforts to date have been minor because education has traditionally been the province of local governments. Further initiatives to improve the equality of education spending both within states and between states seem called for. Federal effort here is important as two-thirds of spending inequality among school districts is from differences across states.[41]

Finally, there are some areas where reforms are needed. The federal government should re-examine its programmes for the disabled to lower the work disincentives and also unify the disparate schemes to make them consistent. The effect of the programme on labour supply remains a controversial subject within the literature, which provides a wide range of estimated supply elasticities. Nonetheless, one study suggests efficiency gains could be realised by converting this programme to an income subsidy scheme.[42] As to aiding the working poor, the minimum wage appears too blunt a policy instrument.[43] It would be better to expand the Earned Income Tax Credit, which is a programme that has proved to be successful in lifting qualifying families with children out of poverty.[44]

Financial markets

Financial markets are evolving rapidly in the United States. New financial products, such as commercial loan-backed securities, are being developed. In the past five years, over-the-counter trading of derivatives has skyrocketed; the notional value of outstanding derivatives is estimated to be $30 trillion, with perhaps $1 trillion of capital at some risk.[45] The share of new credit extended by deposit institutions has fallen from 35 per cent in the mid-1980s to only 15 per cent in 1998. Partially in response to this, the banking sector has started to consolidate, with the number of banks falling by almost one-third. Indeed, since the end of 1996, several large commercial banks have merged to reduce costs. Others have purchased or merged with investment banks and other financial services companies to expand their business. Technical innovations in computing and communications, globalisation, and some regulatory reform – notably a relaxation of prohibitions on inter-state banking – help explain this evolution.

Despite some reforms, the basic laws that establish the regulatory framework of the financial sector have not kept pace with private-sector developments. Some of the most important laws in this regard date back to the Great Depression when the financial environment and range of products were simpler. Then, markets were distinct, and one could tailor regulations to particular institutions to meet policy goals. Now, distinctions among markets have blurred, and this same regulatory framework now inhibits market development and competition. The next two subsections detail these issues with respect to deposit institutions and derivatives trading. The last discusses recent developments in the securities market.

Deposit institutions

Unlike most other OECD countries, associations between banks and other financial institutions are severely restricted. Under the 1933 Glass-Steagall Act and the 1956 Bank Holding Company Act, banking organisations, including bank holding companies, can only engage in a subset of activities such as investment banking to a limited extent. Insurance underwriting is severely limited, and non-financial activities are prohibited. The same acts prohibit other financial and non-financial firms from controlling banks. The acts also make certain distinctions[46] between nationally chartered banks, which are regulated by the Office of the Comptroller of the Currency (OCC) in the Department of the Treasury and state-chartered banks, which are regulated by the Federal Reserve, the Federal Deposit Insurance Corporation and the states.[47]

With the evolution of financial markets, there appears to be a broad consensus that new legislation should reduce these Glass-Steagall barriers. Some analysts argue that financial firms could realise significant efficiency gains through "one-stop shopping" and the sharing of fixed costs. Competition could increase as regulatory barriers between isolated institutions fall. By reducing these barriers that separate various types of institutions, reform of financial regulation can reduce the advantages that a subset of institutions now enjoys. High lobbying expenditures suggest that rents from these advantages are large. Reducing inefficiencies in the banking sector could cut costs up to 20 per cent, if all inefficiencies are removed and those in the life insurance industry could be halved.[48] Moreover, diversifying bank earnings could reduce the probability of default and its associated social costs, rendering the system safer.[49] Consumers would benefit from lower costs and increased product diversity through increased competition among previously segregated portions of the financial services industry.

Regulators have allowed an expansion of banking activities, but because their authority is limited, this has resulted in a patchwork of exemptions that apply to specific institutions. Based on an interpretation of what is meant in Section 20 of the Glass-Steagall Act by "principally engaged" in securities, the Federal Reserve has permitted bank holding companies to own securities firms that provide a limited proportion of their revenues from underwriting and dealing in so-called ineligible securities. In December 1996, it raised that limit to 25 per cent. Consequently, in the past couple of years several banks have expanded the operations of their Section 20 affiliates or purchased securities firms. The largest deal occurred in April 1998 when Citibank and Travelers announced a merger valued at $83 billion. Most of Travelers' securities underwriting operations could fit under Section 20 regulations, but unless Congress amends the Bank Holding Company Act limitations on banking and insurance underwriting affiliation, Citigroup will have to sell Travelers' insurance underwriting business. The OCC also announced new regulations designed to expand the activities of the operating subsidiaries of the nationally chartered banks it regulates. By statute, such banks cannot own any subsidiaries engaged in activities prohibited to the bank itself.[50] However, in November 1996, the OCC eased its interpretation of the statute to allow subsidiaries to engage in activities closely related to banking, though this may be challenged in the courts.

The Glass-Steagall prohibitions do not apply to savings and loans and savings banks, which are depository institutions that operate under a different charter than commercial banks and are regulated by the Office of Thrift Supervision of the Department of Treasury. Instead, the Savings and Loan Holding Company Act similarly circumscribes their operations. Through a legislative loophole, however, savings and loans that are the only such subsidiary of a holding company – so called "unitary thrifts" – may affiliate with other financial and non-financial firms. As a result, in the past year the Office of Thrift Supervision has approved applications for unitary thrifts from several large insurance companies, as well as some non-financial firms. The number of charters is growing rapidly. At the beginning of 1998, there were 102 unitary thrifts engaged in non-banking activities, holding about one-quarter of all thrift assets.[51]

Recently, policymakers have proposed two competing plans to expand the activities of banking institutions. In 1997, the Department of Treasury proposed allowing banks to provide other financial services through bank subsidiaries as well as holding company affiliates,[52] but with additional safeguards that also apply to affiliates. The Federal Reserve objects to this plan. A second proposal, recently embodied in a bill, H.R.10 and opposed by the Treasury Department, would allow such activities only in affiliates through a common holding company while eliminating previous Section 20 limits. This bill passed the House in 1998 but was not taken up by the full Senate. This difference in corporate structure has generated strong debate between proponents of the two plans, as each side suggests their proposal is superior in preserving the safety of the deposit insurance fund and financial system, preventing an inappropriate extension of the federal safety net and improving efficiency in the financial sector. In practice, the differences between the two structures are small (Annex II discusses these issues in greater detail). There are, however, other aspects of the two plans that some have claimed explain the controversy. Under current law, the Federal Reserve regulates all bank holding companies, and so the House bill would enhance its authority. Under the Treasury proposal, banks would not need to set up holding companies, and therefore, more banks could apply for national charters under the purview of the OCC. Some analysts suggest that the controversy is simply a "turf war" between two regulators. In addition, under the Community Reinvestment Act, the assets of bank subsidiaries, but not of holding company affiliates, may be included in estimating a bank 's credit responsibilities to its community.[53] Controversies over this Act were so strong that some legislators reject other bills if they affect the scope of the Act contrary to their preferences.

Plans to reduce the Glass-Steagall and other barriers, however, do not extend to rationalising other aspects of the regulatory framework. Indeed, one piece of legislation increased the advantages enjoyed by credit unions. These deposit institutions compete with banks and thrifts for deposits and loans. While their charter circumscribes their activities even more than the thrift charter does for savings and loans, credit unions do not pay taxes on retained earnings because they are conceptually member-owned, not-for-profit firms. Such a tax exemption gives them a cost-of-capital advantage over other lenders, although as member-owned co-operatives, they do not issue common stock. The Supreme Court ruled in February 1998 that under existing law, membership in a credit union must be restricted to those with a common bond through occupation, association or neighbourhood. This would have restricted the size of credit unions. While most credit unions are small, a few are large. For instance, the John Deere Community Credit Union is bigger than 90 per cent of all commercial banks. The President signed legislation in August overturning the decision by allowing multiple common-bond associations. The same act included safety and soundness reforms – including net worth requirements and the establishment of a prompt corrective action system. In addition, some proposals recently considered by Congress would extend the activities and membership of the Home Loan Bank System. As government-sponsored enterprises, these institutions issue debt securities to finance investment activities unrelated to their original purpose of enhancing home finance. These Home Loan Banks earn security income for its shareholders, which are currently thrifts and commercial banks. Such debt, although not explicitly guaranteed by the Federal government, benefits from a market perception that the latter will prevent the failure of its sponsored enterprises. In the 1980s the government did rescue the Farm Credit System. This market perception operates to the disadvantage of the deposit insurance funds and taxpayers because it diminishes the role of market discipline in curbing risk taking.[54]

Derivatives

In order to protect farmers and small investors and to prohibit the manipulation of agricultural markets, Congress passed the main legislation governing derivatives, the Commodity Exchange Act, in 1936. This Act requires all futures and futures-like instruments to be traded on a (heavily) regulated exchange, overseen since 1974 by the Commodity Futures Trading Commission (CFTC). During the 1980s financial derivatives became increasingly traded, sometimes outside of a regulated exchange. In order to allow the over-the-counter market (OTC) in derivatives to develop, the Congress instructed the CFTC in 1992 to exempt some of them from the exchange-traded requirement of the Commodity Exchange Act. The CFTC subsequently issued such exemptions in its Part 35 rule that created a safe harbour for swap and hybrid contracts. The requirements for swaps to be legally traded over the counter are:

1. The swaps must not be part of a fungible class of instruments that are standardised as to their material economic terms;
2. The creditworthiness of the counterparties must be a material consideration in entering into and determining the terms of the contract;
3. The trade must not be executed through a multilateral execution facility such as an exchange;
4. Both counterparties must be "appropriate persons", *i.e.* institutions or wealthy individuals.

Because the Congress relied on the CFTC to squeeze the over-the-counter market into the existing regulatory framework, instead of modernising the Commodity Exchange Act, two problems have emerged that are now worsening. First, the Congress never firmly established whether swaps and hybrids qualify as futures under the Act. It appears that market participants believe that these contracts are not futures, while the CFTC seems to have always maintained that many of these instruments were subject to the Commodity Exchange Act. The problem is that if the swaps are futures, then those written on non-exempt securities could be deemed illegal because the CFTC does not have the authority to exempt futures contracts from the provisions of the Commodity Exchange Act governing futures contracts on individual securities and narrowly defined securities indices. As an illegal contract, any trader could challenge it in court as unenforceable, which has happened in the past.[55] There is some suggestion that in response to this legal uncertainty, traders are moving activities outside the country, although the CFTC denies it.[56] Some have posited that the United States permanently lost some of the market in exchange rate contracts to London because of a similar ambiguity.

The issue came to a head in May 1998 when the CFTC issued a concept release, asking for comment on whether the Commission's current exemption on swaps and hybrids should be continued and whether the Commission should regulate them. While the release made no explicit recommendations and did not change any existing regulations, many market participants interpreted it as a precursor to regulation of these instruments and as a declaration that the swaps were futures subject to the Commodity Exchange Act. Shortly afterwards, the

Secretary of the Treasury, the Chairman of the Board of Governors of the Federal Reserve and the Chairman of the Securities Exchange Commission issued a joint statement questioning whether the CFTC had authority to regulate the OTC market and expressing concern about the possible implications of the concept release on the legal status of some OTC derivatives. As part of its Omnibus Budget Act, the Congress enjoined the CFTC from issuing any new regulations except in emergencies, and it tried to fix the legal status of existing swaps, but only through 30 May 1999.

The second problem that has developed is that the sharp division between the OTC market, where all any exchange-like characteristics are prohibited, and the existing heavily regulated exchanges, is retarding the natural evolution of the derivatives market. Some swaps are becoming more standard. A London clearinghouse has made an application to start clearing some instruments, while other firms have also expressed an interest. The CFTC granted it limited authority in early 1999. A clearinghouse might have been beneficial in monitoring Long-Term Capital Management whose failure in the autumn of 1998 posed the potential for serious disruption of financial markets (Box 5). There is also some interest in trading these derivative contracts electronically. Under the current regulatory framework, some of these developments are illegal outside regulated exchanges.

With these regulatory imbalances between the organised exchanges and the OTC market leading to the latter gaining market share, there have been renewed calls by the exchanges themselves for a reduction in regulation. They argue that differences in regulatory burdens among the existing exchanges, the over-the-counter market and foreign markets have tilted the competitive field, leading to a loss of business.[57] They note that many of the markets for the financial securities that underpin most financial-based derivatives are too large and liquid to be subject to the same potential for manipulation as agricultural markets. One solution is to allow markets for "professional traders" that would mimic the existing over-the-counter market but with additional features of an organised exchange. Such "ProMarkets" were an element of legislation that a Congressional committee considered in 1997.[58] The CFTC needs re-authorisation by the year 2000, so the Congress may take up a broad review of the Commodity Exchange Act then.

There was a further conflict between regulators over *accounting standards for derivatives*. In June 1997 the Financial Accounting Standards Board, a private entity whose standards are used in legislation and regulations, issued its final standards for accounting for derivatives and hedging that come into effect at the beginning of the first fiscal year after June 1999. They require firms to book their holdings on their balance sheet at fair values. If the firm uses the instrument to hedge risk, accumulated gains or losses would not affect profits until the hedge had

Box 5. Long-Term Capital Management

Long-Term Capital Management (LTCM) is a large hedge fund created in 1994 by a team of highly reputed financial experts. Its basic portfolio strategy was to buy and simultaneously short a range of securities whose prices were fundamentally related but had diverged. As such, the fund was "market neutral" in the sense that the level of interest rates was nearly irrelevant to its expected returns. However, the fund was still practising a risky strategy; it had large positions that would only be profitable if the prices of various securities converged. Because of increasing competition from securities houses and banks, LTCM had to be highly leveraged to generate returns in excess of 40 per cent in 1995 and 1996. Normal leverage ratios were about 25 to 1, with ratios moving above 50 to 1 after the fund started experiencing significant losses.

While the fund's performance in the first half of 1998 was poor, Russia's effective default in August precipitated LTCM's collapse. Unlike many other funds, LTCM had not heavily invested in Russian paper, but the default engendered a general reassessment of risks in the market (see Chapter II). Spreads between securities widened, where LTCM needed them to narrow to make profits. It lost $1.8 billion in August reducing its capital to $2.3 billion. By mid-September its capital base was only $600 million, supporting $80 billion of assets, and LTCM's clearing agent said that it would stop processing its trades if its account fell below $500 million.

The threat of LTCM's immediate demise worried the New York Federal Reserve Bank and LTCM's major creditors for two reasons. *First*, disentangling LTCM with its myriad of lenders in a formal bankruptcy proceeding would have been very costly and possibly damaging to the lenders and to the markets. *Second*, and more importantly, in a default, the lending banks would have been able to net and close out positions with LTCM and may have had recourse to its collateral. The banks would then have taken on derivative positions similar to the ones they had closed out and would have had to sell collateral, if they legally could, to avoid holding the same exposure. The markets at the time, however, were fragile, and dumping a large amount of securities could have lead to severe price movements. The sheer size of LTCM was a problem; the notional value of its derivatives was $1 trillion. Moreover, it held extremely large positions in some thin markets. In one derivative, it had four hundred days of trading volume.

Under the encouragement of the New York Federal Reserve, fourteen banks agreed to inject $3.6 billion into LTCM in exchange for a new issue of shares amounting to a little over 90 per cent of its existing equity. LTCM had refused a last minute offer from a separate group of investors who offered $4 billion for the whole portfolio. No taxpayer money was involved. Eleven banks each put up $300 million with three others injecting smaller amounts, but LTCM's clearing agent declined to participate, arguing it already was exposed for $500 million. As it turned out with spreads between different classes of bonds narrowing once again and the stock market rallying to an all time high, it appears that this rescue has been a profitable investment for the banks.

A review of the events surrounding LTCM suggests four lessons for the regulation of highly leveraged firms:

1. *Bank supervisors need to be more vigilant in ensuring banks perform adequate credit-risk assessments.* Even though a 1994 Federal Reserve supervisory letter had stressed that banks should analyse counterparties such as hedge funds, banks were not

(continued on next page)

(continued)

    aware of LTCM's risk position (McDonough, 1998). Both the OCC and the Fed-
    eral Reserve have since issued letters to their bank supervisors instructing
    them to step up their monitoring of loans to hedge funds.
 2. *Regulations and laws should not discourage market mechanisms such as clearinghouses to
    develop in the OTC market.* A clearinghouse would have had better information on
    LTCM's positions generally and would have prevented it from amassing huge
    positions in specific securities (Born, 1998b). As its clearing agent, Bear Stearns
    had the best information on the Fund's position and put early pressure on it.
 3. *Risk assessment procedures need improvement in two ways.* Banks need to account for
    potential future exposure. Often they calculate their value at risk over short horizons
    such as a couple of weeks, but this does not account for delays that can occur
    as they try to unwind positions. More generally, banks do not account for
    problems that can arise if huge positions need to be unwound simultaneously.
    In addition, all firms need to *stress test* their portfolios. The founder of LTCM
    called August and September "a ten-sigma event", implying that it had effec-
    tively a zero probability. The standard errors of estimated probabilities of
    events that are rarely seen are large. Estimated covariances in "good times"
    may not be a useful guide for what can happen in "bad times". Moreover,
    market evolution may have made historical observations less meaningful.
 4. *Nevertheless, the LTCM experience does not necessarily imply that the OTC market and
    hedge funds need additional regulation.* LTCM was a special case. No other firm
    combined its size, leverage and large positions in specific markets. Moreover,
    the intervention worked well. No public money was involved, and a disorderly
    bankruptcy was avoided. No bad precedent was set; arrangements among
    creditors in lieu of formal proceedings are common. No problems of moral
    hazard were created. Lenders lost money, and investors were nearly wiped out.
    Some partners are reportedly bankrupt.

---

unwound, presumably with little net impact. If, instead, the instrument is regarded as a speculative derivative, the firm must book price changes as net income as they accrue. The Board defines an instrument as a hedge and not speculative if it is "highly effective in achieving offsetting changes in fair value or cash flows". The spectre of more volatile earnings has led many financial institutions to argue against the new rule. The Chairman of the Federal Reserve testified that the rule could significantly curtail hedging. On the other hand, the Securities and Exchange Commission supports it.

Securities

New York Stock Exchange officials have modified some operating rules. The Congress dropped its legislation requiring *pricing stocks in decimals* rather than eighths after the exchange announced in June 1997 that it would begin to implement it voluntarily when systems were in place. Under similar concerns, it modified its *circuit-breaker rules*. Following the change, a 10 per cent drop in the Dow Jones Industrial Average triggers a temporary trading halt, while a 20 per cent drop institutes a longer stoppage, perhaps for the day depending on the timing. A 30 per cent drop ends trading for the day regardless of when it happens.[59] Previously, the exchange set the circuit-breaker thresholds in points. These circuit breaker rules were first instituted in the aftermath of the 1987 stock market crash but were applied only once when the index fell 554 points, or 7.2 per cent, in October 1997. Some controversy among regulators remains, however, as to whether these trading halts serve a useful purpose. Likewise, at the urging of the President's Working Group on Financial Markets, the New York Stock Exchange raised its thresholds before collars are applied on programmed arbitrage trades involving stocks and stock futures in the S&P 500. Previously, limits on such trades were applied when the Dow Jones Industrial Average moved 50 points in either direction. When the rule was originally implemented, 50 points represented $2^{1}/_{2}$ per cent of the value of the index. Now 50 points represent about $^{1}/_{2}$ per cent, and the collars were applied almost daily. The SEC has approved the new rule that sets the thresholds at 2 per cent of the value of the index at the end of the previous quarter, but it has requested that the exchange reconsider whether such rules are needed at all.

In November 1998, the President signed legislation closing a loophole in a 1995 Act on *shareholder lawsuits*. The 1995 Act increased the standards for class action lawsuits alleging securities fraud in federal courts. The Act, however, did not apply to state courts. The new measure moves all such suits involving 50 or more parties to federal court, and it allows 50 or more separate cases filed in the same state court involving a similar complaint to be consolidated and moved to the federal courts.

Concluding remarks

To cope with the rapid changes in the financial industry, the regulatory framework needs to be updated. A useful first step would be to reduce the remaining Glass-Steagall barriers consistent with maintaining the integrity of the financial system. Given the various loopholes, exemptions, grandfather clauses, and regulatory rulings, such reform would be less of a change than some opponents suggest. Nonetheless, by removing these walls, financial institutions would better compete on their merits and no single type of institution would be favoured. The choice of regulatory structure – that is bank holding companies or subsidiaries of banks – is worth debating, but this debate should not continue indefinitely. The competing plans, as embodied by H.R.10 and the Department of Treasury appear to have different effects in only limited circumstances. The Congress could move the debate along by separating explicitly through legislation consideration of the regulatory structure from ancillary issues such as responsibilities of different regulatory agencies and the breadth of the Community Reinvestment Act. For instance, the Congress could consider having the Federal Reserve and the OCC share oversight over all banks, folding the national and state charters into one. It can look to the Federal Trade Commission and the Department of Justice as a model of inter-agency co-operation.

The Congress could consider going further in rationalising the regulation of deposit institutions. Currently, there are five different types of institutions that are regulated by four different federal agencies as well as state governments. Congress could revoke the thrift charter, as previous legislation on the insurance funds assumed would happen, and following the suggestion of the Government Accounting Office, it could merge the Office of Thrift Supervision and the FDIC's oversight of state-chartered non-member banks into the OCC.[60] Indeed, other major OECD countries have at most two regulators. Congress could go even further in levelling the playing field by revoking the credit union charter, or at least its tax exemption, while at the same time removing offsetting restrictions on credit union assets. With reform of Glass-Steagall, there would be little need to continue the privileges that unitary thrift charters and non-bank banks continue to enjoy.[61] In addition, the Congress should consider reducing the scope of the Home Loan Banks – not expanding it.

Policymakers also need to clarify the regulatory framework for derivatives, but the case for substantial regulation of the OTC market is weak. Indeed, there is a stronger case that new laws should provide regulatory relief to the organised exchanges. The current division between the OTC market and the current exchanges is impeding the development of important institutions such as clear-inghouses in derivatives trading. State and federal consumer protections and anti-fraud provisions appear adequate to prevent the routine occurrence of the few high-profile cases already seen. There are some tentative lessons one can draw from Long-Term Capital Management (Box 5), but they would seem to apply more to bank regulators than to policy towards hedge funds and the over-the-counter market.

Product markets

As indicated in the OECD *Survey on Regulatory Reform in the United States*, the hallmark of US economic regulation is its reliance on competition. In this regard, antitrust authorities have increased their level of activity. It appears that a new policy is evolving with greater attention paid to those industries, such as information technology and communications, where so-called "network effects" can inhibit competition. In the aftermath of the Telecommunications Act of 1996, regulators have been struggling to introduce competition in local phone markets, and while there has been some progress, results to date have been disappointing for residential customers. Expectations of immediate progress, however, may have been unfairly high; as technology evolves and communications markets converge, competition will normally increase. Indeed in this regard, policy makers are developing policies for high-speed Internet access where some of the same issues as local phone service arise. Federal-level measures to introduce competition in the electricity market have been lagging, but significant reforms have been introduced by state governments.

Antitrust policy

Antitrust enforcement activity has swelled in the past few years. In FY 1998, the Department of Justice (DoJ) collected $244 million in criminal fines, 15 per cent above the previous year.[62] The Federal Trade Commission (FTC) instituted thirteen enforcement actions challenging anti-competitive conduct, the highest number in a decade. Requests by the authorities for greater detail on merger filings,[63] which is the first step in consideration of a government challenge, rose 42 per cent in the past decade, although much of this is the result of a surge in mergers (Figure 21). They also have pursued a number of high-profile cases. Defence contractors Lockheed-Martin and Northrop Grumman dropped a proposed $9½ billion merger after a DoJ challenge, perhaps slowing recent

Figure 21. **Requests for additional information and reported mergers**

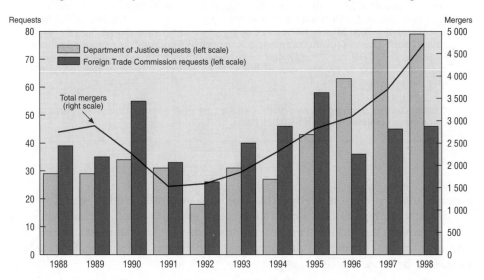

Source: FTC 1997 and 1998, Annual Report to Congress, Hart-Scott-Rodine Act.

Box 6.   United States of America v. Microsoft Corporation

In May 1998 the Department of Justice (DoJ) along with the Attorneys General from twenty states and the District of Columbia filed suit in federal court alleging anticompetitive abuses.* Microsoft denies the charge that it sought to illegally divide the browser market with Netscape in 1995. In response to other allegations, Microsoft argues that it reserves the right to make technical decisions without interference and that it has the right to compete forcefully in a dynamic market. It disputes claims that its actions were targeted to damage its rivals.

Microsoft can point to certain legal precedents in its favour on the argument involving technological advancement. In a court brief, it notes several cases where the courts have apparently declined to become involved in arguments of whether certain technical features were justified or whether they were meant to damage rivals. An Appeals Court reversed a lower court's preliminary injunction and ruled that Microsoft's bundling of its Internet Explorer browser with Windows appeared unlikely to violate the 1995 consent decree. The states later dropped a charge involving Microsoft's office suite.

On its various claims of "competing hard", however, Microsoft appears to be on less firm ground. According to case law, dominant firms must step lightly where firms with little market power can act more aggressively. In court proceedings, the burden of proof can shift to the dominant firm to defend its actions and show they were not predatory.

Thus, a good deal of the case hinges on whether Microsoft's market position qualifies as monopoly power. Microsoft controls 90 per cent of the market of personal computer operating systems, but a high market share does not qualify as market power if potential competition exists to check its exercise. Hence, the DoJ emphasises "network effects" (Box 7) as a justification for its argument that high barriers to entry exist and potential competition is minimal. Microsoft counters with the claim that Sun's computer language Java could weaken network effects specific to the use of Windows and thereby reduce Microsoft's market power. As a result, the charge that Microsoft abused Sun's Java to prevent competition is especially important. In a separate private litigation, a US District Court judge in November issued a preliminary injunction ordering Microsoft to rewrite parts of Windows 98 and other programmes to comply with Sun's version of Java.

---

* South Carolina dropped its participation in the case after America Online and Netscape announced their merger in November 1998.

consolidation in that industry. The DoJ also recently filed a suit to block Northwest's attempt to buy a controlling share in Continental Airlines. While the FTC approved the British Petroleum-Amoco merger, its chairman noted that approval for other mergers, presumably including the announced Exxon-Mobil deal, may be more difficult.

Beyond increased monitoring, both the DoJ and FTC see the need to develop a body of case law and doctrine for the "age of globalisation, deregulation, and technological change".[64] In the international arena, the United States signed a deal with the European Union in June 1998 to strengthen collaboration in international antitrust enforcement. Despite the well-publicised differences over the Boeing-McDonnell Douglas merger, co-operation remains high over such cases as the American Airlines/British Airways alliance and a proposed merger between two large accounting firms. Globalisation is exerting a growing influence on US antitrust enforcement policy. In November 1997, the Antitrust Division of the US Department of Justice formed an International Competition Committee with a two-year mandate to enhance international co-operation among competition agencies. So far, it has concentrated on improving enforcement against international cartels, and on facilitating international co-operation in the review of cross-border mergers. Following on the 1996 Archer Daniels Midlands case, US and EU authorities also agreed to co-operate on cases involving illegal international cartels. Now one-quarter of combined merger and criminal grand jury investigations have international aspects.

Greatest attention has been paid to the high-tech sector, where the DoJ has instituted a high-profile case against Microsoft (Box 6). The FTC had a more narrow complaint against Intel, but the parties settled the case before proceedings began. The authorities believe certain industries in the high-tech sector are characterised by significant "network externalities" (Box 7), which can enable a firm to enjoy a dominant position at a crucial point in the market. The DoJ also sees the possibility of network externalities in less technologically demanding sectors, as the recent suit against Visa and MasterCard attests.

Telecommunications

Some analysts have expressed disappointment over the pace of reform in local phone service after the 1996 Telecommunications Act. A recent study found that consumer cable and in-state long distant rates have risen since passage of the Act, while local rates have not come down.[65] The market shares of the regional bell operating companies[66] (RBOCs) and other incumbent local exchanges remain high and are not falling as fast as the share of AT&T did in the long-distance market after the 1984 divestiture (Figure 22). The RBOCs have used legal action in an attempt to delay implementation of a clause of the Act that requires them to satisfactorily open up their local markets before they can offer long distance services, but they eventually lost.[67] The Federal Communications Commission (FCC) has used this clause to deny the four applications of the RBOCs to enter the long distance market in particular states, finding in each case that they had not sufficiently opened their local markets. Some local operators, along with state regulators, also challenged the FCC's pricing guidelines on unbundled services as an infringement on the rights of the states, but they too lost on appeal.[68] In any case, most states have adopted requirements similar to those of the FCC.

Box 7.   Network effects

Network effects arise in a market when a customer's demand for a product is positively related to the consumption of others due to either technological constraints or market dynamics.* Katz and Shapiro (1994) make a useful distinction between *communication networks* and *hardware/software systems*. In communications networks the consumption of others directly affects a consumer's demand. For instance, if only one consumer owns a fax machine, the machine is useless, but as others buy them, the value of the existing fax machine rises. Such cases generate *network externalities* as the public value of another consumer owning a fax machine is higher than the private value because the consumer does not take into account the impact the purchase has on the value of other fax machines. In hardware/software systems, a consumer's value of the good is not directly affected by the consumption of others. As the *installed base* of equipment grows, innovation of complementary products may accelerate, raising the value of the existing product. For example, as more people buy a new computer, more software may become available. In both systems expectations of the future size of the installed base are an important component of industry dynamics. As such, monopolists may try to forestall entry by pre-announcing future products; in the software industry this is known as *vapourware*. In addition, competition between networks can be unstable. Such markets may exhibit *path dependence* where the detailed history of the market determines its outcome. At an extreme, there can be *tipping* where one network comes to dominate the market and competing networks disappear. Some analysts point to the disappearance of the BetaMax video recording system in favour of VHS as an example.

Antitrust authorities often point to network effects as a large barrier to entry. Firms trying to compete may have to build a whole new communications network, which can be expensive and risky because consumers may be reluctant to be the first to join as they are *locked in* to the old network. Firms may also have to convince consumers that buying the "hardware" is worthwhile as a lot of "software" will become available. At an extreme a firm may have to develop both. Firms that control *network standards* can exploit them at the expense of competitors.

Antitrust authorities, however, need to be mindful that while some network effects may exist, proving that the market is not *contestable* requires a detailed examination. For instance, such effects may be important on a small scale, but once a *critical mass* is reached, additional increases to the installed base have little effect on valuations and dynamics (Liebowitz and Margolis, 1994). Encouraging consumers to switch networks may be difficult, but it should be noted that they sell old durable goods in favour of newer, better ones all the time. Networks have also been overtaken in the market. Although Beta came first, VHS came to dominate (Lopatka, 1995). Indeed, antitrust officials have recognised this point. They sought divestiture of MCI's Internet backbone business to preserve competition in a market that can support several networks, and they are working to introduce competition in local phone markets, which some had previously considered natural monopolies.

---

* This is in contrast to other models that generate a positive relationship. With information cascades, a consumer demands a product after seeing others consuming it because she believes that others may know something she does not. With bandwagon effects or fads, a consumer buys a product because it is fashionable. In both of these models, expected future consumption rates are unimportant.

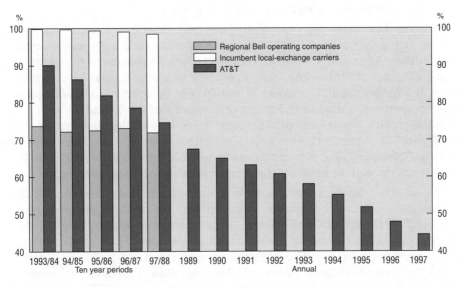

Figure 22.   **Market share of dominant telephone companies**

Legend:
- Regional Bell operating companies
- Incumbent local-exchange carriers
- AT&T

Source: FCC Trends in Telephone Service (1998) and Telecommunications Industry Revenue, 1997.

Interconnecting operations support systems, which track all of the information necessary to operate a phone company, has involved difficult modifications to procedures and computer systems. The problem of allowing customers to keep their phone numbers when they switch providers has proved difficult to resolve as a long-run solution could cost $1 billion a year. Converting implicit subsidies to an explicit, competitively neutral fund to pay for universal phone access, as required by the Act, has also been troublesome.

Nonetheless, progress in opening local markets, although slow, has been made and should accelerate in the future. When completed, deregulation could result in gains of $40-60 billion.[69] The revenue of firms currently competing with the incumbents has grown 73 per cent at an annual rate in the past four years, compared with a 4¼ per cent for the incumbents. As these competitors become stronger through internal expansion or mergers, their market share should grow faster.[70] While residential consumers have not seen many effects to date, competition has increased for high-end business users.[71] The FCC has also used its powers to keep the process moving. When approving the merger of NYNEX and Bell Atlantic, it required that the firm accede to the FCC's interpretation of specific market opening provisions of the Act. Power, satellite, cable and wireless communications companies are beginning to offer high-speed Internet access service in certain cities. In the future they will compete with phone companies in providing a package that includes local phone service.

The FCC must soon formulate rules on high-speed Internet access that involve similar issues that the FCC faced in opening local telephone service to competition. Regional telephone companies are implementing a technology called a digital subscriber line that can provide broadband services over existing wires. It appears the FCC is going to require the companies to resell access to their competitors at discounted prices or to move the services to an arms-length subsidiary. With the review of the recent telephone-cable operator merger of AT&T and TCI, America Online, an on-line Internet service provider, requested that the FCC order TCI to provide access to its cable lines at wholesale prices. The FCC chose, instead, to approve the merger without requiring such access.

In other developments, some local operators have applied to the FCC for permission to merge.[72] Approval, however, may be difficult because the FCC announced in the NYNEX-Bell Atlantic merger that future applications will meet a stricter test. As the number of RBOCs dwindles, the loss of potential competition and innovation increases. The FCC did approve the merger of the second and fourth largest long-distance companies, MCI and WorldCom, given that the companies had already agreed to divest all of MCI's Internet business to secure the approval of the DoJ and the EU's Directorate-General IV. AT&T and British Telecom also have announced that they are forming a joint venture to provide global services to multinational corporations.

Electricity

As of the end of 1998, eighteen states had passed legislation or issued regulations to restructure electricity markets (Table 14). Pilot programmes in retail

Table 14. **State electricity usage and costs by status of deregulation activity[1]**

	Number of States	Per cent consumption	Average price (cents/kwhr)
Legislated reforms[2]	13	25.6	8.2
Regulatory orders[3]	5	11.5	9.2
Ongoing investigations	31	57.1	5.8
None[4]	2	5.8	7.2
Total	51	100.0	6.9

1. As of 1 November 1998 for number of states, 1996 for consumption and prices. The table includes the fifty States and the District of Columbia.
2. Arizona, California, Connecticut, Illinois, Maine, Massachusetts, Montana, Nevada, New Hampshire, Oklahoma, Pennsylvania, Rhode Island and Virginia.
3. Maryland, Michigan, New Jersey, New York and Vermont.
4. Florida and South Dakota.
Source: Energy Information Administration.

competition exist in California, Massachussetts, Montana, Pennsylvania and Rhode Island. High prices represented the main impetus for reform in these states, mostly in the Northeast and the West, where costs were on average 19 per cent more in 1996 than in the country as a whole. The most notable state to restructure is California, which was scheduled to introduce retail competition at the beginning of 1998 but delayed it until the end of March in order to fix a pricing system. Nonetheless, even though only 1 per cent of customers had switched their supplier, a broad range of interests maintains that the process is working and that households have seen a 10 per cent decline in prices. Agencies in five other states issued new regulations, while all the rest but two are conducting investigations or considering legislation.

While the states have taken the lead, the federal government has also envisaged reform. In 1998, the Administration proposed measures that would reduce costs by $20 billion a year, mandating that all consumers would be able to choose their supplier by the beginning of 2003 unless their states formally opt out. Under its plan, the Federal Energy Regulatory Commission could require utilities that transmit electricity to yield operational control of transmission facilities to an independent system operator. In addition, the states would be encouraged to develop proposals to address the problem of stranded costs.[73] In 1999 the Administration plans to propose similar legislation. Congress has only started hearings on electricity restructuring, and it is possible that it will only pass modest legislation in 1999. One such law would clarify the jurisdiction of federal and state regulators, which is consistent with one of the recommendations of the OECD *Report on Regulatory Reform*. In 1998 Congress considered repealing the Public Utility Holding Company Act and this issue may come up again in 1999. This Act broke up interstate utility holding companies, requiring them to limit themselves to one well-defined geographical area and restricted mergers. The Administration, however, opposes wide-scale mergers before competition and deregulation takes hold.

Congress instituted additional hearings on deregulation after wholesale electricity prices in the Midwest spiked due to hot weather and the failure of some wholesale power marketers to meet their delivery contracts. The Federal Energy Regulatory Commission, however, is likely to use this experience to "fine tune" the market structures instead of returning to more regulation such as price ceilings.[74] Despite these problems at the wholesale level, retail delivery markets continued to work well.[75]

International trade

A specific objective of the US government continues to be to negotiate international agreements to reduce trade barriers.[76] To this end, accords on financial services and international bribery were completed, and the United States is pursuing further avenues with the European Union and Latin America. Moreover, several more specific bilateral deals have been struck, and the thorny problem of US sanction laws is slowly being worked out. However, with the current account deficit ballooning and the manufacturing sector experiencing slower growth, some adversely affected interests are urging the authorities to reduce imports and step up pressure to open foreign markets. So far, disputes have remained within lawful international and national bodies, or have been resolved through negotiation. The United States reserved its right to impose sanctions to enforce two WTO panel decisions – one involving the European Union in a dispute over banana trade and another against Canada concerning magazines. It also threatened to impose sanctions against Japan to reduce steel imports. The trading partners, however, view these actions as unilateral and illegal. It will be important for these issues to be resolved within the framework of international law.

Building on earlier successes, a multilateral agreement was signed that will significantly open up trade in *financial services*. The agreement covers 102 countries that represent 95 per cent of financial trade. During earlier phases of the negotiations, the United States significantly improved its final offer and will now give foreign companies virtually unrestricted access to the US market. The United States also signed an OECD agreement to *outlaw international bribery*. In addition, the United States has actively been pushing for broader agreements on *electronic commerce*.

The United States continues to participate actively in the WTO. Of the 125 distinct matters brought to the attention of the Dispute Resolution Body (DSB), the US government has been involved directly in 70 cases (Table 15), while it has retained its third-party rights in a number of others. In those in which it has lost, it has accepted the rulings from the DSB panel or the Appellate Body. In two of the cases in which it was a defendant, the federal government withdrew the challenged measures or allowed them to expire without renewal.[77] In a third case involving regulations on reformulated gasoline, the Environmental Protection Agency revised its regulations. In a fourth case involving protection for sea turtles, the Trade Representative has stated its intention to meet its requirements.[78] In a fifth case, concerning an antidumping finding involving Korean semiconductors, the DSB only recently issued its report, partially in favour of Korea. As a plaintiff, the US government lost a case against Japan involving photographic film and chose not to appeal the decision. Instead, it will continue to monitor market access conditions for film in Japan.

A serious confrontation, however, has erupted over the EU *banana* regime. The United States and several Latin American countries successfully challenged the regime before the WTO who ruled the European Union must come into

Table 15. **WTO cases directly involving the United States**

As of 26 February 1999

	Ongoing		Completed			
	Active panel	Consultations	Won	Lost	Settled	Withdrawn
Plaintiff	5	16	9	2	9	1
Defendant	4	12	0	5[1]	3	4

1.   Includes a case with Korea where the United States has not announced whether it will appeal the DSB's ruling.
Source: WTO.

compliance by 1 January 1999. The European Union maintains it is putting policies into place whereby it will be in compliance, but the United States argues that the changes are minor and the system is illegal. The main difficulty is that the DSB did not specify the measures the European Union must take to comply and instead issued a report open to different interpretations. US frustration is running high as this is the third time the regime has been struck down. It views renewing the appeals process from the start when small changes are made as a delaying tactic that challenges the integrity of the dispute settlement system.[79] As a result, it threatened to impose 100 per cent tariffs on a variety of EU exports worth $520 million by 3 March under Section 301 of the 1974 Trade Act. The two sides agreed to allow the DSB to rule on the various claims, while at the same time, the United States required exporters to post a bond for potential liabilities. In early April the DSB authorised sanctions on goods valued at $191 million; the European Union at that time had not announced whether it would appeal.

Other issues – especially concerning food products – remain an area of conflict between the United States and the European Union, with some of them involving the WTO. In December 1997 the European Union announced that the United States had to improve procedures to guarantee that meat and poultry shipments were free of *hormones and antibodies*. Such an announcement was made after a WTO DSB Panel ruling that held such EU prohibitions were unscientific and thus contravened previous agreements. A few months later an Appellate Body upheld the ruling and an arbitrator found a fifteen-month implementation period was reasonable. The December announcement came on the heels of a US ban on the importation of live cattle and sheep from all EU countries because of *mad cow disease*. A similar dispute over *tallow-based products* sold in Europe was resolved in early 1998, while general issues of *food labelling* and *genetically modified crops* remain an area of concern. A separate issue over *personal data protection* also has arisen. European laws require privacy guarantees before trade can take place, but the United States favours voluntary self-regulation. A disagreement over the regula-tion of *aeroplane noise* has recently developed. The European Union has proposed rules that would ban, as of April 2002, the use of hushkits to reduce jet engine noise. The United States argues that these rules would discriminate against their older models, and the US Congress is now considering removing US landing rights for the Concorde.

The United States has objected to Canada's response to the WTO's ruling on *split-run magazines*. The WTO ruled against previous legislation that placed an 80 per cent excise tax on Canadian-specific advertising in split-run magazines. Canada withdrew that contested measure, but the Canadian parliament is considering new legislation that would simply prevent foreign magazines from carrying advertisements directed at Canadian consumers. The Canadian government has offered to re-submit the dispute to the WTO for an expedited review, which the United States argues is a delaying tactic. In response, the US government has cited its right under the North American Free Trade Agreement to impose trade retaliation of equivalent effort. According to the Agreement, any response to measures adopted with respect to cultural industries shall be governed by the provisions of the Canada-US Free Trade Agreement, which allows equivalent retaliation without recourse to dispute settlement procedures.

There have also been some developments regarding the *application of* U.S. *sanctions law*. In 1996, the European Union filed a case in the WTO against the Libertad (Helms-Burton) Act, which imposes sanctions on companies that "traffic" in property confiscated by the Cuban Government and to which US persons have a claim. The European Union allowed panel proceedings to lapse in April 1998, during negotiation of understandings on laws regarding investment in confiscated property as well as laws creating conflicting requirements. Since the enactment of the Libertad Act, the President has exercised his authority to suspend the right to file lawsuits under the Act, although foreign companies have sometimes felt obliged to negotiate bilateral deals for cover. In a few cases under the Act, the US government has denied visas and entry into the United States by those who were determined to be "trafficking" in such property. The United States and the European Union avoided a confrontation over the Iran-Libya Sanctions Act in May 1998 when the US Government decided to waive the requirement to impose sanctions on certain firms investing in a $2 billion gas deal with Iran. The European Union and Japan initiated dispute settlement proceedings against the United States regarding a Massachusetts law that provides a 10 per cent price preference in favour of any company not doing business in Burma when determining the award of state procurement contracts. In November 1998, however, a US District Court judge declared the Massachusetts law unconstitutional. As a result, the plaintiffs in the WTO case decided to suspend panel proceedings, pending the outcome of the appeal of the decision. Finally, Swiss banks and representatives of *Holocaust* victims came to an agreement over the treatment of their financial accounts.

The United States has also begun talks on two large regional trade agreements. In April 1998 leaders of 34 Western Hemisphere countries agreed to start negotiations on a *Free Trade Area of the Americas* pact in September. Negotiators have a goal of duty-free trade by 2005. Nine negotiating groups are to issue preliminary work by November 1999. In addition, the possibility of a *Transatlantic Economic Partnership* has been proposed that would involve a broad range of issues between the United States and the European Union.

Several smaller bilateral deals have also been struck. The US and Italian governments negotiated an *open-skies treaty*, bringing the number of such treaties to five out of the six largest European markets. Talks with the United Kingdom have broken down, however. The United States reached a similar agreement with Japan, as well as separate agreements on procurement procedures for Nippon Telegraph and Telephone and on insurance retailing.

Other issues remain outstanding with respect to *Canada*. In the spring of 1998, the US and Canadian governments reached agreement on short-term measures for the 1998 fishing season that covered a number of species and areas. Basic disagreements over the 1985 Pacific Salmon Treaty, however, are still unsettled. In July 1998, the United States filed a dispute settlement case against Canada under the US-Canada Softwood Lumber Agreement with respect to the decision of the province of British Columbia to reduce its stumpage rates. Agriculture issues also remain sensitive. Canadian officials requested consultations under the North American Free Trade Agreement and with the WTO after a blockade of Canadian trucks at the boarder. Negotiators reached a new bilateral accord in December 1998 concerning agricultural trade, and a work programme to address outstanding problems is underway.

While the United States continues to have one of the most open trading regimes and has negotiated recently several trade enhancing measures, some people fear that protectionist sentiments are gaining ground. In September 1998, the Congress voted down legislation that would have renewed *fast track trade procedures*, which were in place from 1974 through 1994. These procedures call for the President to consult closely with the Congress regarding major trade negotiations and commit the latter to a straight yes-or-no vote on legislation to implement these agreements. While none of the trade agreements already concluded will be affected, implementation of new pacts could be more difficult if fast track is not renewed. The September vote follows a narrow victory for the President when the Congress rejected by a mere eight votes an amendment that would have prevented the federal government from suing state and local governments to enforce WTO decisions. In early 1999, the President re-instated Super 301 authority that instructs the Trade Representative's office to identify those countries whose practices it deems unfairly restricts US exports. If no quick, remedial action is taken, the office then must initiate a section 301 investigation as a prelude to a challenge before the WTO and possibly other retaliatory action. While by itself, the order does nothing more than require the Trade Representative to step up its investigations, major trading partners have interpreted the move as indicating an increased willingness by the United States to use unilateral trade sanctions. In addition, unfortunately, the Congress has not yet approved the 1994 OECD *Shipbuilding Agreement*, which is designed to reduce government subsidies to that sector.

Private firms have also applied for relief through petitions concerning antidumping and countervailing duties. Half of the active cases before the WTO where the United States is the defendant involve in some way such duties that, in principle, are consistent with WTO agreements. After several years of well-below-average filings, petitions surged in 1998 (Figure 23). Although only 45 per cent of them result in some final order, merely filing one can have a chilling effect on imports. If the authorities issue a positive preliminary ruling, importers must post a bond to cover potential duty liabilities. There is some speculation that this is an important business strategy by the US steel industry to raise prices whenever its market softens.[80] Indeed, about three-quarters of the cases filed in 1997 and 1998 involved steel products, explaining most of the 1998 run up. The International Trade Commission issued a final ruling in favour of the steel companies

Figure 23. **Anti-dumping and countervailing duties petitions**

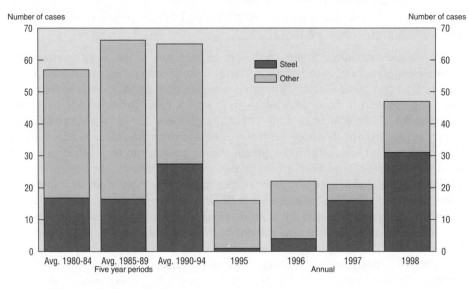

Source: US International Trade Administration, Department of Commerce.

with other cases pending. Furthermore, under pressure from the steel industry, the House of Representatives passed a non-binding resolution calling for a one-year ban on steel imports from countries found dumping steel. The Administration recently settled a pending investigation of Russian steel through a comprehensive agreement with the Russian Federation to limit its steel exports to the United States, while providing increased legal and commercial certainty for Russian exporters. It is also monitoring imports of steel from other sources. In particular, it has advised Japan that it may take action under US trade laws should the dramatic increase in Japanese export levels fail to subside. In addition, the European Union and Japan have raised the issue of whether the Antidumping Act of 1916 is consistent with WTO agreements.

Other structural initiatives

In November 1998, the United States signed the international pact negotiated in *Kyoto* the year before to reduce greenhouse gas emissions to 7 per cent below 1990 levels in 2008-12. Without additional measures, the Administration estimates that US greenhouse gas emissions will be 40 per cent above the targeted level (Figure 24). The last budget sets aside more than $1 billion for climate change initiatives, research on alternative energy sources and energy conservation. The centrepiece of the Administration's strategy to reduce emission, however, is an international permit trading system. Under a plan that includes trading among industrial and key developing countries, it estimates that the costs to reaching the target would be less than 0.1 per cent of GDP, as opposed to 0.6 per cent of GDP if trading were restricted domestically.[81] In addition the Administration estimates that by spurring greater efficiency, its electricity competition plan will reduce 2010 emissions by 2 per cent. Without international permit trading, Wharton Econometrics estimates that the agreement could cost the United States $3\frac{1}{4}$ per cent of GDP and 2.4 million jobs.[82] The treaty still needs to be ratified by the Senate, which will be difficult. Several senators have voiced dissatisfaction with the pact as it does not include developing countries and could be costly.

In other areas, as part of its implementation of the *new national ambient air quality standards* issued in July 1997, the Environmental Protection Agency (EPA) announced final rules aimed at lowering nitrogen oxide emissions in the eastern United States by 28 per cent by 2007.[83] To reduce costs of compliance, the EPA has proposed a regional emissions trading programme. It estimates that its plan will limit costs to $1 500 per tonne of reduction, as opposed to the $2 000-$10 000 per tonne costs that would apply if states rely on local control for compliance. It has also issued final rules on regional haze and has proposed new rules on motor vehicle emissions. Some senators are drafting legislation to encourage

Figure 24. **Actual and projected emissions without new abatement policies**
Millions of metric tonnes of carbon equivalent

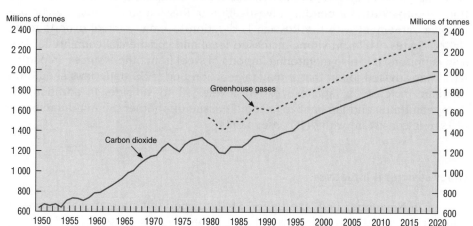

Source: The Kyoto Protocal and the President's Policies to Address Climate Change: Administration Economic
Analysis, July 1998.

companies' early efforts on meeting new pollution standards. Reauthorising the
Superfund programme – that funds the cleanup of polluted land – has proved to be
difficult. By 1997, the fund had spent $17.9 billion and had cleaned up the
504 sites deemed the most dangerous. However, 1 300 sites remain on the
priority list, and unless the taxes are reauthorised, the fund will be depleted by
2000. The Vice President has called for additional initiatives to improve *water
quality*, especially by tackling the difficult problem of pollution from non-specific
sources.[84]

In spite of the 60 per cent increase in *personal bankruptcies* in the past three
years (Figure 25), the Congress and the Administration could not agree on a
reform plan. Under the current system debtors can file a request to absolve their
debts after asset sales. House and Senate Republicans developed a plan that
would require debtors instead to restructure their repayments if they had income
above the median and could pay off one-quarter of their debts in five years.
Democrats, however, balked at the lack of consumer protections in the bill such
as disclosure requirements on credit card statements, and the President objected
to the form of the means test. Passing reform legislation is difficult because
analysts cannot agree on the cause in the rise in personal bankruptcies. The mix
of households filing for bankruptcy has not changed since 1980, leading some

Figure 25.   **Non-business bankruptcies**

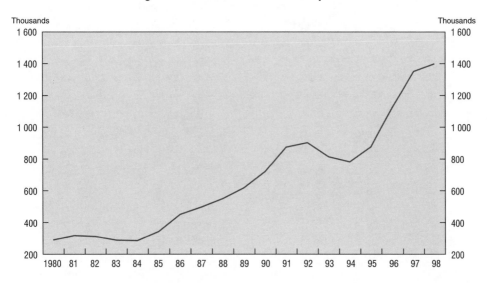

Source: The American Bankrupcy Institute.

to speculate on other societal and cultural changes.[85] As an example of the controversy, the National Bankruptcy Commission issued its final report in October 1997, preserving on a 5-4 vote most of the current system. Indeed, the commissioners in the minority offered a detailed dissent explaining why they feel the recommendations are too lenient.

In other matters, the President signed legislation *reforming the Internal Revenue Service* (IRS), establishing due process requirements and other tax payer rights. In one particularly important change, the law shifts the burden of proof from the taxpayer to the IRS. In June 1998, the Supreme Court voided the *line-item veto* as unconstitutional.[86] The Congress considered, but did not pass, a broad overhaul of the US *product liability code*, which would have included a cap of $250 000 on punitive damages against small businesses. In its place, the President signed more minor legislation making it difficult for suppliers of raw materials to medical device manufacturers to be sued. The Congress also considered a small measure involving *property rights* whereby developers could more easily sue in federal court over local zoning board decisions. This bill, which did not come to a vote in the Senate, follows on a larger effort two years earlier for broader protections and compensation that did not pass.

IV. Coping with ageing

One of the major structural changes facing the US economy is the adjustment to an older and slower growing population. This transition will result in a number of challenges particularly for public-sector institutions that provide for the incomes and social protection of the elderly. There will be increasing strains on government finances that will be felt mainly from health care for the elderly but also in the area of pensions. The economy will also have to adjust to a situation where the growth of the labour force may slacken, private saving may eventually drop, bringing a slackening in the growth of the capital stock. The same challenges are faced by other countries and have been examined in the OECD report "Maintaining Prosperity in an Ageing Society". The key to meeting these challenges will be to ensure that resources available to society grow as quickly as possible. In this way the young could enjoy a growing standard of living while maintaining an adequate living standard for an increasing number of elderly people. The United States is well placed to face the coming challenges. Nonetheless, there are issues that have to be addressed. The present chapter first explores the scale of the demographic changes before looking at the current economic position of the elderly and the institutions that support this position. It then considers the impact that demographic changes will have on the economy and on the institutions that provide income to the elderly. This chapter ends by recommending some of the changes that are needed to increase the resources available in the future so as to cope with ageing.

The scale of the demographic problem

In the next 25 years, the number of elderly people in the United States will grow rapidly, indeed faster than in many countries. According to the estimates of the Social Security Administration (Figure 26), the population aged over 65 will grow by over 2¼ per cent per year in the period 2000 to 2025, broadly the same as in the past 25 years. Such an increase will be almost a percentage point faster than the growth of the elderly population in Europe and Japan and only exceeded

Figure 26.   **Growth in number of elderly people**

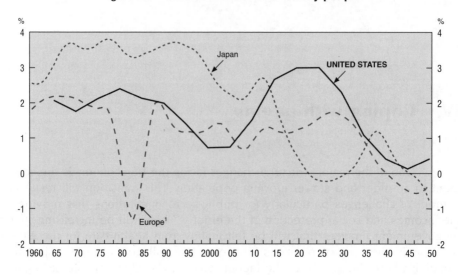

1.   Germany, France, United Kingdom, Italy.
Source: United Nations and Social Security Administration for USA.

by a few other OECD countries that have relatively young populations at the moment. The relatively rapid growth in the number of elderly in the United States is mainly the result of fertility rates that, in the 1950s and 1960s, were much higher than in other OECD countries. Life expectancy is also increasing and, in recent years, has grown at a faster pace than had been foreseen. After 2025, the growth in the number of elderly is expected to slow, however, falling to ¾ per cent annually in the next 50 years, in line with that projected for other countries, though this outcome depends crucially on the assumptions about mortality, especially for those over 80.

The number of people of working age will not increase at the same pace as the number of elderly. Consequently, the aged dependency ratio is projected to show a marked increase as the baby-boom generation retires, though remaining well below that in other OECD countries. In 1998, this ratio (the ratio of the number of people aged over 65 to the number aged between 21 and 64) was 0.21. After remaining relatively stable in the next ten years, it is expected to increase to 0.37 by 2035, an annual average increase of about 1¾ per cent in these years. This increase will mean that a rising share of consumption will be absorbed by the elderly, so limiting the future growth in living standards of the working population. The rise in the dependency rate in the United States is in line with the growth of this ratio in Europe and Japan (Figure 27), as a result of higher population growth, despite the higher growth of the elderly in the United States. After 2035, the dependency ratio almost stabilises growing by only 0.1 per cent annually reflecting increased life expectancy rather than imbalances in the size of different generations. In Europe and Japan, though, the ratio continues to increase by over 1 per cent per year. Such longer-term projections are particularly hazardous as they depend greatly on assumptions about future birth rates that, outside the United States, may be optimistic as they assume a marked rebound in the fertility towards the replacement rate for which there is little evidence.

The rise in the number of elderly is offset, to some extent, by the movement in the number of other dependants. The number of children, relative to the total population will fall, while the number of spouses that are economically active may continue to rise. This latter movement reflects the fact that at each age, successive cohorts of women have had higher participation rates. This seems likely to boost participation rates for some time. Even though the consumption needs of the falling number of children are less than those of the elderly, the retirement of the baby-boom generation will not generate an unusual level of overall dependency in the United States. Rather, the retirement of the baby-boom generation will bring to an end a 50-year period in which there was a temporary improvement in the overall dependency ratio (Figure 28). By 2035, when the baby boom generation will have largely retired, the overall dependency ratio will have risen from its 1998 level but will still be only as high as it was in 1985. The experience of the United States contrasts to that of Europe and Japan where, by 2050, the overall dependency ratio may be between one fifth and one quarter higher than in 1980.

Moreover, with immigration more than compensating for a birth rate slightly below the replacement rate, the Social Security Administration projects that both the working age population and the total US population will continue to grow (Figure 29). For the next 25 years, the expansion should average 3/4 per cent annually while the growth of the working age population will be 1/2 per cent. This contrasts to most other OECD countries where the sum of the birth-rate and the migration rate is markedly below the replacement rate and population may eventually fall, with only six OECD countries having a faster population growth, (Australia, Canada, Luxembourg, Mexico, New Zealand and Turkey). As a result, by the middle of the next century a substantially higher proportion of the population may be working in the United States than in Europe or Japan. Such a development, together with the more moderate rise in the overall dependency ratio suggests that the problem posed by ageing will be markedly less in the United States than elsewhere.

Figure 27. **Elderly dependency ratio**

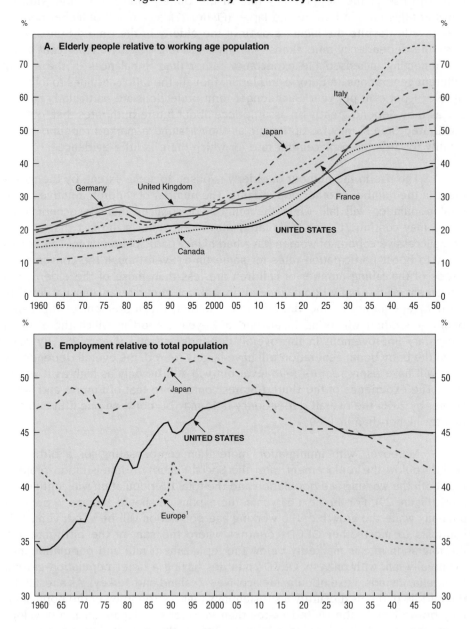

1.   Germany, France, Italy and United Kingdom.
Source: United Nations, US Social Security Administration, national source for Japan and OECD.

Figure 28. **Overall dependency ratio**[1]

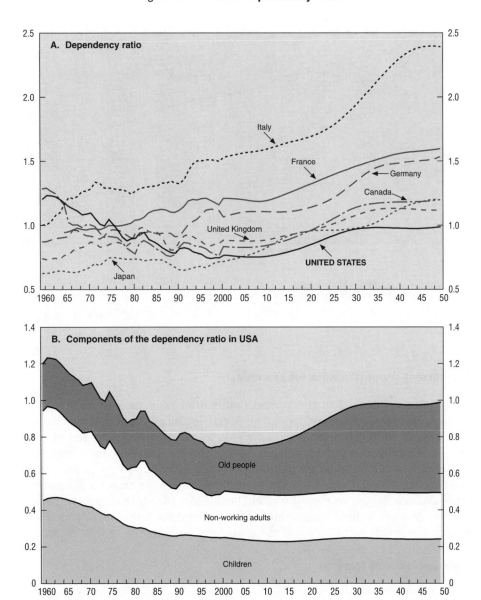

1. In both of these diagrams the weight of children in the overall dependency ratio has been reduced by 60 per cent, relative to their asolute number.
Source: United Nations and OECD.

Figure 29. **Population growth in an international context**

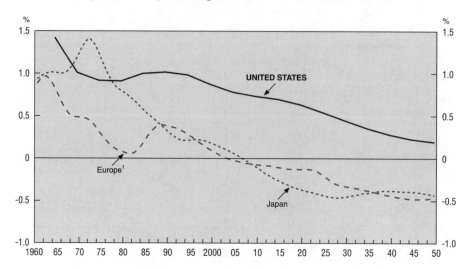

1.   Germany, France, United Kingdom, Italy.
Source: United Nations and Social Security Administration for USA.

The current support system for the elderly

Retired people in the United States draw their income from four main sources, other than continued work. The Social Security system provides pensions to nearly all retired households as well as to the surviving spouses of retired people. Employer-based retirement plans provide benefits to a majority of households, while a significant number of retired individuals rely on income from assets accumulated during their life. In addition, significant transfer payments are made through the government-provided health care plan for the elderly. Finally, a number of other federal programmes provide benefits acting mainly as a safety net for those with no or very low social security benefits.

Main institutional features

Social security

The Social Security system was introduced 64 years ago. It now covers 96 per cent of the workforce, after progressively widening its scope over the years. Now only some state and local government employees and older federal employees are excluded from the system. However, as many of these employees have previously worked in the private sector, even they are covered to some extent. As there is an upper limit on contributions to the system, only 86 per cent of total earnings give rise to a benefit. Although there have been many changes over the years, the level of benefits paid today is broadly equivalent to that envisaged when the system was created (Table 16). The size of the pension in relation to pre-retirement income declines as income increases (see Box 8 for the main details of the system). The decision to grant contributions to many of the early participants and the progressive widening of coverage and benefits, has ensured a very favourable rate of return for the participants in the Social Security system to date as in the pay-go schemes of other countries. Even those retiring in 1995 are estimated to have received a real rate of return of nearly 5 per cent on total contributions.

By 1996, expenditure on Social Security old age and survivors benefits were running at 4 per cent of GDP. Such a spending rate was not out of line with projections made when the system was founded. However, the decision taken soon after the system was founded to abandon the idea of a funded scheme, and operate on a pay-go basis has meant that the level of taxes needed to pay the benefits was substantially higher than originally thought (Figure 30). Contributions to the old age and survivors portion of social security have been at 10.7 per cent of earnings since 1997. Part of this contribution has been used to increase the size of the Social Security Trust fund which now amounts to nearly 10 per cent of GDP and is entirely invested in government securities. This contrasts to the initial estimate of a tax rate of 6 per cent, which was based on the original policy makers assumption that a large fund would be accumulated.

A number of other government programmes provide benefits to a small minority of the elderly population. Notably the Supplemental Security Income

Table 16. **Planned and realised social security benefits**

Date of retirement	Replacement rates		Real rate of return		Transfer
	Planned in 1939	Actual	Planned	Actual	Per cent Lifetime earnings[1]
1940	43	39	183.0	135.1	4.5
1950	47	24	25.0	23.5	8.2
1960	52	49	12.0	14.6	12.5
1970	56	48	7.0	10.3	13.6
1980	60	67	4.7	7.7	14.2
1990	60	61	3.9	5.7	10.3
1995	60	62		4.8	8.7

1.   Uses a real rate of discount of 2 per cent for a married couple with one person earning average pay.
Source: Miron and Weil (1997), Steuerle and Bakija (1994).

Box 8.   The Social Security pension system: principal features

The principal features of the system in 1997 were:
- The standard entitlement age to old-age pensions is 65.
- The early retirement age is 62.
- The earnings base for calculating pensions is the 35 years of highest earnings, indexed to average national earnings up to age 60 and not indexed thereafter. If there are fewer than 35 years of earnings, a value of zero earnings is assigned to the missing years. Once 35 years of contributions have been completed, additional work increases the pension base only to the extent that higher earnings replace lower earnings.
- The value of pensions is related to the pension base in a non-linear way. At an earnings base equal to average earnings in 1997, the replacement rate for a single worker was around 40 per cent at age 65. At an earnings base equal to the minimum wage (a third of male average earnings), the replacement rate is around 60 per cent; whereas it is only around 28 per cent at an earnings base equal to twice the level of average wages. The part of an individual's income above a maximum level (just under $2^{1}/_{2}$ times average earnings) is exempt from contributions and does not give right to a pension.
- Actuarial adjustment is applied to the value of pensions for early and delayed withdrawal. Pensions are permanently reduced by 6.7 per cent for every year of early withdrawal, cumulating to 20 per cent for those who retire at age 62 – almost 60 per cent of workers elect to take this reduction. Delayed withdrawal of benefits was rewarded with a 5 per cent increase in pensions for each year up to 70 and is scheduled to rise by 8 per cent per year after 2004. Only 5 per cent of workers use this option.
- An earnings test is applied to pension benefits. Prior to the standard entitlement age, pension recipients in 1997 could earn up to $8 640 (30 per cent of average earnings) without any reduction in benefits; pensions were reduced by 50 per cent for earnings above this limit, implying that a single person with an earnings base equal to average earnings, and continuing to earn the average wage, would lose nearly all pension entitlements. After the standard age of entitlement, the exempt amount in 1997 was $13 500 (close to 47 per cent of average earnings); pensions were reduced by 33 $1/_{3}$ per cent for earnings above this limit.

The principal arrangements concerning the spouse and widow benefits in the old-age benefit system include:
- The spouse and widow benefit is equal to 50 and 100 per cent of the primary benefit respectively.
- The spouse benefit is available at age 62, but the benefit is subject to an 8.33 per cent actuarial adjustments.
- The widow benefit is available at age 60, but each year of withdrawal prior to the standard entitlement age implied a reduction of 5.7 per cent of benefits.

(SSI) provides, together with food stamps, a safety net for those who have relatively low incomes in retirement. Just under 6 per cent of elderly households received such payments in 1996, with total expenditure amounting to 1.5 per cent of Social Security benefits. A slightly lower proportion of the elderly population also receive food stamps and/or housing assistance. Finally just under 40 per cent of all veterans benefits are paid to elderly households.

Figure 30.   **Social security tax rates: their evolution over time[1]**

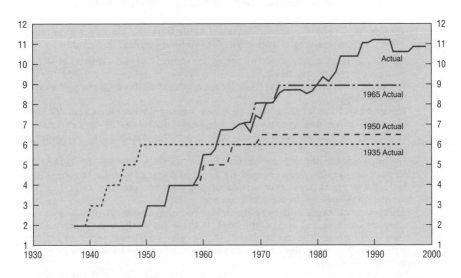

1.   The lines show the level of contributions for old age and survivors benefits and the point in time at which estimates
     of future rates were made.
Source: Miron and Weil (1997).

Private sector pension plans

Around 40 per cent of the private sector labour force are members of a retirement plan. A greater proportion of employees work for a firm that offers a pension scheme but short-stay and young workers often are not eligible to join the scheme. Between ages 31 and 60, participation rises to 60 per cent. These plans take two forms. In the traditional *defined benefit scheme* (DB), the employer undertakes to pay a pension to an employee at retirement that typically amounts to 1 per cent of salary per year worked by the employee (see Box 9 for other details of a typical plan). The employer is responsible for paying the benefit and the employee makes no contribution, though the employer contribution is part of the employees overall compensation package. These schemes must accumulate a fund to secure the payment of the benefit. Funding a defined benefit pension scheme is an attractive option for a company due to tax concessions. The contributions (generally 5 per cent of salary but lower if investment returns are above 3 per cent in real terms)[87] are not considered by the tax authorities as part of the employees' income. On the other hand, the company can treat them as a legitimate business expense. Income tax is not paid on the investment earnings of the trust. This allowed a considerable deferral of tax payments and hence reduced

---

Box 9.   Private defined-benefit plans: principal features

Private defined-benefit plans differ considerably from one employer to another. In 1995, the principal features of such plans for full-time employees included:

– The normal retirement age was 65 and 62 for around half and a quarter of all full-time employees respectively;
– The early retirement age was 55 or less for more than three-quarters of all full-time employees;
– The earnings base for calculating pensions was terminal earnings (usually highest consecutive five years in last ten years) for close to 60 per cent of employees and career earnings for close to a tenth of employees. A quarter of employees had flat rate pensions;
– The pension accrual rate varied by service, earnings and age for more than 60 per cent of employees covered by terminal earnings formula; the remaining had a flat per cent per year of service ranging from less than one to $2\frac{1}{4}$ per cent per year, the average being 1.45 per cent;
– Social-security taxes and benefits influenced the design of private pension schemes covering half of all employees. In these plans, the benefit accrual rate rises with income. The overall result is to ensure consistent replacement rate across incomes, offsetting the declining importance of Social Security pensions as income increases;
– The actuarial reduction factor for access to pensions prior to the normal age varied by age for 60 per cent of employees with defined-benefit plans. Where uniformed percentage reduction was applied, it varied from less than 3 to more than 7 per cent for each year of withdrawal prior to the normal age, the average being 5 per cent per year;
– Participation in a plan gives rise to vested benefits after a maximum of five years or, progressively, between three and seven years.

Deferred withdrawal of a private pension was generally not rewarded with an actuarial increase.

---

costs for the plan sponsor. Income tax is payable by the retiree on the entire pension.

The second form of retirement saving is known as *defined contribution* (DC) plan. In this system, typically both the employee and the employer contribute to the scheme. The contributions accumulate in an investment fund and then at retirement, the employee receives the balance of the plan, including the accumulated income and capital gains. However, there is no compulsory arrangement to pay a pension. The individual is free to use the money as needed. When an employee leaves a firm, the defined contribution is liquidated and the employee has in general to re-invest the proceeds in a new plan or pay a penalty tax. Some DC plans run in addition to defined benefit plans but increasingly the primary retirement saving plan in the private sector is of a defined contribution nature.

Defined contribution schemes appear to be cheaper to run, in terms of record management and compliance. The use of one administrator helps in this regard, while restrictions on the number of funds offered to an employee can reduce investment management costs so raising the returns to investors.[88] Employee stock ownership plans represent another form of retirement saving that were introduced to allow companies to contribute stock in their own company to an employee trust that became available to the employee on retirement. These plans had significant tax advantages for companies especially when they were financed by a loan rather than through the gradual issuance of new stock. Saving plans have also been introduced for the self-employed (Table 17). A large number of other tax-favoured schemes for retirement saving have been introduced, with varying coverage and conditions (Table 17).

The greater tax incentives for employees to use defined contribution retirement plans have resulted in a marked swing towards this type of plan. Another factor has been the increasing regulation of defined benefit plans under the 1974 Employment Retirement Income Security Act (ERISA) legislation. These have raised compliance costs considerably, bearing in mind the need to keep track of ex-employees and to pay insurance premiums to guarantee pensions. Overall, administrative costs of DC plans appear to be two-thirds those of DB plans where there are a large number of members, with the gap being much greater for small plans.[89] In addition, the progressive reduction in the upper ceiling of a pension that can be paid from a tax-favoured pension fund has favoured the move to DC plans.

In 1975, fewer than 4 million employees had a defined contribution scheme as their primary employer provided retirement plan (Figure 31). By 1993, this number had almost quadrupled, with the bulk being members of 401(k) schemes and almost 45 per cent of primary plans were of a defined contribution nature. For firms employing under 100 workers, defined benefit plans fell markedly in this period but the growth of DC plans more than offset this, with the result that 90 per cent of plan provision in small firms was through DC plans in 1993. For larger firms, there was a much less rapid growth of defined contribution plans which represented only one-third of total primary plans by 1993 (Table 18). The members of defined benefit plans have seen a marked rise in the availability of supplementary defined contribution schemes.[90] Despite the increase in DC plans, the total proportion of employees with retirement saving or pension plan provision has remained quite stable – at 43 per cent of private sector employment. This raises the possibility that the growth of DC primary plans essentially represents a change in the form of benefits rather than an increase in total saving for retirement. Indeed, between 1985 and 1992, 20 per cent of employers replaced defined benefit schemes by defined contribution schemes.[91]

Table 17. **Tax preferred retirement saving plans, Part 1**

Plan characteristics	Individual accounts				Small business plans		
	Non-qualified deferred annuity	Deductible IRA	Traditional non-deductible IRA	Roth IRA	SEP-IRA	Salary reduction SEP	SIMPLE IRA
Eligibility	All taxpayers	Taxpayers not in an employer plan, unless earning more than $35 000 for individuals and $50 000 for couples[1]	All taxpayers	Taxpayers with earnings less than $110 000 for individuals and $160 000 for couples[2]	Employees of all employers	Employees of taxable employers with 25 or fewer employees[3]	Employees of employers without another plan and with under 100 employees
Contribution limits							
Overall dollar limit	None	$2 000 reduced by other IRAs	$2 000 reduced by other IRAs	$2 000 reduced by other IRAs[4]	$30 000[5]	$30 000[5]	n.a.
Overall maximum % of pay	n.a.	100	100	100	15	15	n.a.
Employer limits	None	n.a.	n.a.	n.a.	Lesser of $30 000 or 15%	Lesser of $30 000 or 15%	Matching contribution up to 3% of pay or fixed 2%
Employee limits	None	$2 000	$2 000 (after-tax)	$2 000 (after-tax)	n.a.	$9 500	$6 000
Aggregate employer deduction limits	n.a.	n.a.	n.a.	n.a.	15% of aggregate compensation for all qualified plans	15% of aggregate compensation for all qualified plans	None
Exclusion from SS tax	No	No	No	No	Yes[6]	No for employee contribution	No

Table 17. **Tax preferred retirement saving plans, Part 1** (cont.)

Plan characteristics	Individual accounts				Small business plans		
	Non-qualified deferred annuity	Deductible IRA	Traditional non-deductible IRA	Roth IRA	SEP-IRA	Salary reduction SEP	SIMPLE IRA
Distributions							
Subject to early withdrawal penalty tax[7]	No	Yes	Yes	Yes	Yes	Yes	Yes
Penalty tax exceptions[8]	None	Medical expense, first home purchase, higher education expense and health insurance payments for unemployed	Same exceptions as IRA	First-time home buyer (up to $10 000 limit)	Same exceptions as IRA	Same exceptions as IRA	Penalty is increased to 25% if funds are withdrawn in first two years
Conditions for in-service withdrawal	No additional limitations	No additional limitations	No additional limitations	5-year waiting period	No additional limitations	No additional limitations	No additional limitations
Loans available	No	No	No	No	No	No	No
Non-discrimination							
Non-discrimination rules[9]	None	None	None	None	Uniform per cent of pay to all eligible employees	HCEs 125%[10]	Required matching up to 3% or 2% fixed contribution
Salary cap for non-discrimination testing	n.a.	n.a.	n.a.	n.a.	$160 000	$160 000	$160 000

Table 17. **Tax preferred retirement saving plans, Part 1** *(cont.)*

Plan characteristics		Individual accounts				Small business plans		
		Non-qualified deferred annuity	Deductible IRA	Traditional non-deductible IRA	Roth IRA	SEP-IRA	Salary reduction SEP	SIMPLE IRA
Complicating factors	Spousal protection	None	None	None	None	None	None	None
	Vesting	Immediate	Immediate	Immediate	Immediate	Immediate	Immediate	Immediate
	Special restrictions and benefits	None	None	None	Based after-tax contributions	Employer does not have to contribute every year	No new plan may be established after 31.12.96	Employees may direct investment after 2-year waiting period

Note: All dollar values are indexed, and the given figures are as of 1997.

1. IRA phase-out schedule: currently $25 000 to $35 000 for individuals and $40 000 to $50 000 for married couples filing together. These phase-outs are scheduled to increase to $50 000 to $60 000 for individuals and $80 000 to $100 000 for joint filers by 2007 with incremental increases starting in 1998. There are also special limits for non-working spouses.
2. The phase-out schedule for Roth IRAs is $95 000-110 000 for individuals and $150 000-160 000 for married couples filing jointly.
3. Public sector employees and employees of tax-exempt organisations are not allowed to make elective deferrals into a SEP.
4. Deposit limits for contributions to Roth IRAs actually have a greater value than traditional IRAs because it is an after tax contribution.
5. The $30 000 overall dollar limit is a cumulative limit for employers and employees across all qualified plans.
6. Since the employees contributions are only after-tax contributions that are not excludable from social security tax.
7. The general exceptions to the standard IRS 10 per cent penalty for early withdrawal include death, disability, separation from service and plan termination.
8. Withdrawals for medical expenses in excess of 7.5 per cent of AGI are exempt from the IRS penalty for all plans.
9. State and local plans are exempt from all non-discrimination tests.
10. The 125 per cent HCE rule says that a Highly Compensated Employee (HCE), which are defined under the IRC to include employees who are 5 per cent owners during the current or preceding year or who received compensation in excess of $80 000 in the preceding year, may not defer more than 125 per cent of the average deferral of all Non-Highly Compensated Employees (NCHEs).

Source: Harry Conaway, William M. Mercer, and C. Eugene Steuerle and Andrea Barnett, The Urban Institute, 1997.

Table 17. **Tax preferred retirement saving plans, Part 2**

Plan characteristics	Defined contribution plans						Defined benefit
	Eligible 457 plans	403(b)	401(k)	Profit sharing	Employee stock ownership plan	Money purchase	
Eligibility	Employees of state and local government and tax-exempt organisations	Employees of tax-exempt organisations and public schools	All employees except state and local governments	Employees of any employer	Employees of taxable employers	Employees of any employer	Employees of any employer
Contribution limits							
Overall dollar limit	$7 500 ($15 000 limit for last 4 years before retirement as catch-up allowance). Reduced by contributions to 403(b), SEP and 401(k) plans	$30 000[1]	$30 000[1]	$30 000[1]	$30 000 (increased to $60 000 if not more than 1/3 of employer contributions are allocated to HCEs)	$30 000[1]	Benefit limit = $125 000
Overall maximum per cent of pay	33.33	25	25	25	25	25	Benefit limit = 100%* except for state and local government
Employer limits	Lesser of $7 500 or 33⅓ % reduced by employee contribution	Exclusion allowance = 20% of pay times years of service reduced by employer annuity purchase	Lesser of $30 000 or 25% reduced by employee contribution	Lesser of $30 000 or 25% reduced by employee contribution	Lesser of $30 000 or 25% reduced by employee contribution	Lesser of $30 000 or 25% reduced by employee contribution	Normal cost for the year plus amortisation over 10 years or 150% of current liability[2]
Employee limits	Lesser of $7 500 or 33⅓ % reduced by employer contribution	$9 500 (plus catch-up allowance if more than 15 years of service)	$9 500	Only after-tax if not 401(k) plan subject to overall limits	Only after-tax if not 401(k) plan subject to overall limits	Not typically allowed	Subject to DC limits

Table 17. **Tax preferred retirement saving plans, Part 2** (cont.)

Plan characteristics	Defined contribution plans						Defined benefit
	Eligible 457 plans	403(b)	401(k)	Profit sharing	Employee stock ownership plan	Money purchase	
Aggregate employer deduction limits	n.a.	n.a.	15% of taxable compensation	15% of taxable compensation	25% of taxable compensation for leveraged (15% non-leveraged) plus deductions on ESCOP dividends	Based on funding requirement	Based on funding requirement[3]
Exclusion from SS tax	Yes	No	No for employee contributions	Yes[4]	Yes[4]	Yes[4]	Yes
Distributions							
Subject to early withdrawal penalty tax[5]	No	Yes	Yes	Yes	Yes	Yes	Yes
Penalty tax exceptions[6]	None	None	None	None	None	None	None
Conditions for in-service withdrawal	Unforeseeable emergency[7]	Financial hardship[8]	Financial hardship[8]	Minimum 2-year holding period for each contribution	Depends on set-up	Not allowed	Not allowed
Loans available	Yes	Yes	Yes	Yes	None	None	No
Non-discrimination							
Non-discrimination rules[9]	Can favour HCEs	ACP for matching funds, general test for non-elective deferrals, and uniform availability for elective deferrals[11]	$160 000	General rule[10]	General rule[10]	General rule[10]	General rule[10]

Table 17. **Tax preferred retirement saving plans, Part 2** *(cont.)*

Plan characteristics	Eligible 457 plans	Defined contribution plans					Defined benefit
		403(b)	401(k)	Profit sharing	Employee stock ownership plan	Money purchase	
Salary cap for non-discrimination testing	n.a.	$160 000	$160 000	$160 000	$160 000	$160 000	$160 000
Complicating factors							
Spousal protection	None	None	Death benefit[12]	Death benefit[12]	Death benefit[12]	Survival annuity, consent and death benefit	Survival annuity, consent and death benefit
Vesting	Deferred	Immediate	Employer contributions are deferred and elective contributions are vested immediately	Deferred	Deferred	Deferred	Deferred
Special restrictions and benefits	Unfunded plan. All assets part of employer's general assets and subject to creditors until distribution. Must be held in trust after 1.1.99 for public sector. May also be a DB plan	May also be structured as a DB plan	SIMPLE 401(k) follow same regulations except they follow SIMPLE IRA rules for eligibility, employer and employee contribution limits, and vesting	None	*100% employer securities allowed.* Required opportunity for divesture at 55.* Put option and voting rights	Minimum funding required in full each year	*Pension Benefit Guaranty Corporation premium of $19 per employee. *Special rules for multi-employer plans

Table 17. **Tax preferred retirement saving plans, Part 2** *(cont.)*

Note: All dollar values are indexed and the given figures are as of 1997. This table does not include education IRAs because they are not properly viewed as retirement vehicles.

1. The $30 000 overall dollar limit is a cumulative limit for employers and employees across all qualified plans.
2. Under the Taxpayer Relief Act of 1997 the 150 per cent limit for Defined Benefit plans will be increased to 170 per cent by 2005 with incremental increases starting in 1999.
3. There is an additional combined deduction limit of the greater amount of the maximum funding limit for defined plans and 25 per cent of compensation, when an employee participates in both a defined benefit and a defined contribution plan.
4. Since the employees contributions are only after-tax contributions that are not excludable from social security tax.
5. The general exceptions to the standard IRS 10 per cent penalty for early withdrawal include death, disability, separation from service and plan termination.
6. Withdrawals for medical expenses in excess of 7.5 per cent of AGI are exempt from the IRS penalty for all plans.
7. Unforeseeable emergencies are defined as severe financial hardship to the participant as a result of sudden illness or accident to the participant or a dependent, property loss due to casualty or other extraordinary and unforeseeable circumstances beyond the control of the participant. No payment will be made if there are other ways to satisfy the financial need. Specifically not included: college and home purchase.
8. Financial Hardship is defined as, immediate and heavy financial need where the funds are not available from other sources. The need may be either foreseeable or voluntarily incurred. The distribution cannot exceed the amount required to meet the immediate financial need created by the hardship.
9. State and local plans are exempt from all non-discrimination tests.
10. The general non-discrimination rule says that no HCE may receive a contribution or benefit that is a higher percentage of pay than the contribution or benefit of any NHCE.
11. The Aggregate Contribution Percentage test (ACP) applies to employer and after-tax employee contributions. It requires that either 1) the ACP for the group of HCEs I not more than 125 per cent of the ACP for all other eligible employees or 2) the excess of the ACP for the group of HCEs in not more than two times the ACP of all other eligible employees. The Actual Deferral Percentage test (ADP) applies to elective employee contributions and is designed to limit the contributions of HCEs based on the average deferred percentages of NHCEs. It requires that:

For ADP of NHCEs:	ADP of HCEs may be:
Less than 2 per cent	2 times the ADP of NHCEs
2 to 8 per cent	ADP of the NHCEs + 2 per cent
8 per cent or greater	1.25 times the ADP of the NHCEs

Additionally, the 401(k) ADP test is based on an aggregate average of deferrals and therefore allows a higher disparity than the 125 per cent HCE rule for SEP plans.
12. The Death Benefit provides 50 per cent of the remaining value of the plan to the widow in a lump sum payment.

Source: Harry Conaway, William M. Mercer and C. Eugene Steuerle and Andrea Barnett, The Urban Institute. 1997.

Box 10.   401(k) retirement saving plans

The design of these schemes varies considerably. Four types of contributions can be paid to a 401(k) plan:

- An elective contribution in which the employer pays a certain percentage of the employees' earnings to a fund, on a pre-tax basis;
- A matching contribution in which the employer adds a certain percentage of the employees contribution. Both of these contributions are made from pre-tax income and reduce taxable income;
- A voluntary contribution made out of post-tax income by the employee;
- A non-elective contribution made by the employer.

Based on various surveys, it would appear that 80 per cent of employers proposing a scheme offer matching, with a mean match rate of 62 per cent. The upper limit on the employee contribution that is matched varies considerably – from 1 to 20 per cent of pay – but the mean is 5½ per cent, according to one survey. There is a maximum ceiling on tax deductible contributions.

Participation in these plans is voluntary but the scheme only obtains tax-favoured status if a certain proportion of low-income staff join it.

The proportion of households with some pension plan coverage is considerably higher than the proportion of employees with coverage at a given point in time. Many households have pension rights from past employment, or have rolled-over defined contribution accounts from previous employers into other tax-exempt plans, even if their current employer does not provide one. Overall, nearly 62 per cent of households had some form of retirement plan in addition to Social Security, though not necessarily both spouses have an additional benefit. Amongst households ten years away from retirement, 65 per cent had rights to some form of private retirement plan in 1992.[92] Older and better- paid people are more likely to be covered by a plan, with enrolment rising to slightly over 70 per cent in age group 45 to 54 and to around 80 per cent for those earning above $50 000 annually in 1992. Employer provided retirement plan coverage is very limited for those earning under $10 000 per year (about $5 per hour); only 16 per cent are covered. This reflects poor coverage amongst part-time or young workers and other groups with low pay and high staff turnover.

Although the proportion of private employees covered by retirement plans has remained stable, the assets held in these schemes has risen markedly more rapidly than GDP. In 1995, the investments of private sector plans now amounted to over 35 per cent of GDP with defined contribution plans almost equal in size to those of defined benefit schemes (Figure 32).

Figure 31.   **Primary retirement plan by type and number of members**

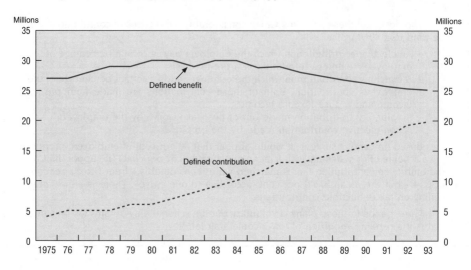

Source: EBRI.

A further source of retirement savings comes from individual retirement accounts (IRAs). Originally authorised by ERISA for employees with no access to defined contribution schemes, their widespread use awaited various clarifying regulations issued in 1981 that widened considerably those who could invest in these plans and also increased contribution limits. The balances invested in such accounts, together with Keogh plans for the self-employed, have grown rapidly in the early 1980s, but subsequent changes in 1986 limited the amounts that could be deposited in such accounts. Nonetheless, the balances of IRA accounts amounted to about 17 per cent of GDP in 1995.[93] Since then the 1997 tax law has increased the contribution ceiling again. These accounts are mainly invested either in stock brokerage accounts or mutual funds which together accounted for 70 per cent of the total, though it is not possible to spit this total between bonds and equities.

Government employee pensions

The various levels of government almost universally provide pensions for their employees. Almost 90 per cent of public sector employees work for an agency that sponsors a retirement plan and nearly 90 per cent of these employees are members of the scheme. Overall, almost one-fifth of pension

Table 18.   **Primary retirement plan by type and size of employer**

1985-1993

	Distribution of employees by type of Primary Retirement Plan (per cent of all plans)				
Number of employees of firm	Defined benefit	Defined contribution	Defined benefit	Defined contribution	Change in share of defined benefit plans
	1985		1993		1985-1993
2-9	29.3	70.7	10.8	89.2	−18.5
10-24	25.9	74.1	8.8	91.2	−17.1
25-49	31.0	69.0	11.6	88.4	−19.4
50-99	39.8	60.2	18.4	81.6	−21.3
100-249	53.0	47.0	27.5	72.5	−25.4
250-499	69.1	30.9	40.7	59.3	−28.5
500-999	73.3	26.7	51.8	48.2	−21.6
1 000-2 499	75.3	24.7	60.5	39.5	−14.8
2 500-4 999	79.6	20.4	68.7	31.3	−10.9
5 000-9 999	82.1	17.9	75.1	24.9	−7.1
10 000-19 999	85.7	14.3	81.9	18.1	−3.8
20 000+	89.1	10.9	83.9	16.1	−5.2
Total	71.9	28.1	55.9	44.1	−15.9

Distribution of Primary Retirement Plans by type of plan
(per cent of all plans)

Number of employees of firm	Defined benefit	Defined contribution	Defined benefit	Defined contribution	Annual growth in number of plans	
					Defined benefit plans	Defined contribution plans
	1985		1993		1985-1993	
2-9	30.6	69.4	10.8	89.2	−11.9	3.7
10-24	25.6	74.4	8.8	91.2	−9.5	6.1
25-49	31.1	68.9	11.6	88.4	−8.0	7.3
50-99	39.1	60.9	18.1	81.9	−5.0	8.5
100-249	51.8	48.2	26.9	73.1	−5.2	8.4
250-499	64.7	35.3	39.9	60.1	−3.7	9.3
500-999	72.7	27.3	50.8	49.2	−3.1	9.1
1 000-2 499	75.1	24.9	60.2	39.8	−1.3	7.5
2 500-4 999	79.5	20.5	68.0	32.0	−0.9	6.8
5 000-9 999	82.4	17.6	74.3	25.7	−0.8	5.4
10 000-19 999	85.3	14.7	81.7	18.3	1.5	4.9
20 000+	85.8	14.2	82.7	17.3	−0.6	2.4
Total	32.4	67.6	13.0	87.0	−9.2	5.1

Source: EBRI (1997).

Figure 32. **Retirement plan assets by type of plan**
Percentage of GDP

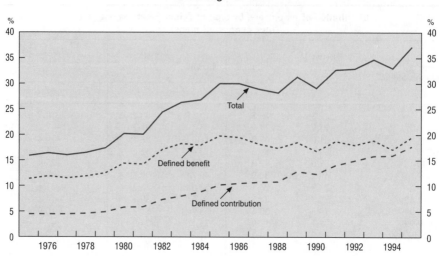

Source: EBRI.

benefits come from this source. The federal government scheme was reformed in 1983, when new hires were put into a scheme that was integrated with the Social Security system. The new scheme has been fully funded since its inception and, in 1993, had assets amounting to 0.6 per cent of GDP. Neither the older scheme nor the plan for military employees are funded, but the government is gradually building up assets as it amortises the past service obligation that, in total amounted to slightly over $1 billion in 1993. Overall, assets represented only 31 per cent of the accrued liability for pension. The assets of the funds are totally invested in Federal securities and so the exercise can be thought of as a purely book-keeping exercise. Nonetheless, such a system does allow the calculation of expenditure more nearly on an accruals basis. These three pension funds are currently accumulating assets at the rate of 0.6 per cent of GDP annually. State and local government schemes are better placed than those of the federal government. Their assets represented 85 per cent of liabilities in 1993, a considerable improvement on the position in the mid-1970s.

As part of the 1983 reform, the federal government has also introduced a voluntary defined contribution scheme. Employees can make a contribution of up to 10 per cent of their income to the thrift plan (subject to a ceiling) and there is an employer match of at least 1 per cent and at most 5 per cent of income.[94] The investment choices open to civil servants are less than those offered in the typical 401(k) funds. The employee can choose between a cash fund, a bond fund and a portfolio designed to mimic a wide average of equities.[95] By 1995, these funds amounted to $35 billion (0.5 per cent of GDP). The funds are managed by Federal Thrift Savings Board and, once vested, are owned by the employees. About one-third of the staff members' own contributions is allocated to equities, but this proportion falls to just 13 per cent once the governments contribution is counted. State government employees and teachers are also eligible for additional defined contribution plans, similar but separate to 401(k)s.

Voluntary saving

Individuals also accumulate assets outside pension plans, partially in preparation for retirement. Indeed, in 1992, the median household aged 55 held $123 000 of assets outside pensions and retirement saving plans (Table 19) and this rose to $230 000 for the mean household[96] (Table 19). A substantial part of non-pension wealth is represented by housing, with nearly 85 per cent of pre-retirement households owning their principal residence. Including pension plans and Social Security wealth, mean wealth was $492 000, representing some 39 per cent of the present value of lifetime earnings (Table 20). This ratio was fairly stable over the middle range of incomes but rose at the lower income levels and fell at higher incomes. If there were no further additions to wealth prior to retirement, and were it possible to completely annuitise this wealth on retirement on

Table 19.   **Types of financial assets held by pre-retirement households**
1992

	Mean	Median	Mean	Median
	Thousand dollars		Per cent of total assets	
House	78.8	63.4	16.0	18.9
Real Estate	39.2	9.5	8.0	2.8
Business assets	39.7	6.8	8.1	2.0
Financial assets	42.1	19.7	8.6	5.9
Retiree Health Insurance	8.5	9.2	1.7	2.7
Other	22.4	14.6	4.6	4.4
IRA assets	19.6	10.3	4.0	3.1
Social Security	116.5	128.1	23.7	38.2
Retirement plans	125.0	73.6	25.4	22.0
All retirement assets	261.1	212.0	47.0	63.3
All other assets	230.7	123.0	53.1	36.7
Total	491.8	335.0	100.0	100.0

Source: Gustman and Steinmeier (1998).

Table 20. **Wealth and life-time earnings of pre-retirement households**

1992

Mean wealth within given a earnings percentile range

Lifetime earnings Percentile	Wealth Thousand dollars			Earnings Thousands dollars	Wealth to earnings ratio			Replacement rate[1]
	Total	Pensions	Other	Lifetime	Total	Pension	Other	
0-5	63.4	1.0	62.4	27.3	2.32	0.04	2.29	0.89
5-10	134.1	7.0	127.1	144.9	0.93	0.05	0.88	0.86
10-25	175.4	21.7	153.7	392.8	0.45	0.06	0.39	0.59
25-50	346.9	70.1	276.8	844.4	0.41	0.08	0.33	0.65
50-75	522.5	138.4	384.1	1 345.4	0.39	0.10	0.29	0.65
75-90	734.3	216.9	517.4	1 886.9	0.39	0.11	0.27	0.66
90-95	950.1	289.1	661.0	2 470.7	0.38	0.12	0.27	0.67
95-100	1 610.7	443.4	1 167.3	5 048.0	0.32	0.09	0.23	0.41
45-55	439.0	93.9	345.1	1 098.1	0.40	0.09	0.31	0.66
0-100	491.8	125.0	366.8	1 274.0	0.39	0.10	0.29	0.60

1. On the basis that all wealth is annuitised at retirement to give a constant real income for the household, with the survivor receiving a pension equal to 60 per cent of that received by the household.
Source: Gustman and Steinmeier (1998).

competitive terms, then the resulting annuity would represent 60 per cent of lifetime earnings (Table 20). Allowing for additional saving between the date of the survey and final retirement, the replacement rate would rise to 62 per cent. This estimate assumes that housing wealth will be completely annuitised, but does not take account of lower taxation, the absence of work-related expenses and child-rearing expenses, the higher utility of leisure compared to work and the absence of the need to save. However, there are some groups with extremely low replacement ratios. These appear to be concentrated amongst those employees with no private pension plan.

Health care

Nearly all retired people have a large part of their medical expenses paid through two government programmes Medicare and Medicaid. Medicare is an insurance programme run by the Federal government for the disabled and those aged 65 and over that provides acute health care and some post-hospital services. Medicaid is a state-run programme that provides health and long-term care services for the poor. A large part of this programme provides for the long-term health and nursing care for the elderly. In 1995, Medicare spending on the elderly was $162.3 billion (2.2 per cent of GDP). Medicaid also provides health care for the elderly, spending about $50 billion (0.6 per cent of GDP) at the state and

---

Box 11. The Medicare health care programme for the elderly

The Medicare system is composed of two parts. The first part, the Hospital Insurance Fund (also known as Part A) pays for inpatient hospital, skilled nursing and hospice services, and it makes direct payments to managed care plans to cover these same services for those enrolled. Medicare Part A receives its income directly from the Hospital Insurance Trust Fund. About 88 per cent of the revenue to this fund comes from a payroll tax of 2.9 per cent,* with the remaining coming from interest on its assets, revenue from taxes on social security benefits and various miscellaneous sources. The other half of the system, the Supplementary Medical Insurance Pro-gramme (also known as Medicare Part B) pays for physician services, out-patient hospital costs, independent laboratory expenses and home health services on a fee-for service basis, and it also makes payments to managed care plans for those enrolled. General federal revenue and monthly premiums pay Part B services. Origi-nally, Congress intended the premiums to cover half of Part B services, but subse-quently the coverage ratio drifted down and was quite variable. The 1997 Balanced Budget Act wrote into law that premiums should cover one-quarter of expected costs after a transition period in which home health care costs will be incorporated into the baseline.

---

* The Health Insurance (HI) payroll tax is collected with the rest of social security payroll taxes. Since 1994, HI taxes have had nomaximum, in contrast to Social Security where there is an upper limit on taxes.

---

federal level in 1995 representing 30 per cent of total spending on this pro-gramme in 1997. Under the programme, the federal government refunds, on average, 57 per cent of the cost of the programme to state governments to match their efforts to provide medical assistance for low-income individuals, most states linking Medicaid payments to eligibility for Supplementary Security Income. The largest share of the expenditure– about $25.6 billion in 1995 – pays for nursing home care. For the elderly poor, Medicaid also pays Medicare's deductibles, premiums and co-payments, as well drugs and spectacles, which are not covered by Medicare. Finally, Medicaid operates intermediate care facilities for the men-tally retarded and makes other payments for mental health, part of which benefit the aged. As well as these government plans, individuals also receive benefits from employer health plans and from medigap insurance purchased to cover shortfalls in Medicare protection.

Nursing home care is a particularly large expense for a number of elderly persons. Medicare makes no provision for such long-term care,[97] with many peo-ple having to finance it themselves. About 43 per cent of persons turning 65 will enter a nursing home before they die, and of those, one-fifth will spend five or more years there at an average annual cost at about $40 000 a year (140 per cent of per capita GDP).[98] Such costs are high relative to those found in other countries.[99] Long-term care insurance is rare.[100] The typical problems of the private insurance market, high administrative charges and adverse selection, mean that private insurance covered only 1 per cent of long-term care expenditures that year.[101] To cover this gap, about two-thirds of nursing home residents in 1994 relied on Medicaid for some support.[102] Medicaid, however has rigorous eligibility rules. There is a strict income rule. In addition, to qualify, in most states, residents without a spouse, cannot have more than $2 000 in liquid assets, excluding a primary residence and an automobile with a modest market value. It is possible for the elderly who think they may need nursing home care, to transfer their assets to children or other beneficiaries prior to their need for Medicaid assistance. States do have prohibitions on "Medicaid estate planning" in the three years before application. One study found that half of Medicaid applicants converted or transferred some of their assets and that the states denied eligibility to half of the people who did transfer some assets.[103] A little over one quarter of residents on Medicaid first entered the nursing home as a private pay resident. For those who stayed more than three years, more than half were on Medicaid.[104]

Their implications for old people

Income

The co-existence of a well-developed private pension system, the social security programme and tax-favoured savings plans means that the elderly receive income from a variety of sources. The bulk of the income of retired people comes from Social Security, with occupational pensions and income from assets and labour well behind (Figure 33, panel A) but a significant part of the income from assets comes from investments that were accumulated in retirement plans. About 57 per cent of occupational pension payments originate in the private sector while the remainder are made by government plans. Social assistance payments, through the SSI programme, account for a small amount of total benefits.

There has been a major transformation of the economic position of the elderly. By 1995, elderly households in the United States had an income just 92 per cent of the average disposable income of all households, once correction had been made for the lower tax burden of the elderly and the fact that they live in smaller households (Figure 34). Such relative prosperity of the elderly was only exceeded elsewhere in the OECD area in France and Japan. Moreover, the position of elderly households is more favourable once account is taken of all their non-monetary income. In the United States, the elderly generally own their own house, so receiving an implicit income from not having to pay rent, and also get substantial transfers to pay for their medical expenditure which has grown rapidly.

Figure 33.   **Income sources of the elderly**
1994

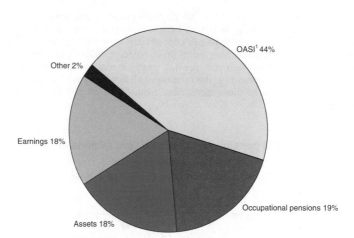

1.   Social Security old age and survivors benefits.
Source: Bureau of Census, Bureau of Economic Analysis.

Figure 34.   **Relative disposable income of elderly and all households**
1995 or a nearby year

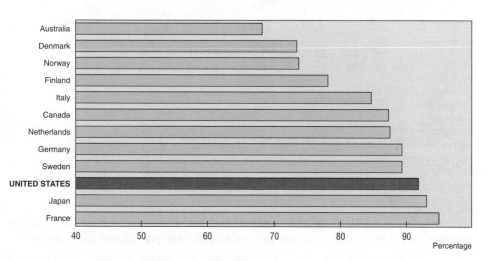

Source: OECD Maintaining Prosperity in an Aged Society.

Box 12. **Pension payments over the past 50 years**

The next 30 years will not be the first period in which the share of GDP devoted to the elderly has risen rapidly. Between 1950 and 1997 pension payments rose from under 2 per cent of GDP in 1950 to 8 per cent of GDP by 1997 (Figure Box). This initially reflected a rapid period of catching up in the incomes of elderly people that occurred between 1966 and 1986 when the pre-tax median real money income of elderly families rose by 75 per cent, while the income of all families rose by only 25 per cent.* As a result, the income of the elderly rose from 45 to 65 per cent of the national median income.

Total pension payments by type of pension
Percentage of GDP
Cumulative payments, summing to total

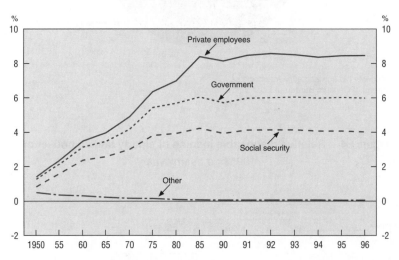

Source: Bureau of Economic Analysis.

---

* US Bureau of the Census Historical Income, 1996, Table F11.

As a result, by 1991, both the median and the mean income of the elderly, adjusted for family size, were above those of the US population as a whole.[105]

Medical benefits have become an increasing portion of the total resources of the elderly over the past two decades. Medical spending has risen to two-thirds of state pension payments by 1997, up from one quarter of social security benefits ten years after the inception of the Medicare programme in 1975. Despite the large scale of the Medicare transfers, the retired still have to finance almost 30 per cent of total medical expenses themselves. Most pay premia either to an employer sponsored medigap programme or a private insurance scheme. Hospital care, for both in and out patient care accounts for only a small proportion of out of pocket expenses. Nonetheless, 15 per cent of the elderly people, ineligible for Medicaid and opting fee for service coverage, have no further insurance cover. Overall, out of pocket expenses amount to 20 per cent of total expenditure – about one-third of social security benefits – mostly reflecting spending on prescription drugs and long-term care.[106]

Redistribution

The improvement in the economic situation of the elderly has been reflected in a marked reduction of the proportion of the elderly experiencing poverty. Social security benefits represent almost the only income of the lowest two quintiles of the income distribution of the elderly. Even for the mid-income range they represent three-quarters of total monetary income. Such payments have reduced the proportion of the elderly living in poverty to 12 per cent in 1990 down from 22 per cent two decades earlier, in contrast to increases in poverty amongst working-age households and children.[107] Poverty was concentrated amongst elderly widows. Almost one-quarter of all widows aged over 85 lived in poverty, with the figure rising to 50 per cent for Hispanics and 60 per cent for African-Americans. In contrast, in 1991, only 5 per cent of elderly married couples were living under the poverty line.[108] Indeed, the income of single elderly females was only 57 per cent that of elderly married couples in the United States in 1986, compared to an average of 80 per cent in the seven other OECD countries.[109] This reflects the fact that in the United States there is no minimum old age benefit for widows in contrast to other countries.[110] However, both the SSI programme and food stamps are available to limit the impact of low Social Security benefits.

The reduction in poverty is partly due to the fact that the progressivity of the social security benefit schedule gives a greater return to low incomes groups that is only slightly offset by the higher mortality rate of low income individuals.[111] A further significant, perhaps unintended, redistribution occurs within the social security system as the result of the interaction of the formula for computing average working life earnings and the progressive nature of the benefit schedule. In calculating benefits, the income of individuals in a period when they are not affiliated with the Social Security is set to zero. This reduces average earnings over the whole working life and such a person benefits from the progressivity of benefits. State and Local government employees gain from this provision as do immigrants.[112] Single-earner families obtain a markedly higher rate of return than a double-earner families and more than a single women or man. Indeed, the redistribution between such families is almost as large as between high and low income households with the same family composition. More controversially, the research also suggests that the rate of return of African-Americans is somewhat lower than that of the population as a whole.[113]

Although the social security system makes no distinction between sexes, the current system nonetheless redistributes contributions considerably towards women. For the generation born between 1917 and 1922, women earned around a return about 300 basis points higher than men.[114] Several factors explain such high returns. First, all individuals receive a minimum benefit equal to 50 per cent of their spouses benefit. In practice, most recipients of this benefit are women. Moreover, given that female earnings are lower than male earnings, the progressive nature of the benefit system benefits women. The longer life expectancy of women also boosts their return. Finally, women are more likely to have an interrupted working career and so benefit from the failure to completely pro-rate pensions according to actual length of contributions.[115] While, in general, women appear to benefit from the social security system, a spouse who works faces a considerable financial disincentive. A major part of the contributions of married women who work are not reflected in a benefit payments.[116] There are other anomalies in the rules, such as the abrupt cut-off period of ten years marriage before which divorcees can qualify for receiving a survivors benefit.

In any year, Medicare expenditures are concentrated on relatively few people. In 1995, slightly more than half of retired people receive less than $1 000 in Medicare benefits but accounted for only 3 per cent of total expenditure. On the other hand, 5 per cent of beneficiaries received benefits of over $25 000 and accounted for 45 per cent of total expenditures.[117] Spending on this group is highly persistent. Beneficiaries who represented the top 5 per cent of *per capita* outlays over a given two-year period, also accounted for more than 20 per cent of total expenditure over a nine-year period, with the top 30 per cent of *per capita* beneficiaries, in a given year, accounting for 78 per cent of expenditure in the same period.[118] Such a concentration of medical spending might make self-insurance, through medical saving plans, difficult to achieve. Moreover, if catastrophe insurance (*i.e.* coverage for very large medical expenses) were combined with such accounts (as it is in many proposals), the ability of the plans to limit expenditure would be markedly reduced.

Incentives to retire

The design of the US public pension scheme influences the timing of retirement, but to a much lesser extent in than in other countries, leading to one of the highest retirement ages in the OECD area. Nonetheless, despite changes, by 1997, the incentive structure embedded in the old-age pension system discourages full-time work at older ages.[119] Continued work results in a reduction in the pension wealth. Thus, the total before-tax gain from continued work is not gross earnings, but gross earnings less the drop in pension wealth. Using these rules in effect, the eventual loss of pension wealth divided by pre-tax earnings, over the 55-69 age span ranges between 5 per cent at age 55 to nearly 25 per cent at age 65[120] (Figure 35, panel A), but this varies considerably across ages and marital status. The impact of this disincentive can be seen at age 62 and 65 – the ages when the implicit tax rate jumps – when the probability of withdrawing from the labour force increases significantly. However, the extent of the withdrawal is greater than can be explained by the economic incentives, indicating that the administratively set dates of 62 and 65 exercise an independent influence on behaviour. Further support for this linkage comes from the fact that the implicit tax on continuing work for people in the age range 60 -64 was increasing until recently and participation rates were falling (Figure 35, panel B). Moreover, inter-national evidence suggests that there is a link between the average age of retire-ment and implicit tax rates (Figure 35, panel C). However, the extent of the discrimination against continued work is much less in the United States than elsewhere. The implicit tax rate is only lower in three countries (Iceland, Switzerland and Canada) and the average retirement age is also high. Moreover, unlike the practice in most other OECD countries,[121] early retirement via entry into disability or unemployment-related programmes is rare in the United States: entitlement to disability benefits is based on strict medical criteria, and unem-ployment benefits are of short duration and conditional on active job search.

Private sector defined-benefit plans can have strong effects on the timing of departure from an employer but do not necessarily imply retirement from the labour force. The provisions of such plans concerning normal and early entitle-ment ages, the specific rules determining pension calculation and the actuarial adjustment to early access to pensions differ from one plan to another. The incentives in private defined benefit plans vary depending on age. They range from being strongly negative until age 55, positive until the standard age of retirement and then strongly negative. While such plans encourage early retire-ment from career jobs with implicit tax rates that are sometimes higher than those in the Social Security system, if the person continues to work with the same employer, they do not discourage continued participation in the labour force. Indeed, more than half of those aged 57 to 61 in receipt of private pensions continue to work, often in part-time jobs.[122] Defined contribution plans run do not distort the retirement decision, at all. Additional years of work are rewarded by higher contributions and a higher stock of wealth at retirement. The growing importance of such defined contribution plans (see above) would thus indicate that a larger proportion of the workforce is not influenced by private pensions in deciding when to quit their employer. Moreover, the cost to the employer of a

Figure 35. **Implicit tax rates and retirement**

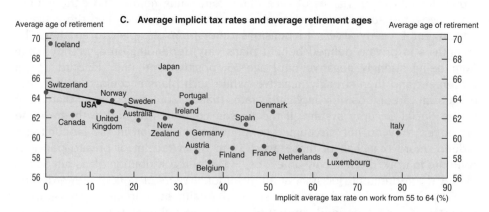

A. Implicit tax rates and labour force withdrawal by age

Implicit tax rate for a single earner (right scale)

Hazard rate (left scale)[1]

Age

B. Implicit tax rates and participation rates of males

Average implicit tax rate for 55-64 years old (right scale)

Participation rates of males aged 55 to 64 (left scale)

C. Average implicit tax rates and average retirement ages

Average age of retirement

Iceland

Japan

Switzerland

Norway

Portugal

USA   Sweden

Denmark

Australia

Ireland

Canada   United   Spain

Kingdom

New   Italy

Zealand   Germany

Austria

Finland   France   Netherlands

Belgium   Luxembourg

Implicit average tax rate on work from 55 to 64 (%)

1. The hazard rate represents the probability of withdrawing from the labour force in a given year.
Source: OECD.

defined contribution scheme does not increase with age, in contrast to defined-benefit schemes, so keeping older employees more competitive.

The Medicare system and private health care systems also interact to influence retirement. To avoid problems associated with co-insurance, the Medicare system mandates that it be the second payer for any insurance offered by employers to their elderly employees. Because firms' insurance costs rise with their workers' ages, companies have a large disincentive to employ the elderly that has been called[123] the "health earnings test." Expensive health insurance probably also encourages firms to avoid employing older workers who are not yet 65. The Administration has proposed offering Medicare coverage to those as young as 55, but under less generous terms. Congress, however, has not started to consider such legislation.

The impact of ageing under current institutional arrangements

Under the present system of support for the elderly, the coming retirement of the baby-boom generation is likely to be associated with a major increase in public health care costs if current demand trends continue. Indeed, the absolute increase in such spending may well be greater than associated with Social Security pensions. If no action is taken public finances will be placed under considerable strain, though the recent improvement in the federal budget position has lessened the future adjustment that is needed. However, the impact of ageing on the macro-economy may be small both relative to other countries and in relation to past changes in the US economy. Aggregate growth may slacken, but the slowdown in per capita living standards may be much less, unless private saving falls to a greater extent than expected. In the private sector, recent changes in the provision of retirement saving may well result in more people having financial assets on retirement. The changes will place greater emphasis on individual decision-making and are likely to result in more emphasis on using savings to finance retirement, rather than drawing a second-tier pension.

The effects on health care

The problems likely to be faced in health-care fall into three groups. *First*, an ageing population means more people will be in the Medicare and Medicaid system. As with the Social Security programme, this increase puts pressure on public finances and raises questions of budgetary priorities, which are considered below. *Second*, such budgetary pressures that arise from the demographics make it all the more important to address inefficiencies in the current system that would in any event need reform. Medicare expenditures have been growing much faster than GDP already, even though members of the baby boom generation have not reached 65 yet. Such growth is due to a combination of factors, including a high income elasticity for health care spending, deficiencies in controlling demand but also the rapidity with which technological change is introduced. *Third*, an ageing population when coupled with the rapid diffusion of medical technologies, could lead to an even greater increase in the demand for medical services – especially that for the chronically sick, though not necessarily the severely disabled – than the simple increase in the number of 65 and over would suggest. Some of this may be already happening as the increase in chronic care expenditures in Medicare may attest. Improvements in the efficiency and quality of such services will be all the more important in the future.

The consequences for public spending

The official estimates of the increase in health care spending for the elderly show expenditure rising much more rapidly than social security spending. Official estimates show Medicare and Medicaid net spending[124] doubling as a share of GDP in the next 30 years (Figure 36) and reaching 7 per cent by the middle of the next century, including both federal and state and local expenditures,[125] up from 2½ percentage points of GDP currently. Federal expenditure alone may rise to around 6½ per cent of GDP, according to the CBO.

Figure 36. **Government health care spending on elderly**[1]
Per cent of GDP

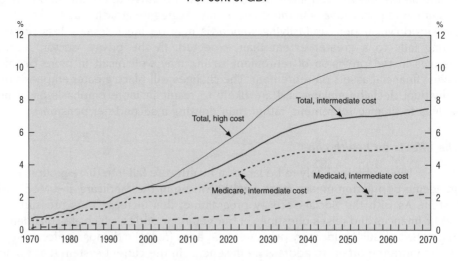

1.   From 1998 onwards the data are official projections using intermediate and high cost assumptions.
Source: Medicare Trustees, HCFA and OECD.

Figure 37. **Factors contributing to growth of medicare spending
on long-term care**[1]

Annual percentage growth rate

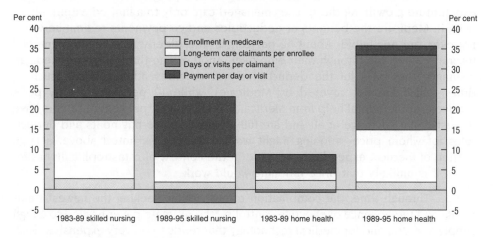

1.   Long-term care consists of medicare skilled nursing facilities services and home health care.
Source: HFCA.

Even this estimate could prove to be optimistic, especially for long-term care. The official projections assume that the growth of Medicare costs per beneficiary will slow to the rate of per capita GDP between 2010 and 2020. No rationale is provided for this assumption, other than that otherwise spending would grow unreasonably fast. Under the high-cost assumptions, where the deceleration of spending still occurs but at a later date, programme expenditure could reach 10 per cent of GDP by 2050. Even to achieve this goal, additional policy initiatives are required that are not yet in place. One particular area of concern over the long-term is chronic and long-term care where demand is already rising. Congress initially intended Medicare only to deliver acute care, but the system has since evolved. Medicare expenditures on home health and skilled nursing care has skyrocketed (Figure 37). Utilisation rates have jumped, both from an increase in the number served per enrollee and in the case of home health care from the number of visits per beneficiary. Such an upsurge may be due to greater need for chronic care, but at least in part, it has also been driven by loosened requirements.[126]

Inefficiencies in acute care

Because there are no effective financial safeguards either on producers or users of health services, more health care may be consumed relative to what an efficient market would produce. In most insurance markets, co-payments and deductibles serve as a partial means of introducing an incentive for the patient. Most private firms have switched to managed care programmes in order to limit expenditure growth. Medicare uses managed care only to a limited extent. Moreover, in Medicare the benefits of deductibles and co-payments to limit services, however, are negligible. About 42 per cent of the elderly receive supplemental insurance coverage through their employer. Another one-third purchase medigap insurance that pays for the deductibles and provides other services (such as drugs, which are not covered by Medicare), while 12 per cent, mostly poor, receives supplemental help from Medicaid. Thus, only 11 per cent of seniors have no first-dollar coverage at all and are fully exposed to co-payments and deductibles for whom price rationing might work. However, as noted above, a large portion of medical expenditure is made in the context of catastrophic illness for which it is unlikely that price rationing would work.

Through time, the combination of individuals seeking the newest treatments and the absence of effective control by the ultimate payer has led to a high supply and demand for medical technology that tends to be very expensive. Such a dynamic sustains cost increases in the long run, which until the early 1990s pushed up the cost of medical services much faster than overall GDP growth. This is not to say that technology is bad or that the solution to the problem is to unilaterally limit the services provided. Medical technology may provide benefits that on *average* greatly exceed its costs.[127] On the *margin*, however, these technologies and services may be extended to people for whom the benefit is much less than its cost. It may be for this reason that most countries do introduce some limitations on the diffusion of new and high cost technologies.[128] In addition, other countries such as Canada and the United Kingdom may have institutional features that prevent such an extension. So far, the public sector in the United States has had more difficulty to restrain its expenditures, in contrast to the private sector where medical spending peaked as a share of GDP in 1993 at 7.7 per cent, and had fallen to an estimated 7.1 per cent by 1998.

Ageing and the demand for chronic care

The way in which longer life expectancy interacts with the ageing population to affect the demand for chronic care is difficult to assess. Since 1982, there has been a 1.3 per cent annual decrease in disabilities.[129] Nonetheless, estimates of the number of disabled elderly in the future range from two to four times the current number.[130] Improvements in acute-care medical technology raise the survival probabilities for various diseases, often leaving patients with long-term chronic care needs. Moreover, medical improvements increase the number of the very old where chronic conditions, such as Alzheimer's disease, are more likely to develop.[131] On the other hand, further advances in medical technology, as well other societal developments reduce the prevalence of disabilities at each age group.

It would appear though that if past trends continue that the increase in life expectancy may only result in an increase in mild rather than severe disability. This emerges from using life tables and disability data for 1970 and 1980. It is possible to calculate the change in expected years of life free from all disabilities, as well as those years with some moderate or severe disabilities.[132] This methodology suggests that most of the increase in life expectancy between 1970 and 1980, has been spent without so severe disability that that the person is confined to bed.[133] Indeed, more recent research suggests that the extent of severe disability has been declining both in the United States and internationally.[134] Thus, increases in demand seem likely to be focused on forms of assistance that could well be provided in the home.

Another way in which demographics will affect the demand for long-term care services is through the relative decline in the availability of informal caregivers. All else equal, the dependency ratio would adequately measure this decline, but other demographic and societal developments could exacerbate the decline, moving more people who previously would have received informal care possibly onto the public rolls. The percentage of those 85 and over living alone with no children or siblings alive is projected to remain constant through 2020[135] but afterwards this number could grow given the decline in fertility rates in the 1970s and 1980s. Indeed, the dependency ratio overstates the amount of familial ties across generations as a greater fraction of the projected working population are expected to be immigrants who have a different mix of old and young than the resident population. Moreover, a disproportionate share of the burden of caring for an elderly parent falls on daughters, though there is a tendency for informal carers to reduce hours worked rather than finding paid work totally incompatible with an informal caring role. There is a tendency for adult daughters to increase their hours worked when an adult parent enters a nursing home.[136]

With the certain increase in demand for chronic care, service delivery needs to improve. Currently, delivery is fragmented between the federally run Medicare programme, the state run Medicaid programme, and various private and not-for-profit facilities. Several agencies have overlapping responsibilities, and consumers have to negotiate through a maze of complicated, disjointed systems to receive the type of services they need.[137] In some circumstances, elderly persons in need of subsidised care do not receive it. Nearly one-quarter of persons 65 or over in 1994 needed some help with either activities of daily living (ADL) or instrumental activities of daily living (IADL).[138] Somewhere between 30 and 55 per cent of those needing assistance did not receive it.[139]

In addition, public support of long-term care is oriented towards institutional care. For instance, in 1995 almost half of Medicare and Medicaid expenditures for long-term care for the elderly went to nursing homes (Figure 38). Nonetheless, demand for access to nursing care facilities outstrips supply; "a bed built is a bed filled". Indeed, to help control costs, most states limit the construction of new facilities, and as of 1995, seventeen states imposed a moratorium. As a result, there are often waiting lists to get in. Such an emphasis on institutional care is odd for two reasons. First, the quality of care is recognised to be poor. In one poll only 18 per cent of policy makers and agency representatives rated the quality of residential services as high, with 42 per cent rating it as low. Second, most people want to remain independent as long as possible and prefer alternative living arrangements that yield more autonomy. Nonetheless, only 14 per cent of Medicaid spending on long-term care for the aged went towards programmes to support home and community-based care. Only six states spent more than a quarter on such programmes.[140] It seems that some residents could thrive in a more independent setting; one study estimates that as a conservative estimate, 15 per cent of nursing home residents could move to a lower level of care.[141] Moreover, in the same poll, policymakers thought that home-based and community-based services were very good.[142] However, control of expenditure levels for home health care is difficult. With little monitoring over the actual activities of the

Figure 38. **Government health care spending on elderly,
by programme**
1995

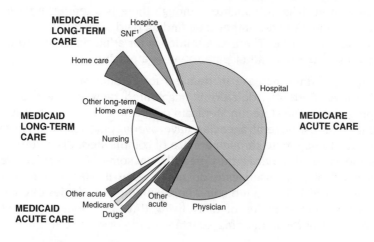

1.   Skilled nursing facilities.
Source: Wiener and Stevenson (1997c), The Urban Institute and HCFA.

helpers, resources may be diverted to unintended uses. An effective programme would require considerable administrative costs.

Public pension benefits

The ageing of the population will boost government spending on pensions. In 1998, social security spending on pensions and disability benefits represented 25 per cent of federal government non-interest spending, equivalent to 4.6 per cent of GDP. The increasing proportion of elderly people in the population will boost spending by around 2 per cent of GDP by 2034 by which time the Social Security Trust Fund will have exhausted its assets. Official projections from the Social Security Administration show that a 1.8 per cent in the increase in the payroll tax will be necessary to ensure that the balance between expenditure, income and the assets of the fund over the 75-year horizon that is set, by legislation, for the evaluation of the balance between social security spending and contributions.[143] In addition, a further 0.4 percentage points increase will be necessary to balance the disability portion of social security. While there are number of detailed areas where the official assumptions are open to question, taken as a whole the assumptions may be reasonable, though the assumed real rate of return on assets is about 75 basis points below the very long-run real rate of return on government bonds.[144] Another concern is that the methodology for evaluating costs does not generate a stable outcome at the end of the evaluation period, indicating that long-run costs are underestimated by the 75-year rule.

In contrast to Social Security, the future liability for the pensions of government employees is not being allowed to expand: since 1983 the pension scheme for new employees operates on a fully-funded basis. The other federal schemes are operating on schedule that will eventually make them fully funded, as appropriate transfers are being made from the budget to the fund to amortise the deficit. Thus even though, federal pensions are the equivalent of 20 per cent of Social Security outlays, the budgetary liability has been properly measured and so costs will be contained even though benefits will rise. However, the overall surplus of the three main federal pension funds is included within the overall budget balance. Unless these funds are used to increase saving, their impact in cushioning future spending will be limited. State and local governments do not aggregate their employee pension fund cash surpluses with their regular budget and so will benefit from the smoothing of expenditure induced by funding.

The overall effect on public finances

The increased spending stemming from ageing will tend to push the budget into deficit. The assets of the health care and social security trust fund will be consumed by 2010 and 2034, respectively. On the, admittedly unrealistic, assumption of continued unchecked borrowing, the unified federal budget

– which includes the health care and pension trust funds as well as all other non-age-related spending – would have a deficit of 4½ per cent of GDP by 2050, with debt amounting to 45 per cent of GDP (Figure 39). Beyond that the deficits and debt might quickly snowball, especially as higher interest rates and other adverse macroeconomic feedbacks could occur if deficits and debt reached these levels. Such projections assume that economic growth slows in line with the population projections and government spending, other than on pensions and health, remains constant as a share of GDP[145] and that real interest rates remain at recent levels.

While these estimates of future deficits appear large, they are mainly the result of the cumulative impact of deficit finance on interest payments and would be less alarming if timely action is taken is to reduce borrowing. Overall, if expenditure were reduced or taxation increased by ¾ per cent of GDP, debt might be no higher over the very long term than currently, though the deficit would likely be on an increasing trend.[146] If the objective were to ensure that the budget balance was stable then the expenditure cut would have to be around 1½ per cent of GDP. While that represents a significant financing gap, it is substantially less than the 4½ per cent of GDP improvement seen in the structural general government balance between 1992 and 1998.

Figure 39. **Public finances over the long-term**[1]
Per cent of GDP

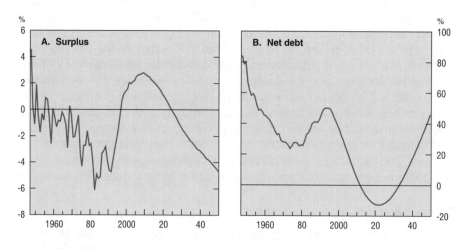

1. The scenario uses the May 1998 CBO long-term projection of public finances with the initial starting point updated to include the January 1999 medium-term projections.
Source: OECD.

From an economic view it is the scale of this overall macroeconomic imbalance that is important. The institutional structure – with earmarked taxation and trust funds – suggests that there is some merit in separating the imbalance into three parts: Social Security, Medicare and the remainder of the budget. Taking the case in which the fiscal position of the budget is stabilised in the very long-term, the overall requirement for expenditure cuts decomposes into cuts of 0.8 and 1.3 per cent of GDP, for Social Security[147] and Medicare, respectively, with a further cut of 0.3 percentage points needed to fund the increase in federal Medicaid spending. On the other hand, the remainder of the budget has room for tax cuts amounting to 1.6 per cent of GDP, illustrating the importance of viewing the government sector as whole, rather than just focusing on the ageing components of the budget. For example, the financial position of social security would be secured by a permanent transfer of 0.8 per cent of GDP from the remainder of the budget. However, the scope of transfers from the rest of the budget rests on the assumption, underlying the current budget, that government spending, other than on pensions and health care, can be reduced by a further percentage point of GDP in the next ten years.

The effects on the macroeconomy

Labour supply

During the next 30 years, changes in the overall growth of the economy seem likely to be dominated by movements in the labour force. The growth of the labour force will be adversely affected by two factors, reduced growth of the working age population as a result of a fall in the birth rate and a shift in the structure of the population towards elderly groups which, with current incentives and given their wealth, have low participation rates (Table 21). Demographic developments would entail an average annual increase in the labour force of only 0.5 and 0.2 per cent in the first and second quarters of the next century. Compared with the average annual growth of the working age population of 1.1 per cent since 1975, the decline is substantial. By 2025, the proportion of those aged between 55 and 64 will rise from 13 to 20 per cent of the total working-age population. This could reduce the aggregate participation rate by close to 2 percentage points in 2025 after which the effects would diminish somewhat, if participation rates by narrow age groups remain at their 1996 level. However, such a reduction in the level of the labour force translates into a very small impact on the annual growth rate of the labour-force (less than 0.1 per cent annually). Thus the main impact on the labour force will come from a falling birth rate rather than ageing. Some part of this slackening could be offset by the increasing experience, and hence productivity, of a more elderly labour force.

Table 21. **Labour force participation rates by age**

1996

Per cent of age-group

Age	Men	Women
16-19	53.2	51.3
20-24	82.5	71.3
25-34	93.2	75.2
35-44	92.4	77.5
45-54	89.1	75.4
55-59	77.9	59.8
60-64	54.3	38.2
65 and over	16.9	8.6
Total	87.0	72.0

Source: Labour Force Statistics, 1997.

Savings

The supply of capital may also be reduced by ageing as the aggregate saving propensity of households could be reduced, but there is little agreement on the magnitude of the effect in the United States. Studies based on aggregate data[148] indicate that the variation in private saving rates across countries and across time is systematically linked to the age structure: a greater proportion of the population above the age of 65 is associated with lower saving rates. This sensitivity of the saving ratio to the age structure of the population is in line with the life-cycle theory of consumption, whereby the middle aged save and build up assets which are then drawn down to finance consumption in excess of disposable income in retirement. The extent of dissaving in retirement will depend on the size of bequests intended to be passed on to survivors and on the need to have sufficient assets to meet unforeseen contingencies. Savings rates appear to be significantly influenced by the receipt or the expectation of a bequest.[149] As the average size of bequests received by the young are directly related to the age structure of the population, the overall household saving rate will be influenced by changes in the age composition, even if households' saving propensities do not drop markedly at older ages.

Overall, on the basis that household behaviour is no different in the United States than in other countries, it would seem that the saving rate may fall by between 0.14 and 1 percentage point for each one percentage point increase in the old-age dependency ratio.[150] The central assumption adopted by the OECD in a recent study[151] was that a reduction in the household saving rate of 0.3 percentage points would occur for every 1 percentage point increase in the old-age dependency ratio. On this basis, the US private saving ratios would fall by

4¹/₂ to 5 percentage points by 2050, reducing the national saving rate by 3 to 3¹/₂ percentage points. However, before turning down the household saving rate could rise up to 2010 as the large baby-boom cohort passes through the peak saving period in their life cycle. The decline would be much less marked than in other countries (Figure 40).

The above estimates of the impact of ageing on saving focus on the impact of changes in the age structure of the population on savings. However, this impact may vary according to the reasons for which the structure changes. The above calculations are based on a change in the age structure that is essentially brought about by a fall in the birth rate.[152] However, if the change in the age structure is brought about by an increase in life expectancy then savings may not fall, even though the elderly dissave and are more numerous.[153] If individuals have to save during their working life to provide for their retirement, then an increase in life expectancy with a constant retirement age requires greater saving during the working life. As a result an older population may be associated with higher saving, higher wealth and a larger capital stock, higher output and faster economic growth during the transition to a longer life expectancy.[154]

Figure 40. **Projected private saving ratios**
Per cent of GDP

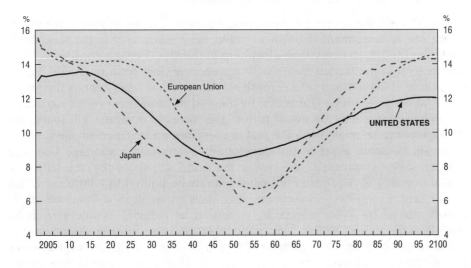

Source: OECD.

Capital requirement and saving-investment imbalances

The reduction in the growth rate of the labour force due to demographic developments may also on its own lower the growth rate of capital requirements. As long as factor prices remain constant, capital-labour ratios should be unchanged. The drop in the growth rate of the labour force would thus permit a reduction in the growth rate of the capital stock. This in turn would require less investment. Indeed, by the middle of the 21st century when the labour force could stagnate, unless there is marked change in the work patterns of the elderly, the investment ratio required to stabilise the capital-output ratio would be around 10 per cent compared with a required ratio of around 12 per cent at present.[155]

The impact of ageing on saving-investment imbalances is particularly uncertain. The scenarios developed by the OECD assume a fall in private saving that might generate an *ex ante* saving shortage, though, for the United States, the impact of ageing may be less than that found in cross-country studies. Ageing-induced imbalances seem unlikely in the shorter run. Household saving may not be negatively affected by ageing for the next three decades or so, and the continued expansion of the labour force will not prompt a major reduction in the investment ratio during this period (Figure 41). Thereafter, both saving and investment could fall. Initially this may not result in an *ex ante* imbalance, as the drop in investment requirements will come through relatively quickly. However, the imbalances would be markedly less than in Europe and Japan.

Macroeconomic aggregates and living standards

Overall, the lowering of labour-force growth induced by lower fertility and *ex ante* saving-investment imbalances could have much smaller macroeconomic effects on the US economy than elsewhere in the OECD area according to OECD scenarios.[156] In the United States GDP growth may slow down to around 1½ per cent, while in Europe and Japan growth may drop below 1 per cent as the growth in the labour force drops (Table 22). By the middle of the next century growth in the United States may be equal to just the increase in labour efficiency. The shortage of capital might push the real interest rate up by 1 percentage point, as there will be some offset to the developed country saving shortage from age-induced saving surpluses in the rest of the world. Consequently, the fall in the capital intensity of production will consequently be limited to a little more than 10 per cent. Such developments are also likely to result in a slowdown in the growth rate of US living standards, measured as national income per capita. Overall, in the period 2000 to 2050, national income per capita could increase by about 1¼ per cent annually, as against 1½ per cent annually in the past 25 years. This contrasts to the over 1 per cent per year slowing in per capita income growth since 1970.

Figure 41.   **Projected savings, investment and current account**
Per cent of GDP

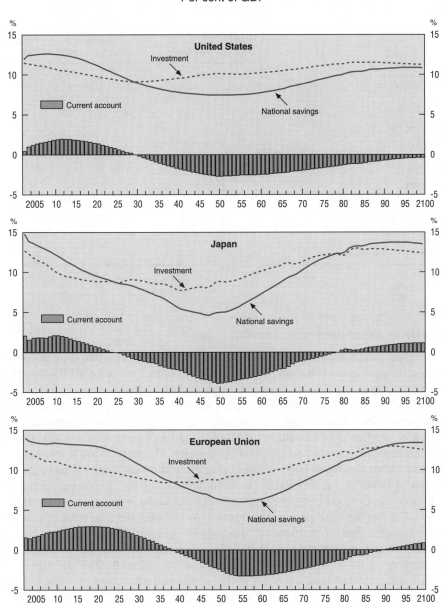

Source: OECD.

Table 22. **Projected long-term economic growth**

Per cent per annum

	Average growth in potential output	Contributions from:			
		Working age population	Participation rate	Labour efficiency	Capital intensity
2000[1]					
United States	2.5	1.1	0.2	1.2	–
Japan	1.9	–0.3	0.9	1.4	–
European Union	2.3	0.1	0.2	2.0	–
2000-2025					
United States	1.6	0.4	0.0	1.3	0.0
Japan	0.9	–0.7	0.2	1.4	0.0
European Union	1.2	–0.4	–0.1	1.7	0.0
2025-2050					
United States	1.4	0.1	0.0	1.4	–0.1
Japan	0.6	–0.9	0.1	1.4	–0.1
European Union	0.5	–0.9	0.0	1.4	–0.1

1. Estimates for 2000 are based on an assumed growth equilibrium path *i.e.* with stable capital intensity.
Source: Tuner *et al.* (1998).

The effects on private sector benefits

The sustainability of private-sector retirement benefits should be less affected by ageing as such than public-sector benefits. Defined contribution plans are not affected directly by ageing though indirect effects could occur if asset values were affected by demographic trends. As to defined benefit schemes, their costing takes into account the demographic profile of the plan members. Nonetheless, a number of uncertainties remain as to the extent to which these plans will act as an effective second pillar as the number of elderly people increases. As outlined above there has been a major change in the way in which private sector retirement benefits are provided. The primary channel for delivering such benefits is now the defined contribution scheme, especially when account is taken of those DC schemes that are supplementary to defined benefit schemes. Such a change means that at retirement, employees will no longer have a monthly income, rather they will have a capital sum. Moreover the size of the capital sum will depend on the investment decisions made by the individual and the extent to which accumulated assets are left in the schemes until retirement. These issues raise the question as to whether this means of providing retirement income will provide sufficient income for the next generation of retired people. At the same time, there still problems with the defined benefit schemes that may need to be addressed.

Defined contribution schemes

The adequacy of these assets in defined contribution funds depends on decisions taken by individuals. Many people, especially those with low incomes, do not even join voluntary defined contributions when they are offered by the employer. As to those who do join, several fears have been expressed about the use of defined contribution schemes. *First*, the individuals may be unable to manage financial market risk, *second* the individual may withdraw savings from these plans or may not rollover plan balances when changing job, *third* defined contribution schemes may offer inadequate protection to spouses and *finally*, there is concern about the difficulty that the individual may face in finding competitively priced annuities on retirement.

It has often been argued that individuals are risk-averse and so will tend to invest a smaller proportion of their plan investments in equities than may be regarded as optimal and certainly less than held by the professional mangers of defined benefit schemes. Available evidence does not support this view[157] (Table 23). In 1993, the proportion of DC schemes assets invested in equities represented a 5 percentage point lower share of DC schemes than DB schemes.[158] This gap appears to have been largely eliminated by end 1996, with both holding almost 63 per cent in equities. As individuals become older there is evidence is that they lower the risk profile of their plan by holding a progressively higher proportion of assets in fixed income securities.[159] Nonetheless, there is some evidence that some part of the equity investment in DC plans represents holdings of the equity of the company for which the employees work, which may represent an undue concentration of risk. Indeed, DB plans face limits on their holdings of debt or equity issued by their sponsor or real estate rented to the sponsor. These limits are not applied to DC schemes.

Table 23. **Class of assets in different types of retirement plans**

Per cent of total assets

	Year	Equities	Bonds	Cash	Other
Defined benefit plans					
Major 1 000 plans	1996	57	33	n.a.	n.a.
All DB plans for employers with over 100 employees	1993	46	38	6	10
Trusteed single employer schemes	1993	42	27	9	21
Defined contribution plans					
Major 1000 plans	1996	60	30	n.a.	n.a.
All DB plans for employers with over 100 employees	1993	45	33	8	14
Trusteed single employer schemes	1993	45	23	13	19

Source: Mitchell (1997), EBRI (1997), Williams (1997).

While the overall averages indicate similar asset allocations for individual and professional managers, there remain a significant group of participants who do not invest in equities. Indeed about 20 per cent of all investors had no equity exposure and this rose to 41 per cent of low income young plan participants. On the other hand, over one-quarter of higher earners (over $100 000 annual income) appear to have over 80 per cent investment in equities. Another common view is that women are more conservative investors and that hence will obtain lower returns than men. This certainly appears to be the case for women investors in the civil service thrift plan. However, it does not appear to be the case for women in the private sector[160] who appear to allocate a similar portion of new contributions to equities as do men.[161]

In recent years, there has been a growing tendency for employees who leave jobs to receive lump-sum distributions from their retirement plans. In part this has been due to the growing proportion of DC plans where, after a vesting period, the fund balance is the property of the employee.[162] Public policy has had an objective of ensuring that these lump-sum distributions are used to generate retirement income. The government imposes significant tax penalties[163] if the cash-outs are not re-invested in approved investment vehicles linked to retire-ment. Overall, this objective appears to be met, as an analysis[164] of all cash distributions in 1996, from the plans managed by a large firm of pension consultants,[165] showed that almost 80 per cent of the cash value of distributions were rolled over to tax approved vehicles even though almost 60 per cent of individuals took a cash payment, as most of the people who took cash payments were young with very low balances.

At retirement, though, the private market has some difficulties in turning a given stock of assets into an income stream that is guaranteed to last until the individual dies. In particular, the annuities market suffers from the fact that indi-viduals generally have a better appreciation of their life expectancy than do insurance companies. Thus, the mortality rate of men taking out annuities at age 65 is almost half that of the general population. Even at 85 the difference is one-third.[166] As a result, the average person does not buy an annuity and if he were to then the return on his investment would be between 260 and 380 basis points below that on corporate bonds[167] (Table 24). For those people who do choose to buy, the management costs reduce the return by about 1¾ percentage points, absorbing 20 per cent of the premium (or capital sum) paid to purchase the annuity. As a result, the classic annuity market is extremely small, the annual income flow for this group amounted to $0.5 billion.[168] International experience suggests that the expenses seen in the United States annuity market are not abnormal. In the United Kingdom financial market, returns paid to savers are reduced by between 1 and 3½ percentage points by costs.[169] Moreover, the expenses are regressive, with quite substantial fixed costs per account.[170] Such cost levels are also seen in the mutual fund industry, thus costs are relatively high

Table 24. **The annuity market**

	Men	Women	Couple
Mortality rates at age 65			
General population	22.2	13.4	n.a.
Annuitant population	11.5	7.3	n.a.
Yield reduction[1]			
General population	3.4	3.9	2.6
Annuitant population	1.7	1.8	1.9
Costs relative to premiums			
Annuitant population	17.5	20.3	21.2

1.   Reduction in yield between a theoritical annuity based on average mortality and the actual observed yields.
Source: Mitchell *et al.* (1998).

for Individual Retirement Accounts (IRAs) where financial service providers compete to attract clients. For defined contribution accounts in the United States, fund management costs are about 50 basis points lower than for retail mutual funds.

It would seem that the spread of employer-related defined contribution schemes is likely to lead an improvement in the wealth of a large number of groups at retirement. It has led to an increase in the extent to which job leavers receive full value from the employer contribution to a retirement scheme. With defined benefit schemes, an early leaver obtains a deferred pension based on the current salary of the individual or a lump sum distribution based on the present value of that deferred pension. Either way, the early leaver makes a substantial loss, compared to the contributions that have been made to the scheme. High job turnover thus quickly erodes benefits under a DB scheme. Moreover, vesting periods are as long as five years for DB plans. DC schemes, such as 401(k)s, also offer the prospect of better benefits to long-term employees. A recent study suggested that DC schemes appear to provide markedly higher benefits for early leavers, though the effect is less clear for long-term participants in DC plans.[171] The long-term DC participant may benefit if the rate of return on the DC fund exceeds that used in calculating the value of the defined benefit scheme (typically based on a 3 per cent real return) given that any excess in a DB scheme reverts to the employer. Based on historic real yields, a DC plan should obtain returns of 4½ per cent;[172] this would be reduced by management costs that average some 90 basis points for large defined contribution equity accounts. However, management costs for an account invested 60 per cent in bonds and 40 per cent in an index tracking stock portfolio would only be 27 basis points.[173] The difference in returns between the defined benefit and defined contribution scheme reflects also the fact the employee bears financial risk in the latter but not in the former. The absence of inflation protection in DB schemes is a risk that goes in the other direction. It is also the case that more low-income staff are likely to accumulate more financial assets under these schemes than they would through a combination of a defined benefit scheme and voluntary saving. The element of compulsory matching of employee and employer contributions[174] will also likely boost saving and it is this that allows the benefits under DC schemes to dominate those under DB schemes.[175] This is the more so since it appears that DC plans are held by many people who previously had no financial saving. This is partially the consequence of non-discrimination regulations which insist that a certain proportion of 401(k) members in a company come from low-income groups.

Defined benefit schemes

Private sector defined benefit funds should not be adversely affected by ageing, though sponsors may have to increase contributions from current low levels if past returns fall. Such schemes are regularly valued and have to comply with strict requirements about the adequacy of benefits. As these valuations are forward looking, adequate financing is in place. However, contribution rates may have to increase in the future. In recent years the high value of financial assets has allowed companies to reduce actual cash payments to their pension plans. Contribution rates (paid by the employer) have averaged only 2.9 per cent of payroll between 1990 and 1994.[176] Such a low contribution rate can only be maintained if the returns on the asset portfolios of the pension funds remain relatively high.[177] With no post-retirement inflation adjustment, the almost universal case, in the 1990s, the required contribution would rise to 5.0 per cent of payroll for the typical pension of 1 per cent of final salary per year of service.

One problem for defined benefit schemes is that current regulations introduced, in the Omnibus Budget Reconciliation Act of 1987, force companies to fund a pension relatively late in the career of an individual and so reduce the scope for the accumulation of interest income in the pension fund. Indeed contributions have to offset the lost interest so boosting the average contribution rate.[178] The objective of these regulations was to limit the extent to which companies were able to shield interest earnings in a pension fund from corporation tax. On the other hand, the tax regulations allow payment of a uniform percentage of payroll for all employees, regardless of age, into defined contribution plans, so pushing employers to choose defined contribution schemes.

Reforming the current system

Problems and challenges

The progressive ageing of the population will generate a number of problems for the US economy though relative to the difficulties facing many other

OECD countries, and the changes that have occurred in the economy in the past decades, the problems are manageable. If no action were to be taken, ageing would have adverse consequences for public finances. By the time the baby boom generation is fully retired, in 2050, the budget deficit could have risen to 4½ per cent of GDP and public debt increased to 45 per cent of GDP, providing that discretionary spendings are held constant as a proportion of GDP after 2009. Such increases will be the result of pension benefits rising by 2 per cent of GDP and medical spending jumping by 4 per cent of output. Moreover, health spending could easily expand even faster, if the current high rate of increase of medical costs continues unabated.

For social security pensions, the mechanisms for solving the financial problem are evident: expenditures could be reduced in several different ways, contributions increased or the rate of return on trust fund assets improved. The challenge is find a combination of policies that can be implemented quickly. For health, the problem is more complicated. Medicare is expensive, and even if projections are close to target, the system will absorb a large fraction of GDP by today's standards. Reform is complicated because of the interaction between consumers who, as in most countries, are not cost-constrained and suppliers who have every incentive to expand supply and diffuse expensive medical technology quickly.

Economic growth is likely to slow down as the baby-boom generation retires, though to a much lesser extent than in other countries. This slowdown may not generate much of a fall in per capita living standards. The major problem will be to avoid too large an increase in taxation on the working generation. As indicated in the OECD study "Maintaining Prosperity in an Ageing Society", persuading some of the baby-boom generation to work for longer would reduce the tax-burden on others. That will require getting the incentives right, in particular reducing the cost to individuals of staying in work between the ages of 60 and 70. As that report also indicated, increasing national savings now can also help to increase resources for future consumption. A number of changes to social security and health care legislation have been introduced in past years and these have been complemented by a new official plan to buttress Social Security.

Presently legislated changes

Measures have been taken to prepare for future fiscal challenges related to ageing. The 1983 pension reform raised contributions and is gradually phasing in an increase in retirement age to 67 by 2027. This reform changed the Social Security into a partially pre-funded system. The annual cash surplus is around $100 billion which has now accumulated to form a fund that now amounts to almost 10 per cent of GDP. In 1996, steps were taken to improve incentives that when fully implemented in 2004, will result in a reduction in implicit marginal tax rates for people who continue to work after age 65.

In the area of health, reform efforts have been directed at developing effective means to limit spending where the marginal benefit falls short of its cost and have generally been undertaken every four years. The most recent reform came in 1997, when Congress passed the BBA, which cuts expected Medicare expenditures by $116 billion over five years and $200 billion over ten years.[179] Nonetheless, the Medicare Trust Fund will be exhausted by 2010. Most of the projected savings come from reducing the reimbursement rate it provides hospitals and physicians. It also provides more choice in the types of managed care systems that can be offered, including a demonstration project for medical savings accounts. Following past patterns, the payment cuts to providers envisaged under the 1997 BBA should have temporary success in reducing the level of costs for a short while, but will likely be unsuccessful in restraining long-term growth in costs. Medical service providers are adept at offsetting the price cuts through volume increases or charging for more expensive procedures, perhaps offsetting half of the percentage reductions in prices.[180] Restraining expenditure through HMOs is already being tried. The CBO expects that enrolment in Medicare managed care providers will rise from 13 per cent to 25 per cent in 2002. In the short run, however, increases in managed care enrolees are expected to raise costs as adverse selection problems and the inefficient method by which HMOs are compensated more than offsets any savings that can be realised, even after cutting reimbursement rates to HMOs.

Recent reform proposals

The Administration opened a national debate on the consequences of ageing some five years ago with the appointment of an Advisory Council for the reform of Social Security. A similar process has started for the reform of Medicare. As an interim measure the President proposed that the budget surplus expected in FY 1999 should not be spent but kept in reserve. Plans for the reform of Social Security have now been announced.

Social security

In his State of the Union address, the President has proposed the outlines of his own programme "Save Social Security Now". The proposal draws on elements of many of the existing plans for reform, notably those of the Advisory Council on Social Security that were discussed in the last Survey. The principal features of this plan are:

- 62 per cent of the unified budget surplus over the period until 2014 will be reserved to save Social Security;
- One-fifth of this reserve will be invested in the equity market;

- Universal Savings Accounts (USAs) will be established. The government will pay $20 billion annually to these accounts in the period 2000-2004. In addition, the government will match a portion of any voluntary individual contribution that is made to these accounts, with a greater match for low-income workers. The amounts to be paid to each account, the population to be covered and the size of the government match have yet to be decided;
- The earnings test for people over 65 who work after drawing pension benefits will be abolished;
- The financial position of widows will be improved by raising the survivors benefit.

These proposals can be judged under four heads:[181] their impact on national saving, diversification, improving incentives and expenditure reduction. In the first respect, the Administration's proposal to reserve part of the unified budget surplus (which includes the current surplus of the Social Security System) to save social security should ensure that the social security surplus does generate an overall budget surplus and so increase national saving. The Administration proposes to transfer money from general revenue to the Social Security Fund. These transfers are planned to amount to 0.9 per cent of GDP in the next five years, rising progressively to 1.8 per cent of GDP between 2010 and 2014. Allowing for a possible higher return from equity investment, the Administration estimates that such a transfer would push back the date at which the Trust Fund was exhausted to 2059. In addition, the balances contained in the USA plans will gradually accumulate on top of the foreseen path of the Trust Fund. If the programme were successful in stimulating private saving, it would go some way to complementing social security benefits in the period beyond 2059 when the future of Social Security is still uncertain.

There is some possibility though that the apparent increase in saving brought about by this plan might be offset by individuals. The risk is greatest in the case of USA plans held by high-income households, where evidence from IRA accounts suggests that a considerable degree of substitution may occur. For lower-income people this is less likely to be the case. In addition, there is a possibility that the personal sector could offset some of the increase in public saving. For this to happen, individuals would have had to set saving plans on the basis of a cut in future benefits. However, evidence for such Ricardian behaviour is mixed, suggesting that the possibility of offset is limited.

The President's proposal does promise overall economic gains through the increase in the budget surplus and private saving. On the basis of a return of $8\frac{1}{2}$ per cent,[182] for each sustained increase in national savings of 1 percentage point of GDP, the level of GDP might be raised by $2\frac{3}{4}$ per cent by 2030, with corporate and property tax yields up by over $1\frac{1}{4}$ per cent of GDP. An increase in

GDP of such a magnitude would be sufficient to more than cover the expected jump in social security costs. Such an increase in investment would represent about one sixth of average net investment in the private sector and would raise capital stock growth by 0.4 per cent per year. By 2030, the capital stock would have risen by 12 per cent. However, such calculations represent only a partial equilibrium. They do not take into account feedback effects, most notably the likely increase in foreign rather than domestic investment. Full economic model simulations generate results of a smaller magnitude (Table 25). For instance, a reduction in the debt ratio of 10 percentage points, spread over the next 20 years (achieved through an *ex ante* increase in government saving of 1 per cent of GDP per year) might raise GNP by 1.3 percentage points by 2040, according to Secretariat simulations. Since 1997, the Administration has raised its target for the medium-term public finances from a balanced budget to a surplus of 2 per cent. On the basis of these simulations, this change in fiscal policy may have raised the future level of GNP by as much as the increased cost of social security pensions.

The President's proposal relies on *diversification* of the financial assets held by social security funds. To be sure, past returns from equities have been high,

Table 25. **Impact of an increase of the budget surplus by one per cent of GDP**

Difference from the reference case

	2010	2020	2030	2040
	Per cent			
GDP level (per cent)	0.5	0.9	0.9	0.8
GNP level (per cent)	0.6	1.2	1.3	1.3
	Per cent of GDP			
Capital stock	2.7	4.3	4.4	4.0
Net government debt	−7.7	−10.6	−10.3	−10.0
Net foreign assets	2.8	6.0	8.1	9.0
Trade balance	0.3	0.1	−0.1	−0.3
Investment income balance	0.1	0.3	0.4	0.5
Private consumption	0.1	0.5	0.9	1.2
Investment	−1.0	−1.0	−1.0	−1.0
Private investment	0.5	0.3	0.2	0.2
Current balance	0.4	0.4	0.3	0.2
Real effective exchange rate (per cent)	−0.6	−0.4	−0.1	0.2
Real interest rates (percentage point)	−0.2	−0.3	−0.3	−0.3
Change in budget deficit[1]	1.0	1.0	1.0	1.0

1. The federal budget surplus has been increased *ex ante* by 1 per cent of GDP.
Source: Turner *et al.* (1998).

both absolutely and in relation to riskiness of equity returns.[183] Over the past two centuries, the rate of return on equities has been 3.5 percentage points higher than that on bonds and the differential has been even higher in the period after 1945 (Table 26). The extent of this post-war gap between the yields on equities and bonds has generally been seen as an anomaly, in that normal degrees of risk aversion would have generated a markedly lower excess return for equities. It may be that the widespread publicity given to this finding, and the related spread of diversified equity investment, has reduced the equity premium which now appears lower. If the anomalous part of the equity premium has been largely eliminated, then it would follow that, on a risk-adjusted basis, there would be much less of a case for investing in equities. The Social Security Fund, in risk-adjusted terms, might not gain from investing more in equities and less in bonds, despite the higher return of the former because of the lower risk of the latter. However, on the basis that past returns are repeated, investing one-fifth of the reserve in equities would thus raise the return by about 50 basis points annually, lengthening the life of the Fund by about five years.

There are, in any case, a number of reasons that suggest the overall results of such a policy would be subject to a number of offsets. Substitutions would have to take place in portfolios. Increasing the income from the equity Social Security funds will require reducing income of existing equity holders. This will require raising equity prices and lowering bond prices. The return to the Social Security Fund might rise, but that would be balanced by an increase in the cost of bond financing for the rest of the economy. The impact on the budget of high bond yields would be limited, as if the scenarios on which the Administration's plans are realised, then the government debt would be com-pletely paid off, at least temporarily. Nonetheless, finances would still suffer, to

Table 26. **Real rates of return on different asset classes**

	Equities	Long-term government bonds	Short-term government bonds
Total period			
1802-1997	7.0	3.5	2.9
Sub periods			
1802-1870	7.0	4.8	5.1
1871-1925	6.6	3.7	3.2
1926-1997	7.2	2.0	0.6
Postwar			
1946-1997	7.5	1.1	0.5

Source: Siegel (1998).

some extent, as the return of private bonds – that the government would have to hold as it became a net creditor – would be lowered.

There is also a practical problem that the distribution of future returns is not known with certainty. Consequently the riskiness of any future government financial balance will also have increased subjecting individuals to increased tax risk. Moreover, the initial generation holding equities might promise themselves benefits based on returns that could not be sustained over the long term.[184] Finally, problems of corporate governance might also occur under this proposal, as governments might try use the equity funds of the Social Security Fund for public policy purposes. It is true that there has been no tendency for this to happen with the equity holdings of the Federal Employees Thrift Fund. However, the Trust Fund would have much larger holdings, amounting to perhaps 4 per cent of all shares outstanding. On the one hand, government might avoid holding certain shares for political reasons. It might be difficult to hold shares in a company that was under an anti-trust prosecution, or was being sued for health reasons – even if these companies were part of an overall market index. On the other hand, the government might decide not to vote its shares at all, but this would amount to tacit support for existing management.

There could be gains from diversification. However, if the expected return were estimated correctly, then sharing the riskiness across generations could be positive factor. The equity premium might fall and capital formation increase. Moreover, some groups, however, might benefit from diversification. Not all households hold equities, as they are inadequately informed about returns or because the costs of small investments are higher than average. Moreover, some groups might like to be short on bonds and over-invested in equities but cannot borrow in existing capital markets. Finally, there is the large group that has no financial assets at retirement. These groups might benefit and so provide some rationale for diversification.

The USA accounts would also *improve incentives* to save, so increasing the capital stock and the resources available for consumption. But they would only go part of the way to a full defined-contribution system which would have a much greater impact on incentives by reducing the extent to which social security contributions are seen as a tax, so improving the work-leisure trade-off and boosting saving. A large number of points remain to be settled as to the design of these plans, notably concerning their management. Private sector administration of these plans is unlikely to be economic: for instance, if the initial $20 billion transfer were split amongst the entire population the annual allocation per account would be less than $100. Such a sum would be below the average annual administration costs of a private sector defined contribution plan,[185] which, for a small fund, amount to $120 per participant plus investment management costs. The pledge to remove the earnings test over 65 is welcome, given the relationship between implicit tax rates and the participation of the elderly in the labour force. Given that this limit is already slated to be substantially eased by 2004 for those over 65, it might be desirable to go further removing the disincentive at earlier ages. This would require ensuring that there is full actuarial equivalence between postponing retirement, contributions that are paid and the eventual pension that is paid, as well as removing the earnings limit between the early and standard retirement age. In this way, the decision to withdraw from the labour force would not be influenced by the design of the Social Security system.

The plan contains no proposals for benefit reductions. Three broad categories of reductions can be identified: lower initial benefits, lower benefit increases after retirement and finally delaying the date at which benefits are paid and so increasing the retirement age. The time path of the savings from these options is different and so comparison can only be made by converting the expenditure savings into an equivalent constant annual share of GDP, using present value techniques. Three possible plans can be identified: reducing initial benefits by 0.5 per cent per year below what they would have otherwise been; reducing the cost-of-living adjustments by 1 percentage point per year on the grounds that the CPI overstates true inflation; and speeding up the envisaged increase in the retirement age and increasing it by one month per year if life expectancy continues to increase. These three options are broadly equivalent in terms of the likely saving, the first two reducing the fiscal gap by 0.5 per cent of GDP and the latter lowering it by 0.4 per cent of GDP. Any one of these plans would suffice to significantly reduce the long-run fiscal gap identified above. Alternatively payroll taxes tax rates could be increased. The choice between these options depends on the importance that is attached to the welfare of different generations. While reducing the growth of future pensions would affect current as well as future retirees lowering the initial level of benefits would impact on the former whereas a gradual further increase the retirement age only affects new retirees well into the future, and would give people adequate time to adjust saving plans. Increasing taxation bears on the current workforce. In terms of intergenerational equity, the first might be preferable as large transfers have been made to existing retirees. An increase in payroll taxation would be more difficult to support in terms of intergenerational equity and would also have the disadvantages of introducing further distortion into the economy.

Overall, the new plan represents a step towards preparing the US economy for the ageing of the population. The preservation of budget surpluses may help to increase national saving. It may also delay the point at which overall government finances move into deficit. In narrower accounting terms, it should also ensure that the life of the Social Security Trust Fund is prolonged. The precise legislative form of the transfer has not yet been decided. Moreover, as indicated above a global solution will require benefit reductions or tax increases, above those contained in the current medium-term budget projections, rather than just reallocating resources between government funds.

The Administration has, indeed, indicated that further work will be required to ensure the longer-term future of social security. One promising avenue would be to explore the interaction of the Universal Saving Accounts and the Social Security System. If these accounts were made mandatory then eventually they would provide a complement to social security benefits that are to be reduced somewhat in the longer term under existing legislation and are likely to have to be reduced again eventually. For instance, with life expectancy steadily increasing some further increase in the age at which benefits are to be paid in full might be envisaged. Individuals would then be able to choose whether to use these balances to retire at presently planned dates or to wait until the standard entitlement date.

Over the longer term it would appear that building on the "USA" plans in order to develop a complement to the Social Security system would have substantial benefits. A minimum guarantee could be built into the system but the precise extent of transfers that are made would have to be explicitly costed and legislated. In any case, some reconsideration of perhaps unintended transfers that occur within social security, notably through the method by which average incomes are calculated and through the spouse benefit rules that transfer income from two-earner couple to single earner couples. With such a system, though some degree of compulsory annuitisation would be needed to overcome problems of self-selection. Greater use of defined contributions would involve switching the liability for existing pension rights to the general budget. The benefits paid to the first 60 age cohorts to pass through the social security system are estimated to have been around $10 trillion (in 1998 present value terms) higher than the contributions they paid.[186] As over a longer time period, the income and expenditure of the social security system has to balance, this earlier transfer has become a debt that has to be serviced in the future. About one-quarter of social security contributions (1¼ per cent of GDP) is used to stabilise this debt relative to GDP.[187] The Administration's proposals, which would appear to involve transferring some money from general taxation to social security, represent a first step in this direction.

Health care

Within the Medicare system, several steps policy makers could take to improve efficiency have already been mooted. The Senate's means-testing plan administered by the HCFA could have saved $4 billion over five years.[188] Larger savings, perhaps double, could be realised, however, if the Internal Revenue System administers the means testing programme instead. Raising the eligibility age along with Social Security would save a small amount initially, but over ten years, it could save $10 billion but could leave 3½ million seniors without insurance,[189] about half of whom might not be able to afford privately purchased insurance. Moreover, if health care costs continue to grow, these estimates may be too low if companies quicken the pace that they shed older workers to save on private health insurance costs. In addition, lawmakers could give HCFA expanded authority to introduce other means of price competition in the system.[190] Currently, HCFA is running one demonstration project in Denver. Leading up to the passage of the BBA, the Senate proposed three additional reforms that were eventually dropped from the final act. They suggested that Medicare benefit should be means tested, some home health beneficiaries should make a small co-payment, and the eligibility age for Medicare should increase in line with Social Security.

In the State of the Union speech, the President proposed making fiscal transfers to the Medicare Hospital Funds amounting to about ¼ per cent of GDP annually. This would prolong the life of the Medicare Trust Funds by ten years until 2020. However, he indicated that the Administration would be looking carefully at the forthcoming report of the bipartisan Medicare Commission. In the event, the Medicare Commission did not issue a report, as the Chairman's proposal did not gather a sufficient majority. Nevertheless, some of its congressional members are likely to introduce legislation based on the Chairman's proposal.

His proposal recommended a change in the emphasis of Medicare away from a fee-for-service programme towards managed care provided by many competing suppliers. Hospital and general practitioner services would be provided by the same plan (so combining Medicare Part A and B). The government would determine a standard package of benefits, in line with current Medicare services with the addition of outpatient prescription drugs and an upper limit on co-payments. Additional benefits could be offered as an option. Private medical companies would then sell annual contracts for cover based on this standard package. Individuals would be free to choose between the various providers and would pay only 12 per cent of the annual premium for this level of coverage, provided that it cost between 85 and 100 per cent of the national average for a standard plan, the remainder being paid by the government. If the scheme were more expensive, the individual would pay all of the excess. On the other hand, if the scheme cost less than 85 per cent of the average, the individual would pay nothing. Additional higher levels of service, over the government set standard, would be paid for entirely by the individual. The current fee-for-service scheme would be available as a separate option, run by the government. The basis of its funding would be changed, so that its annual premium income was sufficient to ensure that it broke even. The payment by the individual would be calculated in the same fashion as for the managed care plans, but in addition there would be a minimum 10 per cent co-payment except for hospital stays and preventive medicine.

Proposals by the Chairman of the Medicare Commission also envisaged guaranteeing free prescription drugs for people with an income below 135 per cent of the poverty line and reducing the deductible associated with serious illness. Despite these proposals, and the introduction of prescription drug coverage in all plans, the staff of the Commission estimate that the move towards managed care could reduce the growth rate of Medicare expenditure by between 1 and 1½ per cent annually. This would be enough to significantly improve the fiscal integrity of the Medicare programme. The Chairman also recommended that further study should be made of the issue of long-term care, covering long-term insurance, tax policy and community-based programmes.

In the long run it does indeed seem likely that Medicare is going to have to increase the number of enrolled persons in managed care programmes, as the private sector already has. In the private sector, there appears to be evidence that this move has raised productivity of medical services.[191] The above proposals are similar to the current system for federal employees.[192] In that system, during the open enrolment period, the government prints a catalogue of certified plans, and employees pick their plan. The government pays a fixed percentage of the insurance costs up to some limit. It also negotiates with plans during a certification process to try to obtain the best price for its employees as well as constrain the number of options to avoid problems of adverse selection. Problems of adverse selection are limited because employees can only switch during the open enrolment period and because employees pay at least a fraction of the marginal dollar for more generous insurance packages. The catalogue and the co-ordinated enrolment period also limit the ability of insurers to choose the best risks, a problem that has hindered the development of managed care, so far, in Medicare. In addition, the extension of managed care to a potentially sick population will require that considerable attention be paid to risk adjustment mechanisms. To be sure such a reform for Medicare would have to include additional consumer protections to address the same concerns that arise in the private sector for non-elderly health insurance (see Chapter III).

The problems associated with chronic and long-term care for the elderly are different from those for acute care. By themselves, costs are not large as a fraction of GDP, although expenditures on certain programmes are growing rapidly. Instead, the quality of services is spotty, and there is a general concern that the elderly are not receiving the right level and type of care. Indeed, the structure of the system makes co-ordination difficult among the several federal and state agencies that are involved. As the number of elderly increase and as they become older on average through lengthening life expectancies, such problems could worsen.

In order to reduce expenditure growth and inefficiencies in some programmes where costs are already escalating, a few reforms have been proposed.

At the federal level the BBA extends the prospective payment system, to home health providers, skilled nursing facilities, outpatient service departments, rehabilitation facilities and ambulance service providers. This reform was especially needed to close a loophole that some hospitals exploited.[193] It also increases anti-fraud and abuse measures, especially in the home health care programme. The Senate considered a proposal to levy a $5 co-payment on home health visits after the first 100 for those without a prior three-day hospital stay, but it was excluded from the final bill. Such a proposal would have fallen on the sickest who are the least in position to pay. Instead, Congress could impose a co-payment only on the first several visits,[194] which may limit marginal benefits while limiting the burden. For long-term and chronic care, however, states need to implement a series of reforms. Reimbursement policies for nursing home care vary by state, and some states still pay for certain services, especially ancillary services such as physical therapy are based on costs.[195] At a minimum state governments should be more aggressive in developing payment systems that encourage savings. It is noticeable that countries with comprehensive long-term care programmes (such as Germany) not only have co-payments on home visits but also enforce strict screening of needs.

One particularly useful programme is to use Medicaid money to support home and community-based systems. Such programmes allow the elderly to live in settings more suitable to their needs, while costing less than nursing homes.[196] Currently all states operate a waiver programme under HCFA rules to run such programmes, but they are now modest in most states. The federal government could encourage their growth by making them a standard part of Medicaid, instead of a waiver programme. It could also encourage private programmes by making them mandatory in long-term insurance policies to qualify for tax-exempt status.

In the long run, other reforms may be worthwhile. First, federal and state governments need to integrate acute and long-term care services, especially for those who are eligible for both Medicare and Medicaid. There is some suggestive evidence that combining acute and long-term care under a managed care provider can produce some savings. It would also lessen the amount of resources each system devotes to maximising the amount of funds that the other system provides.[197] From the view of society as a whole, at best, such policies are a zero-sum game, and probably lead to some inefficiencies. In addition, integration of some Medicare and Medicaid services also would make it easier for consumers to find the services they need.

The second important reform is to encourage private insurance for long-term care. While growing, the market is still small.[198] The 1996 Health Insurance Portability Act[199] clarified the tax-exempt status of employer contributions for long-term care insurance, which previously was ambiguous, and mandated that benefits under some limits were not personal income. Because Medicaid exists as a stop gap measure and perhaps from myopia, people do not save enough for their long-term needs. Some states are experimenting with programmes to encourage the purchase of long-term care insurance through relaxed eligibility standards for Medicaid. Currently, participation in the programmes is modest[200] but in the long run, however, such programmes should aid the development of the long-term care insurance market, bringing down costs and prices. How successful these programmes[201] are and their effects on state budgets will not be known for several years. Some people argue that the benefits of these programmes cannot be large because a large fraction of people takes measures to avoid Medicaid in the first place.[202] The prospect of being on Medicaid with assets that they could otherwise use to avoid Medicaid is not worth much to them.

Nonetheless, it is clear that other people do take Medicaid into account when they plan for retirement. Some go so far as to transfer assets to qualify for Medicaid earlier. Thus, another strategy federal and state governments can take to encourage Americans to start long-term planning is to tighten asset transfer rules and estate recovery programmes. While such programmes are not likely to significantly increase revenue,[203] together with a public awareness programme, more Americans may choose to plan for long-term care. A Nebraska task force, for instance, has recommended extending the look back period for asset transfers to five years, from its current three-year requirement.[204] In addition, the states should expand their estate recovery programmes. In 1995, the states recovered less than 0.5 per cent of nursing home expenditures for the elderly. Based on the collection rates in 1993 for the ten most active states, at least 1 per cent could be collected. Collection rates could be further improved and administrative costs lowered if applicants were required to purchase reverse mortgages on their homes before they entered the programme. On its face, strict eligibility rules and estate recovery programmes would seem to be fairer to current taxpayers who should not fund long-term care to protect inheritances. However, such programmes are unlikely to be publicly popular and result in reductions in the incentive to save.

Summary and conclusions

The next 40 years will see a major change in the structure of the population in the United States. The number of elderly will increase markedly and the growth of the working population will slacken. As a result, the number of retired people relative to that of working age adults will rise substantially, but will be offset, to a certain extent, by less rapid growth of other dependant groups such as children and economically inactive people of working age. Indeed, the ratio of the total number of dependants to the numbers employed should not be any higher in 2035 than it was in 1985. Moreover, in the long run, the expected continued increase in life expectancy is a positive development given that the increased longevity has not been associated with an increase in severe disability.

The ageing of the population will be less marked in the United States than in many other OECD countries. With a relatively high birth rate and substantial immigration, there appears little danger that the US population will fall, as seems likely to occur in some other OECD countries. On current trends, by 2035 the United States will have the lowest ratio of elderly to working age people amongst the major seven economies. Moreover, by 2035, 45 per cent the total population should be working in the United States – only slightly lower than the current proportion – as against only 35 per cent in the major European countries. As a result, there should less of a drop in aggregate economic expansion and only a slight slowdown in the growth of living standards provided that the private saving does not fall to a greater extent than expected.

The recent OECD study "Maintaining Prosperity in an Ageing Society" indicated that were a number of key areas where change was needed in may countries in order to minimise the extent of the burden on the working population that might be generated by an ageing population. These focused on increasing the resources available to economy over the next thirty years, while at the same time reducing the dependence of individuals on the state for their retirement income and focussing on cost-effectiveness in the area of health and long-term health care.

In many respects, the United States is well placed to meet the challenge of ageing. The disincentives to continued work beyond the age of 60 are amongst the lowest in OECD area, the general government budget is in surplus and the likely scale of the necessary fiscal adjustment appears relatively small compared to that which has taken place in the past few years. Moreover, the resources of the elderly are drawn from diverse sources. Nonetheless, improvements still need to be made in all of these areas most notably in health care.

Previous sections of this chapter contain a number of detailed recommendations, in this regard, that are drawn together in Box 13. Two of them can be singled out, maintaining and building on the current budget surplus and restraining the growth of medical expenses under Medicare and Medicaid. The Social Security system is not well prepared for the future. The Trust Fund may be exhausted by 2032. The 1983 reforms has resulted in the buildup of assets and has lowered future benefits but did not achieve their goal of stabilising the system. A new reform of Social Security needs to address several issues: prefunding the likely growth in benefits in order to increase the future capital stock and improving incentives to work at older. More generally, the provision of supplementary pension arrangements for younger people, as well as those that

Box 13. Maintaining prosperity in an ageing society: recommendations for the United States

Public pension systems should remove disincentives to later retirement

- Remove earnings test for people drawing benefits;
- Set reductions/increases in net benefits for work before and after the standard entitlement age on an actuarially fair base;
- Ensure that contributions paid after the maximum computation period result in increased benefits.

Fiscal consolidation should be pursued

Overall

- Restrain public expenditure (except on health and pensions) to a constant share of GDP over the medium and longer term;
- Increase the current federal budget surplus.

Social Security

- Transfer funds from general taxation to the Social Security Fund;
- In order to balance Social Security over the very long term, focus on slowing the growth of expenditure. Structural changes should be made to programme entitlements. Amongst possible changes are: an acceleration in the move to a higher retirement age with a link to life expectancy; a reduction in cost-of-living increases; no longer count years where earnings are zero as part of career-average earnings; a widening of coverage so that all state and local government employees are included in the system;
- In addition, a number of further areas should be reviewed, including: the level of benefits paid to one-income households, relative to households with two incomes; the treatment of benefits paid to divorced people; and finally the possibility of improving the benefits paid to widows.

Health care for the elderly

- Increase the number of people enrolled in managed care systems by making special provision for the chronically sick;
- Increase competition between HMOs by giving more choice of plans, using the federal employees system as a base;
- Allow the HCFA greater freedom to obtain competitive prices for Medicare patients;
- Consider a degree of co-payment for wealthier patients.

The provision of retirement income should be diversified

- Implement the proposed voluntary "USA" saving plans quickly;
- Consider redesigning such plans as mandatory scheme so that saving in these plans could become an adequate complement for Social Security benefits in the long run.

(continued on next page)

(continued)

Focus health and long-term care on cost effectiveness

- Federal and state governments should better integrate acute and long-term care services;
- Use Medicaid money to support home and community based systems;
- Verify the medical need for home-care assistance for frail older people;
- Introduce co-payments for home care visits subject to an income-related annual ceiling;
- Encourage purchase of long-term care insurance through relaxed eligibility standards;
- Tighten asset transfer and estate recovery programmes for long-term care.

---

work part time or in occupations with high labour turnover, could be improved, as current private sector schemes often miss these categories of people.

The Administration's new proposal addresses some of these issues. An increase in the budget surplus is planned, with a significant transfer to the Social Security Fund from general revenue. Such a transfer should not destabilise the rest of the budget that is moving progressively into surplus. Nonetheless, the overall budgetary position will be deteriorating by the middle of the next century and further action is likely to be required perhaps involving traditional avenues of reducing expenditure.

The proposals do represent a step towards the use of some private management of public-sector pension assets. However, the overall benefit of holding equities among the assets of the Trust Fund remains uncertain. Moreover, diversification of Trust Fund assets is likely to involve the government holding 4 per cent of the equity of US companies, raising issues of corporate governance that may be difficult of resolve. The proposal to create voluntary "Universal Savings Accounts" to ensure that individuals accumulate assets for their retirement could help the minority of individuals who retire with no financial assets. A number of practical points need to be solved, notably how to administer relatively small accounts at a reasonable cost. There are, though, already many tax-favoured voluntary savings schemes for retirement and not all the population uses them. While the incentive for low-income groups will be greater than under existing tax-favoured saving plans, the new scheme may, nevertheless, need to be mandatory to be effective, with the contribution rate set at a level that would ensure the balances could be used to complement Social Security benefits that might, in the long-run, not be increasing as rapidly as projected at the moment. For instance, earlier proposals for individual accounts set the contribution rate at

1.6 per cent of income. The "Universal Saving Accounts" could be used as the basis to build a defined contribution system that would complement a basic pension, especially as the design of these accounts has shown that a second-tier defined contribution system is not incompatible with redistributive goals.

Excluding social security, the longer-term financial position of the remainder of the government budget is likely to be adversely affected by health care expenditure. Pushed by the combined effect of ageing and some increase in prices of health care and increased technology, outlays may rise twice as rapidly as social security spending. A substantial reduction in benefits, the quantity of services used and their price will be needed, if increases in taxation are to be avoided.

Attempts to date to reduce Medicare expenditure have focused on lowering the payments made to hospitals and doctors, but more fundamental reform is required. In the short-term, co-payments for hospital treatment could be introduced and some element of means-testing benefits might be needed. However, in the past, medical enterprises have proved adept, at limiting the impact of cuts in fee levels by increasing the volume of treatments. As a result, in the long run, though, a pronounced movement away from the fee-for-service paradigm may be necessary. The private sector has moved towards managed care, so achieving some slackening in the growth of spending as has the federal government in its health care programme for its own employees. Indeed, this latter plan may represent a good base for reform of Medicare, in that the government puts an upper limit on costs, requires co-payment up to a certain ceiling and offers a choice of plans. However, any programme that offers a choice of health plans, with an obligation to accept all candidates, will be faced with the problems of adverse selection that will result in the plan with the best service level tending to attract the individuals with the worst health. To stand some chance of overcoming this problem careful risk-adjustments would be required.

Outside the area of acute medical care, it will also be necessary to try to limit the growth of expenditure on long-term care in the home. There has been little political support for introducing a co-payment for home nursing care but either some more effective gate-keeping will be required to ration care, or price will have to play a larger part. Better integration of the services provided by the federal and state governments in this area is needed. The federal government should encourage states to make programmes that allow the elderly to live in settings suitable to their needs rather than in nursing homes. Private insurance for long-term health care should also be encouraged through raising the exemption limits for Medicaid provided that individuals have insurance to cover a relatively long period of nursing home care. However, many people ensure that they have no assets prior to entry into long-term care so that they qualify for Medicaid. In this area, stricter rules and estate recovery programmes should be introduced.

Notes

1. Includes all sectors, not just investment. For some sectors computer parts are included also.

2. Hong Kong-China, Indonesia, Korea, Malaysia, the Philippines and Thailand.

3. China, China-Taipei and Singapore.

4. Table 5.1 in the National Income and Product Accounts does not split private saving and investment between the business and personal sectors, but with a few assumptions, such estimates are possible. In this survey, business net lending is defined as undistributed corporate profits, with adjustments for capital consumption and inventory valuations, plus corporate consumption of fixed capital less corporate fixed investment. Personal net lending is defined as personal saving plus non-corporate consumption of fixed capital plus wage accruals less disbursements and investment by the personal sector. The Flow-of-Funds accounts give a breakdown of gross investment between the corporate and personal sectors.

5. The Flow of Funds data are adjusted to make them comparable to the NIPA figures. This adjustment excludes flows into government pensions and net saving by farm corporations from net financial flows in the personal sector. This measure has been negative in every quarter starting at the end of 1994. When including these two, flows have still been negative in all but one quarter since the middle of 1996. Asset levels are similarly adjusted by accumulating net saving by farm corporations back to 1952.

6. The Flow-of-Funds accounts present financial statistics for the household and non-profit organisations sector, as well as the personal sector. The latter includes non-corporate businesses and corporate farms. When modelling the NIPA saving rate, data on the personal sector are used as it more closely corresponds to the NIPA saving rate. The accounts do not provide data on tangible assets in the personal sector, however, so table 1.2.2 emphasises households.

7. See Boone, Giorno and Richardson (1998). A further equation was estimated using a modified definition of net financial assets, to exclude the accumulated net savings of corporate farms as well as the level of government pension reserves in order to conform more closely to the NIPA saving concept. The equation regresses the NIPA saving rate (save) on lags of adjusted net financial assets of the personal sector as measured in the Federal Reserve's Flow-of-Funds Accounts divided by disposable income (nfa) and lags of the difference between the unemployment rate and the NAIRU (ugap):

$$save_t - 13.9 - .015\,nfa_{t-1} - .024\,nfa_{t-5} - .021\,nfa_{t-9} + .211\,ugap_{t-1} + .238\,(ugap_{t-1} - ugap_{t-5}).$$
$$R2 = .94,\ Sample:1989:Q1 - 1998:Q3.$$

Other lag structures give qualitatively similar results.

8. For instance, Starr-McCluer (1998) reports a range for the marginal propensity to consume of 3 to 7 per cent out of equity market wealth.

9. Including net external flows, saving equals investment. Pieces of this identity such as investment and consumption are components of the expenditure-side measure of output, GDP. Other pieces, such as personal income and corporate profits, make up national income. Because the income and expenditure-side measures of output do not coincide due to different source data, there is a statistical discrepancy.

10. Returns are measured as investment income as a percentage of assets held at year end the year before. They do not include valuation changes that are not counted as income.

11. OECD (1997a) suggests that the global gains from the recently signed WTO agreement on telecommunication could be as much as one trillion dollars, cumulatively over the next decade. Likewise, the windfall from the accord on information technology could be $50 billion a year when fully implemented. A significant share of these gains would likely accrue to the United Sates.

12. Using the consumption deflator to measure price increases.

13. There are three tiers in the mortgage section of this market. The tiers are distinguish by different levels of guaranties from government sponsored enterprises in the financial sector. The first consists of repackaged mortgages that already carry a government guarantee from the Federal Housing Administration or the Veterans Administration. For these mortgages, the principal is guaranteed by the government and timely payment of the coupons is guaranteed by Ginnie Mae (Government National Mortgage Association). The second tier consists of standard condition ("conforming mortgages") whose interest payments (but not principal) are guaranteed by Fannie Mae (formerly the Federal National Mortgage Association) or Freddie Mac (Federal Home Loan Mortgage Corporation). The last tier represents large ("jumbo") mortgages that carry no guarantee.

14. Such estimates are derived from sampling techniques more than one year after the event.

15. Actual data are not yet available for FY 1998.

16. Spending for this purpose is booked through the Highways Fund that also receives the proceeds of the federal gasoline tax.

17. Child credits will reduce the tax bill of families receiving the Earned Income Tax Credit (EITC) and increase the proportion of the EITC that is refundable for families with two or fewer and making it refundable for families with three or more children.

18. The precise year when the improvement in public finances started varies between 1990 and 1995 according to the country concerned.

19. In one three-month period in 1997, 38 per cent left welfare because of sanctions. Shalala (1998), however, maintains that many households see a rise in incomes shortly after losing benefits.

20. GAO (1998).

21. Anderson and Levine (1998) suggest that child care subsidies could lead to relatively large gains in labour force participation among less skilled, unmarried women.

22. OECD (1998a).

23. National Governors Association (1998).

24. Alabama, Arizona, Arkansas, California, Connecticut, Kentucky, Massachusetts, Missouri, Montana, New Hampshire, New Jersey, Ohio, Tennessee, Texas, Vermont, Washington, West Virginia and Wyoming.

25. Murray *et al.* (1998).

26. The Wisconsin Supreme Court in June 1998 declared the programme constitutional, and the US Supreme Court in November 1998 refused to hear an appeal, letting the decision stand.

27. Farber and Levy (1998).

28. Currie and Yelowitz (1998).

29. Louis Harris & Associates polled 2 000 persons, as well as physicians, employers and legislative officials on behalf of Baylor College of Medicine and Texas Children's Hospital between January and May 1998. This is a significant rise from the 38 million cited in OECD (1994).

30. In 1996, expenditures on health care by private insurers were $4\frac{1}{2}$ per cent of GDP, while private out-of-pocket costs were another $2\frac{1}{4}$ per cent.

31. CBO (1997*b*).

32. See Baker and Shankarkumar (1997) CBO (1997*a*), Cutler and Sheiner (1997) and Newhouse (1992).

33. National Governors Association (1998*b*).

34. The Employee Retirement Income Security Act of 1974 was designed to govern pension plans for large corporations, but the courts have interpreted its statutes as applying to employer-sponsored health plans as well. The President issued an Executive Order in February 1998 mandating the Department of Labor to issue implementing regulations where possible. It promulgated two minor ones in September.

35. The Employee Retirement Income Security Act of 1974 mandates that employees covered by company health plans that are self-insured, usually large companies, be regulated by the federal government. State governments regulate the rest. Because the plans that fall under the Act are not regulated by the states, they are not subject to state malpractice laws.

36. An earlier agreement, reported in OECD (1997*a*), required Congressional approval, and as it moved through the legislature, the implementing bill evolved away from the original settlement. As a result, groups opposed to the final bill, including the tobacco companies, successfully defeated it by the middle of 1998.

37. The settlement covers 46 states. Thirty-nine of them have outstanding suits, so the courts also have to ratify the settlement. Seven states had not yet brought suits, but joining the agreement precludes them from suing in the future. Mississippi, Florida, Texas and Minnesota had already settled separately.

38. OECD (1996).

39. The interpretation of the level and the movements in the poverty rate over long periods of time, however, should be made with caution. These rates do not adjust for in-kind transfers and other in-kind programmes and are based on an out-dated measure of required consumption. They are adjusted by the CPI that may be biased (OECD, 1997*a*). A measure that adjusts for transfers, however, also shows a sharp decline in 1997 (CEA, 1998*a*).

40. Oxley and MacFarlan (1994).

41. Murray *et al.* (1998).

42. Haynes and Moffit (1997).

43. There was no change in the minimum wage in 1998.

44. See for instance OECD (1994).

45. $1 trillion represents 6½ per cent of all outstanding credit at the end of 1997. A stylised interest rate swap would involve one party trading fixed interest payments on a principal of $1 million for variable interest payments on the same principal tied to the LIBOR. This principal of $1 million is the *notional* value of this derivative. Because the parties do not actually exchange this principal in this example, the notional value overstates the amount of money at risk. In one sense, the interest payments also overstate the risk as most contracts include netting and grossing provisions to protect a counterparty from default on the other side of the contract.

46. For instance, national banks can act as insurance agents only from headquarters in towns with a population of 5 000 or less.

47. Some state-chartered banks are not members of the Federal Reserve System and are not controlled by holding companies. As such the Federal Reserve does not have authority over them.

48. Litan and Rauch, 1998.

49. Litan (1987).

50. In the absence of an amendment to the Glass-Steagall Act, the Securities Industry Association (1998) has contended that operating subsidiaries are limited by statute to the activities permissible for national banks. In the 1960s the Comptroller sought to expand the activities of national banks through its operating subsidiaries, but the courts quickly overturned all of them. In December 1997 the OCC approved an application by Zions Bank to operate a subsidiary trading in municipal revenue bonds, which nationally chartered banks are prohibited from handling directly.

51. Kwan (1998). Such growth is reminiscent of the increase of banks' attempts to take advantage of a similar loophole that allowed unitary banks to circumvent bank regulations in the last half the 1960s. The affiliation prohibitions originally applied only to multiple-bank holding companies. For a while, this loophole was insignificant, but starting in the mid-1960s, banks began aggressively seeking unitary thrift charters in order to raise funds in the commercial paper market. At that time regulation Q ceilings on deposit interest prevented these banks from generating enough loanable funds. Between 1965 and 1970 the share of all commercial banking assets in unitary banks rose from 3 to 40 per cent. Congress closed this loophole in 1970.

52. This plan is described in OECD (1997a).

53. The 1997 Community Reinvestment Act requires that banking agencies periodically evaluate how each deposit institution is meeting the credit needs of the entire community. A high rating is necessary to win approval for an expansion in facilities or a merger. The larger the institution, the more credit it has to extend to disadvantaged areas to win a sufficient rating. Banks may now choose to include their subsidiaries in this calculation.

54. See Carnell (1998) and CBO (1993).

55. This raises the possibility that a losing counterparty would claim the initial contract was illegal and therefore unenforceable. In 1991 the London borough of Hammersmith and Fulham convinced the UK House of Lords that its contracts were outside the law, albeit for a completely different reason. Currently a US company, MG Refining and Marketing, Inc. and MG Futures, Inc., is attempting to use a CFTC ruling that its trading was illegal to nullify its contracts.

56. See Summers (1998) and Born (1998a) respectively.

57. Sander (1997).

58. See OECD (1997a) for a description of the proposed legislation.

59. Specifically, the exchange announces these cut-offs in points each quarter where the values depend on the closing value of the index the quarter before.

60. GAO (1996a).

61. Non-bank banks are another curious institution. They were first created in 1980 by exploiting a loophole in the Bank Holding Company Act that defined a bank as one that accepts demand deposits *and* makes commercial loans. Starting with Gulf and Western's acquisition of a bank, the OCC approved over 50 charters for limited-purpose banks that only had one of the two characteristics that defined a bank. Congress closed this loophole in 1987, but it grandfathered the existing 57 institutions under strict regulations. Currently fewer than 25 non-bank banks currently claim these rights, and their assets are small relative to the entire industry.

62. Moreover, of the $205 million collected in FY 1997, half was from a $100 million fine from Archer Daniels Midland involving international price fixing that was settled in late 1996.

63. In the parlance of the antitrust authorities, such investigations are called "second requests".

64. See Klein (1998) and Pitofsky (1998).

65. Report from the Consumers Union and Consumer Federation of America.

66. Currently five of the original seven RBOCs remain: Bell Atlantic, Bell South, Ameritech, SBC Communications (formerly Southwestern Bell) and US West. Bell Atlantic and NYNEX merged, while SBC bought Pacific Telesis.

67. In SBC *et al. v.* FCC a district court judge in Texas ruled that the prohibition on the RBOCs entering the long distance market unconstitutionally singled out individuals in the law. The 5th Circuit Court of Appeals in New Orleans, however, overturned the decision in September 1998, arguing that the portion of the Act was not a bill of attainder because it applied only temporarily. The Supreme Court effectively upheld the 5th Circuit Court's decision by declining to hear arguments on the issue.

68. The 8th Circuit Court of Appeals in St. Louis ruled in favour of the RBOCs in *Iowa Utilities Board, et al. v. AT&T Corp.* in July 1997, but the US Supreme Court overturned the decision on a 5-3 vote in January 1999.

69. The *Survey on Regulatory Reform in the United States* (1999) describes the institutional settings and the important issues in greater detail for the telecommunications sector, as well as the electricity and transportation sectors, and policies related to basic regulation, antitrust and international trade.

70. AT&T's purchase of such a firm, TCI, in July 1998 is a merger of complementary assets that could create a stronger competitor to incumbents in local phone service.

71. Reportedly, NYNEX's market share in Manhattan below 59th Street is only 40 per cent.

72. SBC and Ameritech announced their intention to merge in May 1998; Bell Atlantic and GTE declared in July 1998.

73. Stranded costs are those that a utility legitimately incurred while it was regulated, such as a substantial investment in a plant, that it reasonably expected would earn a

fair return but could no longer generate adequate returns in a new market environment.

74. FERC (1998).

75. OECD (1999).

76. See for instance the FY 1999 *Performance Plan* for the US Trade Representative's Office.

77. One case was brought by Costa Rica involving cotton and man-made fibre underwear; the other was filed by India involving woven woolshirts and blouses.

78. The Appellate Body ruled in October 1998 that US requirements for shrimp exporters to have satisfactory protection for sea turtles were consistent with WTO rules but that US implementation of its law was unfair.

79. See for instance Barshefsky (1998).

80. See for example Adams (1998).

81. Council of Economic Advisers (1998*b*).

82. Novak (1998).

83. The 1997 standards are described in OECD (1997*a*).

84. Non-specific pollution comes from sources that are difficult to identify, such as pesticide runoff from farms. In contrast, it is easier to monitor pollution from a drainage pipe attached to a factory.

85. See Council of Economic Advisers (1997) and National Bankruptcy Commission (1997).

86. Clinton *et al.* v. New York City *et al.*

87. Private-sector actuaries generally use a real discount rate of 3 per cent in evaluating the soundness of a defined benefit pension scheme.

88. For instance, the passively managed equity portion of the Federal Thrift Fund has investment management costs of only 7 basis points.

89. Mitchell (1996).

90. Between 1985 and 1992, the proportion of large employers offering a 401(k) plan in addition to a DB plan rose from 13 to 38 per cent, while the proportion of employees being offered other DC plans rose from 17 to 29 per cent Papke (1998) p. 14.

91. Papake (1998) suggests that the addition of a 401(k) plan raises the probability of the DB scheme being terminated. Overall, for every three new 401(k) plans offered by large employers, one DB plan was closed.

92. Gustman and Steinmeier (1998*a*) p. 8.

93. EBRI databook table 16.2.

94. The employer match is only available to staff in the new scheme. It amounts to 1 per cent of income for the first dollar of staff contribution, 100 per cent of the next 2 per cent of staff income and 50 per cent of the next 2 per cent. Staff who remained in the previous scheme are able to contribute 5 per cent of income to the fund on a tax-deferred basis. In contrast to private sector schemes there are no non-discrimination rules, so that as many high-earners can contribute as want to.

95. Prior to 1990, participants were restricted to holding at least 40 per cent of their own contribution in government bonds. This restriction has now been lifted. GAO (1996).

96. Gustman and Steinmeier (1998*a*).

97. It only covers short-term chronic care for a three-month period.

98. GAO/T-HEHS-98-107 (1998).

99. Jacobzone (1999).

100. At the end of 1995, insurance companies had sold only 4.3 million policies, and of that, far fewer were in force. Policies are expensive; the average premium of a standard policy bought at 65 was $2 560, rising to $8 146 if purchased at age 75. Coronel and Kitchman, (1997).

101. See Cutler (1993).

102. GAO/T-HEHS-98-107 (1998).

103. GAO/HRD-93-29R (1993) Converted assets averaged $5 600 and often involved making burial arrangements. Transfers were less common but averaged more money.

104. GAO/T-HEHS-98-107 (1998).

105. Quinn and Smeeding (1993).

106. Op. cit., Figure 40.

107. With the rates rising from from 9 to 11 per cent and 15 to 22 per cent, respectively in the same period.

108. Quinn and Smeeding (1993).

109. Smeeding et al. (1993). The data is drawn from the Luxembourg Income Survey (LIS) and is adjusted using the LIS equivalence scale.

110. Quinn and Smeeding p. 12.

111. Research by Duggan et al. (1995) found that, based on a continuous longitudinal sample of people affiliated to the social security, showed that the rate of return on contributions averaged around 5.5 per cent for the whole of the cohort of contributors born between 1917 and 1922. The return for low income males was around 76 basis points higher while that for high income males was some 48 basis points lower – a spread of 124 basis points. However, the spread narrowed only very slightly – to 113 basis points – once an empirically determined correction for life expectancy was introduced.

112. Older immigrants, though, benefit little from Social Security and rely on the SSI programme. The current benefit rules also generate a redistribution from long-term US residents towards immigrants Gustman and Steimneier (1998b).

113. Part of the lower life expectancy of the African-American population may reflect a greater concentration of low-income household with low life expectancy. Nonetheless, the research (Duggan op. cit.) based on a continuous longitudinal sample of social security contributors does suggest that considerable differences in life expectancy persist, after controlling for differences in income – a finding that has been replicated elsewhere Rogers (1992), Menchik (1993).

114. Duggan op. cit.

115. According to GAO (1997a), the median number of zero years for workers turning 62 in 1993 was four for men and fifteen for women.

116. A hypothetical – but typical example, would be that the wife earned 80 per cent of the husband's pay and worked for eleven years less. In such a case, the wife's contributions would be 53 per cent of the husband contributions but the benefit received would only be 7 per cent more than if she had not worked and hence made no contributions.

117. HFCA (1998) Figure 19.

118. Garber et al. (1997), p. 11.

119. See Gruber and Wise (1998).

120. Due to the spouse and widow supplements, the implicit tax rate was lower for an earner with a dependent spouse. Reflecting the progressivity of pension benefits, the implicit tax rate was also somewhat higher for those on low earnings than for those on high earnings. As spouse supplements are not available when the spouse is entitled to and draws own pension, the tax rate for an earner in this case is equal to that of a single person.

121. For an overview of early retirement option in OECD countries, see Blöndal and Scarpetta (1998).

122. See Quinn et al. (1998).

123. Steurle (1997).

124. Excluding revenue from Medicare premiums that are expected to average one-quarter of Part B disbursements.

125. Through 2008 the Medicaid projections are based on projections by HCFA for the entire Medicaid programme and are adjusted to include only estimated expenditures on the aged. Afterwards, the Medicaid figures grow in line with Medicare expenditures after adjusting for projected increases in the share of the elderly that are 85 and over. The very elderly are likely to require a greater fraction of nursing care.

126. In a 1989 settlement to a class-action lawsuit, Duggan v. Bowen, HHS modified its procedures for determining eligibility for home health and skilled nursing benefits, greatly expanding access. Currently there is a high rate of reversal when administrators review service requirements and deny benefits, but only 3 per cent of claims are now reviewed, compared to a 60 per cent review rate before the Duggan case.

127. See for instance Cutler and Richardson (1998).

128. McClellan and Kessler (1999) looks at the impact of differing cross-country regulatory control on the diffusion of heart attack technology.

129. Health Interview Survey and the Survey of Income and Program Participation and the National Long-term Care Survey support this view.

130. GAO/T-HEHS-98-107 (1998).

131. One government body suggested that the incidence may double by 2055, GAO/HEHS-98-16 (1998).

132. Crimmins, Saito and Ingegneri (1989).

133. Op. cit. p. 255.

134. Jacobzone et al. (1998) shows this internationally, while Waidman and Manton (1998) show this to be true for the United States.

135. Siegel, (1996).

136. Kreiser and Lo Sallo (1998). The increase in daughters' earnings amounts to 20 per cent of the cost of the nursing home.

137. NLCS (1997).

138. ADLs and IDLs are common measures of a person's ability to function independently and the need for long-term care assistance. ADL refers to basic functions of self care

such as bathing, dressing, toileting, eating, or getting out of a chair or bed. IDLs describe more difficult chores or social interactions such as cooking, cleaning and shopping. GAO/T-HEHS-98-107.

139.   NLCS, (1997).

140.   *Op. cit.*

141.   Spector, Reschovsky and Cohen (1996).

142.   Rabiner, *et al.*, (1997).

143.   Annual report of the Board of Trustees (1998). The evaluations are made on a present value basis that applies a significant discount to events as far away as those in 2075.

144.   Seyel (1998) puts the very long-run real yield on government bonds at 3.5 per cent.

145.   Nominal discretionary expenditure is held constant for the next two budgets, so respecting existing caps, real expenditure is held constant for the following five years and then allowed to increase in line with GDP, as in the latest CBO projections (see Chapter II).

146.   The projections are based on those of the CBO made in May 1998 and January 1999 and the intermediate projections for health and social security spending. The CBO assumed average economic growth of 1.5 per cent over the period to 2050. Beyond 2009, taxation and spending (other than health and pensions) was held constant as a proportion of GDP.

147.   The above calculations of the expenditure cuts required to secure the future of Social Security suggest that more adjustment is required than suggested in the last report of the Social Security trustees. The official method of calculation understates the ongoing cost of the system as equates costs and revenues over a 75-year period, but does not impose a requirement for a stable financial position by the end of the evaluation period. Indeed, this is one reason why there is always a tendency to underestimate the scale of the required increase in the payroll tax that is necessary to balance the system.

148.   For a survey of these studies, see Kohl and O'Brien (1998) and Turner *et al.* (1998).

149.   Weil (1994).

150.   The lower response is based on a pooled cross-country time-series regression reported in Masson *et al.* (1995), while the higher one is based on Masson and Tryon (1990).

151.   Turner *et al.* (1998).

152.   It should be noted, though, that increases in proportion of elderly brought about by changes in the birth-rate also generate marked changes in the proportion of children. A lower proportion of children is generally expected to raise the savings rate. Higgins (1997) found this effect to be marked, especially for developing countries.

153.   Turner *et al.* (1998) discuss this possibility but their model does not incorporate such a feature.

154.   See Pecchenino (1998) for a model incorporating this effect.

155.   This is based on the steady-state investment requirements for keeping the capital-output ratio constant: $i = [(g + s)/(1 + g)].k$, where g is the growth rate of output, s is the economic depreciation rate of capital and k is the capital-output ratio. The growth rate of output in steady state is determined as $g = (1 + n).(1 + e)$, where n is

the growth rate of the labour force and e is the growth rate of labour efficiency. In the calculation k is set at 2.1, e at 1.4, s at 3.5 and n at 1.0 for the current situation and 0.1 in 2050.

156. See Turner *et al.* (1998).

157. Mitchell (1997).

158. Williams (1997).

159. Goodfellow and Scheiber cited in Poterba and Wise (1996).

160. Yakoboski (1996).

161. Bajtelsmit and Vanderhei (forthcoming).

162. Scott and Shoven (1996) found that between 1988 and 1993, the proportion of DB plans with a distribution possibility rose from 58 to 64 per cent, while the proportion of employees entitled to a payment form a DC plan rose to 87 per cent from 75 per cent. Overall, the entitlement to a distribution on leaving rose from 48 per cent in 1983 to 60 per cent in 1988 and 72 per cent by 1993.

163. There is a withholding tax of 20 per cent on all distributions. The eventual tax liability amounts to the marginal tax rate plus and an excise tax of 10 per cent. Typically, the approved vehicle is the new employers pension plan or an IRA account.

164. Yakoboski (1997).

165. Hewitt Associates.

166. Mitchell *et al.* (1998).

167. The gap would be about 100 basis points less when compared to government bonds but an annuity stream comes from a private sector company and not the government. Even if the company invests in government bonds there is still a default risk.

168. Walliser (1998).

169. King (1992).

170. United Kingdom Government Actuary (1996).

171. Samwick and Skinner (1998).

172. Based on a portfolio consisting of one-third equities, two-thirds bonds.

173. Pension and Welfare Benefits Administration (1998), Table IV-3. The quoted figures are based on the costs of an investment of $25 million in an institutional fund.

174. Thus in a typical private sector DB scheme the employer cost is around 5 per cent of payroll, whereas under a typical DC scheme the employer pays 5 per cent and the employee adds a further 5 per cent.

175. *Op. cit.* p. 22.

176. See EBRI (1997) p. 154.

177. Schieber and Shoven (1994).

178. *Op. cit.* p. 116.

179. OECD (1997).

180. CBO (1996).

181. See Genakoplos *et al.* (1998) for a fuller development of these arguments.

182. Poterba (1997). Moreover, this paper also shows that the financial market pre-tax return on a debt-equity portfolio (weights were determined capitalising interest and dividend payments using the Baa bond yield and the S&P dividend yield) in the same period (1959-96) would have been 6.6 per cent. As the post tax return to capital was 5.5 per cent, with a standard error of 1 percentage point, the hypothesis that the financial market and the national accounts return were equal cannot be rejected. However, it should be noted that the standard error of the financial market return was 14 percentage points.

183. See the literature on the equity premium anomaly: Seigel and Thaler (1997), Bansall and Coleman (1996).

184. Mariger (1997) makes this point.

185. PWBA (1998).

186. See Leimer (1994).

187. Stabilising the debt requires funding interest payments equivalent to the difference between the real interest rate on bonds and the rate of technical progress, as the population projections are based on a stable population. With the implicit debt at $9 000 billion, about one-quarter of social security contributions of $400 billion are needed to stabilise the debt.

188. Under the original plan, premiums would gradually rise starting at income levels at $75 000 to 100 per cent of costs at an income of $125 000 a year for married couples.

189. According to estimates by Moon *et al.* (1997).

190. Specific proposals include: *centres of excellence contracting* where HCFA would pay selected, high-quality facilities a flat fee for all services associated with a particular procedure and *competitive bidding* where Medicare would solicit market-based payment rates for non-physician Part B services such as medical equipment and laboratory services, as other countries with single-payer health systems routinely do. Vladeck, (1997).

191. Cutler, McClellan and Newhouse (1998).

192. Butler and Moffit (1997).

193. Hospitals with skilled nursing facilities would transfer people from the hospital to their skilled nursing facility after a few days. By doing this, they would reap the full diagnosis-related groups payment for the hospital stay as well as additional charges for the stay at the nursing facility. The BBA reduces payments to these facilities for patients who are discharged after relatively short hospital stays. Komisar and Feder, (1998) and GAO/T-HEHS-97-90.

194. CBO (1996).

195. NLCS (1997).

196. GAO/HEHS-94-167.

197. Some states, including New York, Wisconsin and Massachusetts have aggressive "Medicare maximisation" efforts, Wiener and Stevenson, (1997) and one study has even found a negative relationship between Medicare and Medicaid spending, Kenney, Rajan and Sosica (1997).

198. As of 1995 firms had sold only one-half million policies through employers, and most policies required employees to pay all the premiums. Coronel and Kitchman, (1997).

199. The Kennedy-Kassebaum Act.

200. Wiener (1998).

201. In one version of the programme (Connecticut, California, Indiana and Iowa) consumers can enter the Medicaid programme with assets equal to the payout of the policy. A $100 000 policy means the elderly can qualify for Medicaid while holding $100 000 of assets. In a second version (New York) consumers can protect any level of assets as long as they purchase a policy that pays at least three years of care.

202. Norton (1995).

203. Liu and Moon (1995).

204. NCSL (1997).

Bibliography

Adams, Chris (1998),
    "Paper Victories: U.S. Steel Mils Win Even When They Lose Trade Cases", Wall Street
    Journal, 30 March, 1A.

Anderson, Patricia M. and Phillip B. Levine (1998),
    "Child Care and Mothers' Employment Decisions", Mimeo, Dartmouth College,
    October.

Baker, Laurence C. and Sharmila Shankarkumar (1997),
    "Managed Care and Health Expenditures: Evidence from Medicare, 1990-1994", NBER
    Working Paper # 6187, September.

Bansal, R. and W. J. Colman II (1996),
    "A Monetary Explanation of the Equity Premium", Journal of Political Economy.

Barshefsky, Charlene (1998),
    "Press Round-Table", London, 22 October (www.ustr.gov/speeches/index.html).

Blondal, S. and S. Scarpetta (1998),
    "The Retirement Decision in OECD Countries", OECD Economics Department Working
    Paper.

Board of Trustees (1998),
    The 1998 Annual Report of the Board of Trustees of the OASDI Trust Fund, US Government
    Printing Office, Washington, DC.

Boone, Laurence, C. Giorno and P. Richardson (1998),
    "Stock Market Fluctuations and Consumption Behaviour: Some Recent Evidence",
    OECD Economic Department Working Paper.

Born, Brooksley (1998a),
    "Testimony Concerning the Over-the-Counter Derivatives Market before the U.S. Sen-
    ate Committee on Agriculture, Nutrition and Forestry", 30 July.

Born, Brooksley (1998b),
    "Testimony of the Commodity Futures Trading Commission before the United States
    Senate Committee on Agriculture, Nutrition and Forestry", 16 December.

Butler, Stuart M. And Robert E. Moffit (1997),
    "Congress's Own Health plan as a Model for Medicare Reform", The Heritage Founda-
    tion, Roe Backgrounder No. 1123, 12 June.

Carnell, Richard S. (1998),
    "Twelve Banks in Search of a Purpose", Remarks to the American Enterprise Institute,
    Washington, DC, 2 December.

Chandrasekaran, Rajiv and Stephen Barr (1999),
    "U.S. Is Ready for the Bug", International Herald Tribune, 2-3 January, p. 1.

Congressional Budget Office (1993),
"The Federal Home Loan Banks in the Housing Finance System", A CBO *Study*, July.

Congressional Budget Office (1996),
Reducing the Deficit: Spending and Revenue Options, A Report to the Senate and House Committees on the Budget , Washington, DC.

Congressional Budget Office (1997a),
"Predicting How Changes in Medicare's Payment Rates Would Affect Risk-sector Enrolment and Costs", March.

Congressional Budget Office (1997b),
"Trends in Health Care Spending by the Private Sector", April.

Coronel, Susan and Michelle Kitchman (1977),
Long-Term Care Insurance in 1995, Health Insurance Association of America, Washington DC, May.

Council of Economic Advisers (1997),
The Economic Report of the President, Washington DC, February.

Council of Economic Advisers (1998a),
The Economic Report of the President, Washington DC, February.

Council of Economic Advisers (1998b),
"The Kyoto Protocol and the President's Policies to Address Climate Change", Washington DC, July.

Crimmins, Eileen M., Yasuhiko Saito and Dominique Ingegneri (1989),
"Changes in Life Expectancy and Disability-Free Life Expectancy in the United States", *Population and Development Review* 15, 2, June.

Culhane, Marianne B. and Michaela M. White (1998),
"Means-testing for Chapter 7 Debtors: Repayment Capacity Untapped? ", Study prepared for the American Bankruptcy Institute, December.

Currie, Janet and Aaron Yelowitz (1998),
"Health Insurance and Less Skilled Workers", Mimeo, UCLA, October.

Cutler, D. (1993),
'Why Does Not the Market Fully Insure Long Term Care?", NBER Working Paper #4301, March.

Cutler, D. and E. Richardson (1997),
"Measuring the Health of the U.S. Population", *Brookings Papers on Economic Activity: Microeconomics.*

Cutler, D., M. McClellan and J. Newhouse (1998),
"Prices and Productivity in Managed Care Insurance", NBER Working Paper #6677.

Cutler, David M. and Louise Sheiner (1997),
"Managed Care and the Growth of Medical Expenditures", NBER Working Paper #6140, August.

Disney, R., M. Mira d'Ercole and P. Scherer (1998),
"Resources During Retirement", OECD, Ageing Working Papers, AWP4.3.

Duggan, J.E, R. Gillingham and J. S. Greenlees (1995),
"Progresive Returns to Social Security?", US Treasury Research Paper #9501.

Employee Benefits Research Institute (1997),
Databook, Washington DC.

Farber, Henry S. and Helen Levy (1998),
    "Recent Trends in Employer-Sponsored Health Insurance Coverage: Are bad jobs
    getting worse?", NBER Working Paper #6709, August.

Federal Communications Commission (1998a),
    "Telecommunications Industry Revenue: 1997", October.

Federal Communications Commission (1998b),
    "Trends in Telephone Service", July.

Federal Energy Regulatory Commission (1998),
    "Staff Report to the Federal Energy Regulatory Commission on the Causes of Whole-
    sale Electric Pricing Abnormalities in the Midwest during June 1998", 22 September.

Federal Trade Commission (1997),
    "Annual Report to Congress, Fiscal Year 1997: Pursuant to Subsection (j) of Section 7A
    of the Clayton Act, Hart-Scott-Rodino Antitrust Improvements Act of 1976", Washington
    DC.

Gallagher, L. Jerome, et al. (1998),
    "One Year after Federal Welfare Reform: A description of state temporary assistance
    for needy families (TANF) decisions as of October 1997", The Urban Institute, Occa-
    sional Paper Number 6.

Garber, Alan M., Thomas E. MaCurdy and Mark C. McClellan (1998),
    "Medical Care at the End of Life: Diseases, Treatment Patterns, and Costs", NBER
    Working Paper #6748, October.

Genakoplos J., O.S. Mitchell and S.P. Zeldes (1998),
    "Would a Privatised Social Security System Really Pay a Higher Rate of Return?",
    NBER Working Paper #6713.

General Accounting Office (1993),
    "Medicaid Estate Planning", GAO-93-29R, July.

General Accounting Office (1994),
    "Medicaid Long-Term Care: Successful state efforts to expand home services while
    limiting costs", GAO/HEHS-94-167.

General Accounting Office (1996a),
    "Bank Oversight: Fundamental Principles for Moderizing the U.S. Structure", May,
    GAO/GGD-96-117.

General Accounting Office (1996b),
    "Thrift Savings Plan Has a Key Role in Retirement Benefits", GAO/HEHS 96-1.

General Accounting Office (1997a),
    "Medicare Post-Acute Care: Home health and skilled nursing facility cost growth and
    proposals for prospective payment", Testimony by William J. Scanlon before the
    House Ways and Means Committee, US House of Representatives, GAO/T-
    HEHS-97-90.

General Accounting Office (1997b),
    "Social Security Reform: Implications for women's retirement income", GAO/
    HEHS-98-42, December.

General Accounting Office (1998a),
    "Alzheimer's Disease: Estimates of prevalence in the United States", GAO/
    HEHS-98-16.

General Accounting Office (1998b),
"Long-Term Care: Baby boom generation presents financing challenges", Testimony by William J. Scanlon before the Special Committee on Aging, US Senate, GAO/T-HEHS-98-107.

General Accounting Office (1998c),
"Medicare Computer Systems: Year 2000 challenges put benefits and services in jeopardy", AIMD-98-24, September.

General Accounting Office (1998d),
"Welfare Reform: Early fiscal effects of the TANF block grant", GAO/AIMD-98-137, August.

General Accounting Office (1999),
"State Welfare Programs", GAO/AIMD-99-28, January.

Gustman A.L. and T.L. Steinmeier (1998a),
"Effects of Savings on Pensions", NBER Working Paper #6681, August.

Gustman A.L. and T.L. Steinmeier (1998b),
"Social Security Benefits of Immigrants and U.S. Born", NBER Working Paper #6478, March.

Health Care Financing Administration (1998),
Chartbook, www/hcfa.gov.

Higgins, Matthew (1997),
"Demography, National Savings and International Capital Flows", Federal Reserve Bank of New York.

Hoynes, Hilary Wiliamson and Robert Moffitt,
"Tax Rates and Work Incentives in the Social Security Disability Program: Current law and alternative reforms", NBER Working Paper # 6058 (June).

International Trade Commission, United States (1998),
"Overview and Analysis of Current U.S. Unilateral Economic Sanctions", Investigation No. 332-391, August.

Jacobzone, S. (1999),
"An Overview of International Perspectives in the Field of Ageing and Care for Frail Elderly Persons", OECD, Labour Market and Social Policy Occasional Papers, forthcoming.

Jacobzone, S., E. Cambois E., E. Chaplain E. and J.M. Robine (1998),
"The Health of Older Persons in OECD Countries: Is it improving fast enough to compensate for population ageing? Labour Market and Social Policy Occasional Papers forthcoming, OECD.

Jost, Kenneth (1998),
"Managed Care and Its Discontents", CQ Outlook: Supplement to CQ Weekly, (30 May), 5-28.

Katz, Michael L. and Carl Shapiro (1994),
"Systems Competition and Network Effects", Journal of Economic Perspectives, 8, 2, Spring.

Kenney, Genevieve, Shruti Rajan and Stephanie Soscia (1997),
Interactions between the Medicare and Medicaid Home Care Programs: Insights from the states, The Urban Institute, Washington, DC, November.

Kessler, D. and M. McClellan (1999),
   A *Global Analysis of Technological Change in Health Care*, University of Michigan Press, Ann Arbor, MI (in press).

King, Tom (1992),
   "Expenses and the Impact to Disclosure", *Money Management*, December.

Klein, Joel (1998),
   "The Importance of Antitrust Enforcement in the New Economy", Address before the New York Bar Association Antitrust Law Section Program, New York, NY, 29 January.

Kniesner, Thomas J. and Anthony T. LoSasso (1998),
   'New Evidence on Intergenerational Risk Sharing', Mimeo, Indiana University, December.

Kohl, R. and P. O'Brien (1997),
   "The Macroeconomics of Ageing, Pensions and Saving: A survey", OECD Economics Department Working Paper.

Komisar, Harriet L. and Judith Feder (1998),
   "The Balanced Budget Act of 1997: Effect on Medicare's home health benefit and beneficiaries who need long-term care", Mimeo, Institute for Health Care Research and Policy, Georgetown University, February.

Kwan, Simon (1998),
   "Bank Charters Vs. Thrift Charters", Federal Reserve Bank of San Francisco Economic Letter, # 98-13, April.

Leimer D. Cohort (1994),
   "Specific Measures of Lifetime Net Social Security Transfers", Office of Research and Statistics, Social Security Administration, Working Paper #59.

Leiner, D. (1994),
   "Cohort Specific Measures of Lifetime Net Social Secutity Transfers", Office of Research and Statistics, Working Paper.

Liebowitz, S.J. and Stephen E. Margolis (1994),
   "Network Externality: An uncommon tragedy", *Journal of Economic Perspectives*, 8, 2, Spring.

Litan, Robert E. (1987),
   What Should Banks Do?, Washington DC: The Brookings Institution.

Litan, Robert E. with Jonathan Rauch (1998),
   American Finance for the 21st Century, The Brookings Institution, Washington DC.

Liu, Korbin and Marilyn Moon (1995),
   "Recovering Hidden Assets: The magic bullet for medicaid savings?", The Urban Institute, Occasional Opinion Piece, #23, September.

Lopatka, John E. (1995),
   "Microsoft, Monopolization, and Network Externalities", *Antitrust Bulletin* 40, 3.

Mariger, R.P. (1997),
   "Social Security Privatisation: What it can and cannot acheive", Mimeo, Board of Governors of the Federal Reserve System.

Masson, P.R., T. Bayoumi and H. Samiei (1995),
   "International Evidence on the Determinants of Private Savings", IMF Working Paper, May.

Masson, Paul R. and Ralph W. Tryon (1990),
"Macroeconomic Effects of Projected Population Aging in Industrial Countries" International Monetary Fund Working Paper, WP/90/5, January.

McDonough, William J. (1998),
"Statement before the Committee on Banking and Financial Services, U.S. House of Representatives", 1 October.

Menchik, P. (1993),
"Economic Status as a Determinant of Mortality amongst White and Non-white Elderly Males", Population Studies, 47.

Miron, J. and D. Weil (1997),
"The Genesis and Evolution of Social Security, NBER Working Paper #5949.

Mitchell, B. (1997),
"Social Securities Retirement Rate of Return", Heritage Foundation.

Mitchell, O. (1996),
"Administrative Costs in Public and Private Retirement Systems", NBER Working Paper 5734.

Mitchell, O. et al. (1997),
"New Evidence on the Money's Worth of Invidual Annuities", NBER Working Paper (6002).

Moon, Marilyn, Barbara Gage and Alison Evans (1997),
"An Examination of Key Medicare Provisions in the Balanced Budget Act of 1997", The Urban Institute and The Commonwealth Fund, September.

Murray, Sheila E., William N. Evans and Robert M. Schwab (1998),
"Education-Finance Reform and the Distribution of Education Resources", American Economic Review 88, 4 (September) 789-812.

National Bankruptcy Review Commission (1997),
Bankruptcy: The Next Twenty Years, Washington DC, October.

National Conference of State Legislatures (1997),
"The Task Force Report: Long-term care reform in the states", July.

National Governors Association (1998a),
"Financing America's Public Schools", NGA Issue Brief, 1 September.

National Governors Association (1998b),
"Strategies to Improve Managed Care Quality and Oversight in a Competitive Market", Policy Issue Brief #9802, 20 February.

Newhouse, Joseph P. (1992),
"Medical Care Costs: How much welfare loss?", Journal of Economic Perspectives, 6, 3, Summer.

Norton, Edward C. (1995),
"Elderly Assets, Medicaid Policy, and Spenddown in Nursing Homes", The Review of Income and Wealth, 41, 3, September.

Novak, Mary H. (1998),
"Implementing the Kyoto Protocol: Severe economic consequences" Testimony before the House Committee on Government Reform and Oversight, Washington DC, 23 April.

OECD (1992),
Economic Survey of the United States 1991-92, Paris, November.

OECD (1994),
   Economic Survey of the United States 1994, Paris, November.

OECD (1996),
   Economic Survey of the United States 1996, Paris, November.

OECD (1997a),
   Economic Survey of the United States 1997, Paris, November.

OECD (1997b),
   Report on Regulatory Reform, Paris, June.

OECD (1998a),
   Education at a Glance: OECD *Indicators*, Paris.

OECD (1998b),
   Maintaining Prosperity in an Ageing Society, Paris.

OECD (1998c),
   OECD *Economic Outlook*, Paris, December.

OECD (1999),
   Draft of *Survey of Regulatory Reform in the United States*.

Office of the United States Trade Representative (1998),
   FY 1999 *Performance Plan: Under the Government Performance and Results Act*, Washington DC,
   February.

Oxley, Howard and Maitland MacFarlan (1994),
   "Health Care Reform: Controlling spending and increasing efficiency", OECD Economics Department Working Paper #149.

Papke, L.E. (1996),
   "Are 401(k) Plans Replaceing Other Employer Provided Pensions?", NBER Working
   Paper # 5736.

Pecchenino, Rowena A. and Patricia S. Pollard (1997),
   "Reforming Social Security: A Welfare Analysis" in *Reforming Social Security in Theory and
   Practice*, Proceedings of a Symposium held at the Federal Reserve Bank of St. Louis,
   April 11, 1997.

Pension Welfare Benefits Administration (1998),
   "Study of 401(k) Plan Fees and Expenses", Contract Report JP70046, Washington DC.

Pitofsky, Robert (1998),
   "Statement of the Federal Trade Commission before the Committee on the Judiciary,
   United States Senate Concerning Mergers and Corporate Consolidation in the New
   Economy", Washington DC, (16 June).

Pope, Charles (1999),
   "Senate Backs Y2K Loans for Small Businesses; Liability Protections Advance", CQ
   Weekly, 6 March 1999, p. 555.

Poterba J.M. and D.A. Wise (1996),
   "Individual Financial Decisions and the Provision of Resources for Retirement", NBER
   Working Paper #5762, September.

Poterba, James M (1997),
   "The Rate of Return to Corporate Capital and Factor Shares: New estimates using
   revised national income accounts and capital stock data", NBER Working Paper #6263,
   November.

Quinn, J.F., *et al.* (1998),
"A Microeconomic Analysis of the Retirement Decision in the U.S.", OECD Economics Department Working Paper.

Quinn, Joseph F. and Timothy M. Smeeding, (1993),
"The Present and Future Economic Well-Being of the Aged" in *Pensions in a Changing Economy*, Richard V. Burkhauser and Dallas L. Salisbury Eds., Employee Benefit Research Institute, Washington DC.

Rabiner, Donna J., Thomas A. Arcury, Hidla A. Howard, and Kristen A. Copeland (1997),
"The Perceived Availability, Quality, and Cost of Long-Term Care Services in America", *Journal of Aging & Social Policy*, 9,3.

Rivlin, Alice M. and Joshua M. Wiener, with Raymond J. Hanley and Denise A. Spence (1988),
Caring for the Disabled Elderly: Who will pay? The Brookings Institution, Washington DC.

Rogers, R. G. (1992),
"Living and Dying in the U.S.A.: Sociodemographic determinants of death amongst blacks and whites", *Demography*, 29.

Samwick, A.A. and J. Skinner (1998),
"How Will Defined Contribution Pension Plans Affect Retirement Income", NBER Working Paper # 6645.

Sandner, John F. (1997),
"Testimony before the U.S. House of Representatives Committee on Agriculture, Subcommittee on Risk Management and Specialty Crops", 15 April.

Schieber, Sylvester and John Shoven (1994),
"The Consequences of Population Aging on Private Pension Fund Saving and Asset Markets", NBER Working Paper #4665, March.

Scott J.S. and J.B. Shoven (1996),
Lump Sum Distirbutions Fulfilling Portability or Eroding Security, Employment Benefits Research Institute.

Securities Industry Association (1997),
"Comment Letter to the Office of Comptroller of the Currency on Operating Subsidiary Notice", 19 May.

Shalala, Donna E. (1998),
"Remarks to the American Enterprise Institute", Washington DC, 6 February.

Siegel, J.J. and R.H. Thaler (1997),
"The Equity Premium Puzzle", *Journal of Economic Perspectives*, Winter.

Siegel, Jacob (1996),
"Aging into the 21st Century", Report to the Administration on Aging, US Department of Health and Human Services, May.

Siegel, Jeremy J. (1998),
Stocks for the Long Run, McGraw Hill, New York.

Skinner, Jonathan and Mark McClellan (1997),
"The Incidence of Medicare", NBER Working Paper #6013, April.

Smeeding, Timothy, Barbara Torrey and Lee Rainwater (1997),
"Going to Extremes: Income Inequality, Poverty and the U.S. Aged from an International Perspective", Mimeo, Syracuse University.

Spector, W.D., J. Reschovsky and J.D. Cohen (1996),
   "Appropriate Placement of Nursing Home Residents in Lower levels of Care", *Milbank Quarterly*, 74,1.

Starr-McCluer, Martha (1998),
   "Stock Market Wealth and Consumer Spending", Federal Reserve Board, Finance and Economics Discussion Series, 1998-20 (May).

Steuerle, C. E. (1997),
   "Plans for a Comprehensive Reform package", Federal Reserve of Boston Conference Series, 41.

Steurle, C.E. and J.M. Bakija (1994),
   Retooling Social Security for the 21st Century, The Urban Institute Press, Washington DC.

Summers, Lawrence H. (1998),
   "Testimony Before the Senate Committee on Agriculture, Nutrition, and Forestry", 30 July.

Turner, D. *et al.* (1998),
   "The Macroeconomic Implications of Ageing in a Global Context", OECD Economics Department.

United Kingdom Government Actuary (1996),
   "Occupational and Personal Pension Schemes, a review of contracting out terms", Paper prepared for Parliament, London, March.

Walliser, J. (1998),
   "Social Security Privatisation and the Annuities Market", Mimeo, CBO.

Wiener, Joshua M. (1998),
   "Can Private Insurance Solve the Long-Term Care Problems of the Baby Boom Generation?", The Urban Institute, Testimony before the Special Committee on Aging, US Senate, 9 March.

Wiener, Joshua M. and David g. Stevenson (1997),
   "Long-Term Care for the Elderly and State Health Policy", #A-17 in Series, "New Federalism: Issues and Options for States", The Urban Institute.

Williams, F. (1997),
   "Equities Top 62 per cent of 401(k) Assets", *Pensions and Investments*, 20 January.

Yaboboski, P. (1997),
   Large Plan Lump Sums: Rollovers and Cashouts, Employment Benefits Research Institute, Washington DC.

Annex I

Integrating financial asset stocks and flows

Recent econometric estimates made by the OECD have indicated that increases in personal sector wealth clearly boost consumer spending. Such movements cannot, however, be seen as generating a permanent boost to the level of demand. Over the longer run, some of the increase will be reversed, as the reduced flow of saving lowers the stock of net financial assets. Eventually, this process will result in households reducing their wealth, relative to income, so bringing saving back to a new higher equilibrium rate. The pace at which net financial assets are depleted will depend, negatively, on the extent of housing investment and positively on capital gains, as well as the extent of the fall in the saving ratio. The strength of these feedback effects is, however, small and it would seem that the recovery in the saving rate will be a slow process.

The precise nature of this relationship can be seen in the two equations relate the ratio of net financial assets to disposable income and the saving rate. The *first equation*, the "stock relationship" is the identity that relates changes in net assets to capital gains on the existing stock and net flows through saving and investment in tangible assets such as housing. Denote net financial assets in quarter t by A_t, annualised saving by S_t and annualised investment net of depreciation by I_t. Suppose, that before net saving, A_t increases at the gross rate of $(1 + k_t)$ due to capital gains. Then, because saving and investment are annualised, the following relationship holds:

$$A_t = (1 + k) A_{t-1} + S_t/4 - I_t/4 \tag{1}$$

Let lower case letters denote their values as a per cent of annualised disposable income, and suppose that income grows at rate v_t. Equation (1) becomes:

$$a_t = (1 + r_t) a_{t-1} + s_t/4 - i_t/4, \tag{1*}$$

$$\text{where} \quad 1 + r_t = \frac{1 + k_t}{1 + v_t}. \tag{2}$$

In equation (1*), s_t denotes the Flow-of-Funds measure of the saving rate. Over a period of years, data suggest that this measure is about 0.15 percentage point above the National Accounts measure, so if s_t is to denote the National Accounts measure, then it is necessary to add 0.15 to the right-hand side of equation (1*). The *second equation*, the "saving flow relationship" is the estimated econometric equation that links the saving rate to lagged values of the ratio of net financial assets to disposable income and the difference between the unemployment rate and the NAWRU:

$$s_t = \beta_0 + \beta_1 a_{t-1} + \beta_2 a_{t-5} + \beta_3 a_{t-9} + \beta_4 ugap_{t-1} + \beta_5 (ugap_{t-1} - ugap_{t-5}) \tag{3}$$

$$s_t = 13.9 - .015 a_{t-1} - .024 a_{t-5} - .021 a_{t-9} - .0211 ugap_{t-1} + .238 (ugap_{t-1} - ugap_{t-5})$$

where $ugap_t$ denotes the unemployment gap.

   On the basis of assumptions for the values of net investment in housing, capital gains
and disposable income growth, these two equations can be solved to yield implied
projections for net financial assets and the saving rate. For instance, even with moderate
growth rate in the stock market in the near term, the past run up in net assets implies
further declines in the saving rate into 2000.

   Such a fall raises the issue of whether these low saving rates are sustainable. A useful
way to formulate the answer is to see what the above equations imply for long-term
behaviour. In steady state, the values of a and s are constant, and $ugap = 0$. With this in
mind, equations (1*) and (2) can be rearranged to give three equations that determine the
steady state values:

$$S = -4r^*a + i \tag{1**}$$

$$r = \frac{(k - v)}{1 + v} \tag{2**}$$

$$s = \beta_0 + (\beta_1 + \beta_2 + \beta_3)a \tag{3**}$$

   The combination of the first and second equation determine the extent to which the
savings ratio is augmented by capital gains when these exceed the growth of personal
disposable income. The third equation shows the negative relationship between saving
and financial wealth.

   Given the growth of incomes (v) and the extent of net investment in housing (i), the
combination of the equations determines the extent to which the equilibrium ratio of net
financial assets to income varies with the rate of capital gains. In fact, the equilibrium ratio

Figure A1.   **Asset and saving equilibria**[1]

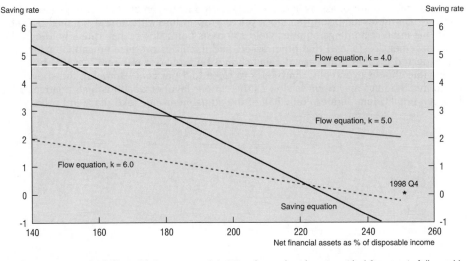

1.   Chart assumes annual disposable income growth is 3.9 and annual net investment is 4.9 per cent of disposable
     income.
Source: OECD.

Annex Table 1.   **Calculating long-run returns on net financial assets**

	Assets				Liabilities		Liabilities to assets
	Direct equities	Indirect equities[1]	Deposits[2]	Other assets	Mortgage	Other liabilities	
Expected capital gain (annual rate)	4.7	3.2	0.0	0.1	−0.3	0.0	
Per cent share of assets or liabilities 1998 average	15.8	42.7	15.6	16.0	65.9	34.1	34.7

1. Includes mutual funds, life insurance, private pensions and bank trusts. The share of equities in these holdings is assumed to rise from 36.8 per cent in 1998 to 40 per cent.
2. Includes foreign deposits, cheques and currencies, and time and saving deposits.

appears to be sensitive to small changes in the growth of capital gains, as is shown in Figure A1, where the equilibrium financial wealth ratio varies between 150 and 225 per cent of disposable income, as the rate of capital gain accumulation increases from 4 to 6 per cent of net assets, annually. These estimates are based on nominal personal income growing at 3.9 per cent annually and net housing investment of 4.9 per cent – broadly equivalent to the expected values of these variables in the longer term.

Thus, the extent to which the saving rate may eventually increase, and the ratio of financial assets decline, will depend crucially on the rate of future capital gains. Estimates of the expected long-run value of capital gains on financial assets depends on three factors: the long-run capital gain on the stock market, the return on other assets and liabilities and the mix of assets and liabilities, including the amount of leverage (see Annex Table 1). On the assumption that stock prices grow in line with current nominal potential GDP, that indirect holdings equities yield 150 basis points lower than direct holdings, due to management costs, and that other assets and liabilities produce no capital gains, then the expected income from capital gains should be around 4 per cent. On this base, the saving rate should eventually climb back to close to 5 per cent. However, the speed with which this rebound may occur is slow as the current level of wealth is high relative to the long-run equilibrium. Indeed, only half of the adjustment may take place in twelve years.

Annex II

The corporate structure of expanded banking powers: holding company affiliates versus bank subsidiaries

Banking regulators from the Federal Reserve Board and the Department of Treasury are debating the best corporate structure for commercial banks. The Federal Reserve favours the holding company model that is currently in place, where banks and other financial firms affiliate through a common parent. The Treasury Department believes that it would be better to allow banks the option to control other enterprises as subsidiaries, but with added protections. The debate revolves around three issues. *First*, do deposit insurance and access to the discount window and to the payments system provide a subsidy that banks could employ in other financial markets? If so, policymakers should prevent its exploitation. *Second*, will expanded bank powers put the deposit insurance fund and the banking system at greater risk? If reform adds risk, then Congress should reduce it, if possible. *Third*, would the competing plans make a difference for these issues?

That banks enjoy some advantages in raising funds is clear from theory. The deposit insurance fund, backed by the federal government, insures deposits up to $100 000. Thus, banks only have to pay a riskless rate of return to these lenders. The government may also bail out large depositors and other creditors in the case of a bank failure as it did for Continental Illinois. If a bank runs into trouble, it can borrow from the discount window at the Federal Reserve, which could prevent a default, lowering the risk creditors face. In addition, banks can hold overdrafts in the payments system during business hours, a facility that businesses without access do not have.

Some analysts argue that there are other costs that banks face so that if any net subsidy exists it is small. Banks have to pay insurance premiums on their deposits. They must hold balances at the Federal Reserve, for which currently they receive no interest. Meeting the various demands of banking regulators is costly. Whalen (1997b) estimates that the value of the subsidy net of regulatory costs was negative in 1996, a result consistent with some other estimates at different time periods. The theoretical value of the subsidy depends on the condition of the bank, and the year the author considered was a good year for banks. In relatively good times, the chance the bank will need to call on its backup credit is small, while the costs may not be commensurately lower. In testimony to Congress Chairman Greenspan (1998) asked:

> "What was it worth in the late 1980s and early 1990s for a bank with a troubled loan portfolio to have deposit liabilities guaranteed by the FDIC, to be assured that it could turn illiquid assets at once through the Federal Reserve discount window, and to tell its customers that payment transfers would be settled on a riskless Federal Reserve Bank? For many, it was worth not basis points but percentage points. For some it meant the difference between survival and failure."

There is other evidence that a subsidy does exist. Debt ratings are almost always higher at banks than at holding company parents.[1] In addition, non-bank financial firms have higher capital ratios for the same debt rating (Kwast and Passmore, 1997), although direct comparisons are difficult because the risk characteristics may vary across institutions. Previous prohibitions on interstate banking had encouraged the holding company structure, but now that these prohibitions are gone, banks are rapidly moving their activities out of holding company affiliates and into the bank or into subsidiaries (Kwast and Passmore, 1997). Banks report that one of the reasons they have been moving activities from holding company affiliates into the bank or a subsidiary when given the chance is to obtain cheaper funding (Greenspan, 1998).[2] Finally, if the net subsidy to banks was really negative, one would expect to see banks dropping their charters, which they are not.

More importantly, the total value of the net subsidy is not the issue. As Kwast and Passmore (1997) stress, what is important is whether banks can raise the marginal dollar more cheaply than other firms. When measuring any net subsidy that banks can potentially pass to their non-banking operations, one should not net out any costs of regulation that do not vary with deposits. There is some evidence that such fixed costs are a sizeable fraction of total costs (Elliehausen, 1997). Nonetheless, US banks do not appear to dominate the securities businesses in which they are currently eligible to underwrite (Whalen, 1997b).

Another question is whether expanding banking powers will add risk to the system. There is a prima facie case that such an expansion could reduce risk through diversification. Using industry data, Litan (1987) emphasises that banks can move to a more efficient mean-variance point through diversifying financial activities. In a study of the overseas activities of individual US banks, Whalen (1998) shows that diversification into securities activities would not appear to significantly increase the probability of failure. Other studies also suggest that diversification reduces risk, although some simulation studies evaluating prospective rates of return of various combinations paint a more mixed picture (Berger et al., 1999).

While suggestive, these results do not necessarily prove that diversification will reduce the probability of failure. It is not necessarily the case that moving to a diversified portfolio lowers the chances of bankruptcy, nor is it the case that banks would necessarily hold an efficient portfolio of activities. Complete evidence of how US banks would diversify their activities is unavailable, because until recently, regulations limited their ability to do so. Nonetheless, what evidence does exist from the operations of foreign affiliates and subsidiaries (Whalen, 1998) and from the period before the passage of Glass-Steagall (White, 1986) suggests default risks are not significantly greater under expanded activities.

Still, even if diversification decreases the overall probability of a failure, there are some circumstances where a non-banking unit could bring down an otherwise healthy bank. This could happen in two different ways. First, the assets of a non-banking unit could deteriorate far enough to absorb its equity and other capital in the bank. If the bank is responsible for that unit's debt, it would fail, although limited corporate liability would typically contain a bank's losses on investment in a failing subsidiary. Second, a bank could try to prop up a failing unit by extending loans or buying its assets at a favourable price. Existing firewalls for bank affiliates prevent this and the Treasury proposes extending these rules to subsidiaries. Regardless, an affiliated bank may be encouraged to illegally circumvent them. Whalen (1997a), for instance, describes the case of Hamilton Bancshares who illegally purchased mortgage loans from a troubled affiliate; in spite of orders to correct the problem, the bank failed. Greenspan (1999) notes that Continental Illinois suffered significant capital losses by attempting to support a failing bank subsidiary. Greenspan (1998) also reports that the second reason banks have been moving some of their operations out affiliates and into subsidiaries or into the bank itself is to avoid Section 23A and 23B regulations.[3] Thus, there is an opportunity for regulation to improve upon the benefits of diversification from the standpoint of protecting the deposit fund and the soundness of the banking system.

Whether the corporate form matters from a regulatory standpoint is also of interest. Within the OECD area, there are three types of structures, although specific exceptions make these distinctions fuzzy and the regulatory burden varies on a continuum. The least restrictive model is universal banking, which is popular in some European countries (Annex Table 2). Under this system, the bank can offer a wide range of services, such as investment banking, insurance and real estate investment inside the bank. The second intermediate model, for which Canada is a good example, prohibits banks from offering these other services. Instead, the bank directly controls a subsidiary that operates in the various markets. Because the subsidiary is separate from its banking parent, accounting regulations can overcome some of the subsidy and risk problems discussed above. The third model is the bank holding company system, which is roughly the dominant structure in the United States and which the Federal Reserve favours keeping. In this structure banks and other enterprises can only affiliate through a common holding company parent. Accounting regulations and conventions make this system a stronger form of separation than the subsidiary model.

Proponents of the holding company structure prefer the stronger separation of activities. Under that system a bank can only provide capital to the non-bank affiliate by paying out dividends to its parent. Such transactions are easy for bank regulators to track and its effects on bank capital do not require any changes to accounting regulations. In the event of a failure by the non-banking affiliate, creditors would not have any recourse to the bank's capital, except for perhaps a claim to some of the parent's stock holdings. Only in an unusual circumstance could a bankruptcy court order a bank to pay out capital to the creditors of a failed affiliate. The opposite is not the case as, if a bank falls into trouble, there are no prohibitions on the non-banking affiliate through the holding company parent to put extra capital into the bank.

For subsidiaries, the regulatory separation is not as tight. Through transfer and internal accounting pricing, banks can more easily downstream at least some funds to their subsidiary than banks in a holding company can upstream to their parent company. The proponents of the holding company structure fear that rumoured troubles at a subsidiary could cause a run on the parent bank: in 1973 problems in a real estate affiliate of a bank holding company provoked a deposit run, even though the bank's exposure was modest. Greenspan (1988) suggests that such events would be more common for banks with subsidiaries. On the other hand, weaker separation can also be a blessing to the deposit fund. In the case of a bank failure arising from problems not linked to an affiliate, the assets of a strong non-banking subsidiary can be used to make good some of the liabilities to the insurance fund.

Proponents of the subsidiary model argue that the costs from regulatory separation are higher than the benefits. They point to the potential efficiency gains from expanding the opportunities of banks and maintain that each of these gains would be smaller if the banks were required to set up a holding company structure.[4] Indeed Greenspan (1998) notes that another reason why banks have been moving some of their operations into subsidiaries is to increase efficiency. Setting up a holding company is also costly and may prevent small banks from expanding their services (Rubin, 1998).

Annex Table 2. **Banking structure in selected countries**[1]

	Securities		Insurance		Real estate investment
	Other	Underwrite stocks	Underwrite	Other	
Universal banking					
Belgium	Bank	Prohibited	Bank	Bank	Restricted to premises
France	Bank	Bank	Subsidiaries	Bank	Restricted to 10% of income
Germany	Bank	Bank	Subsidiaries	Bank	In bank restricted to liable capital. In subsidiaries unrestricted
Netherlands	Bank	Bank	Subsidiaries	Bank	Restricted to 25% of bank funds
Spain	Bank	Bank	Subsidiaries	Bank	Restricted to 75% of bank funds
Sweden	Bank	Bank	Affiliates	Bank	Restricted to premises
Switzerland	Bank	Bank	Subsidiaries	Subsidiaries	1 project limited to 20% of capital
United Kingdom	Bank	Bank	Subsidiaries	Bank	Bank
Subsidiary structure					
Canada	Subsidiaries	Subsidiaries	Subsidiaries	Subsidiaries	Subsidiaries
Italy (firewalls)	government securities bank rest in subsidiaries	Subsidiaries	Subsidiaries	Bank	Restricted to premises
Holding company/restrictive structure					
Japan (firewalls)	Subsidiaries	Prohibited	Prohibited	Prohibited	Restricted to premises
United States (firewalls)	Limited securities in bank, restricted in affiliates	Restricted in affiliates	Restricted in bank	Restricted in bank	Restricted to premises

1. The table reports whether activities are generally allowed in the bank, only in subsidiaries, only in affiliates, or if the activity is prohibited. It also reports in the first column whether firewalls are generally required.
Source : Barth, Nolle and Rice (1997).

The relevant question for policymakers today, however, is how the competing plans, as embodied in H.R. 10 and the Treasury plan, differ. The Treasury's proposal is far from the typical subsidiary model, such as Canada has in place.[5] The Treasury proposes to deduct all of the bank's investment in its subsidiary for regulatory capital purposes and to require that the bank remain well-capitalised afterwards. The proposal prohibits a bank from making good any of the debts of its failed subsidiary. Whether this rule could survive a legal challenge is unclear, though. The Treasury would also continue to apply current regulations on affiliate loans and other financial flows to subsidiaries in its new plan.

Thus, it would seem that for practical purposes the two approaches are very similar. The Treasury proposal is designed to only allow financial flows between a bank and its subsidiary that would be permitted by holding companies. Because a bank's options and incentives[6] are the same under either case, the two systems should be similar in the subsidy it imparts and the threat it engenders for the insurance fund and payments system. Indeed, the Treasury and the FDIC argue that a benefit of the proposal is that a court can use a subsidiary's assets to pay off the debts of the bank, suggesting that it is superior to the holding company structure. Although that too is not as clearcut as the Treasury argues because, under the Federal Reserve's "Source of Strength" doctrine, regulators can make some claims on a holding company parent. Recent cases, such as that of the Bank of New England, suggest, however, that the FDIC may not be able to rely on this doctrine to limit deposit insurance losses. In a bankruptcy law suit settled in 1999, the trustees of the Bank of New England recovered $140 million from the FDIC in assets that the holding company had downstreamed to its bank that failed (Tanoue, 1999). Moreover, to the extent that Treasury maintains various firewalls, the differences in efficiency gains and the cost of compliance between the two structures are also smaller.

As a result, the remaining differences between the two approaches, while hard to measure, appear to be small. The Treasury's summary argument is that where there is no public policy issue, businesses should be free to structure their operations as they see fit. The Federal Reserve's summary argument is that one should not substitute a well working regulatory system for one that tries to accomplish the same thing but whose track record is uncertain. Indeed, an open question is whether the operating-subsidiary model would make the bank regulator's job more difficult. The agencies in the United States with such experience to offer an opinion appear to differ on the answer.

Notes

1. This difference could also be the result of the effective subordination structure of debt. In the case of trouble, holders of securities issued by the bank would usually have recourse to remaining funds before holders of securities issued by the parent holding company.

2. The Federal Reserve Chairman testified that banks report three reasons to move their operations closer to the bank: 1) to obtain cheaper funding; 2) to avoid Section 23A and 23B restrictions on financial flows; and 3) for efficiency gains. These other two reasons are discussed below.

3. These sections of the Federal Reserve Act impose limits on interactions between banks and affiliates. Banks cannot lend more than 10 per cent of their capital surplus to any single affiliate and no more than 20 per cent to all affiliates. All loans must be collateralised and on market terms (arms-length transactions). The bank cannot purchase low quality assets from an affiliate, and holding companies must file quarterly reports on inter-affiliate transactions.

4. Santos (1996) describes five sources of economies of scope: 1) spreading the fixed costs of managing a client, especially the costs of developing and maintaining information; 2) more easily moving resources within the organisation as demand for various products changes; 3) spreading marketing and distribution costs; 4) developing and capitalising on reputation; and 5) providing one-stop shopping for customers.

5. Unlike the Treasury proposal, Canada uses consolidated figures to measure capital adequacy. It does not apply firewalls between banks and their subsidiaries, though it has some limitations on the share of regulatory capital devoted to equities and real estate.

6. Managers' incentives to engage in illegal activities in case of failure, however, could differ between these two proposals.

Bibliography

Barth, James R., Daniel E. Nolle, and Tara N. Rice (1997),
"Commercial Banking Structure, Regulation, and Performance: An international comparison", Office of the Comptroller of the Currency, Economics Working Paper 97-6, February.

Berger, Allen N., Rebecca S. Demsetz and Philip E. Strahan (1999),
"The Consolidtion of the Financial Services Industry: Causes, Consequences, and Implications for the Future", forthcoming Journal of Banking and Finance, 23.

Elliehausen, Gregory (1997),
"The Cost of Bank Regulation: A Review of the Evidence", Mimeo, Board of Governors of the Federal Reserve System, April.

Greenspan, Alan (1999),
"Questions and Answers in Testimony before the Committee on Banking and Financial Services", U.S. House of Representatives, 11 February.

Greenspan, Alan (1998),
"Testimony before the Committee on Banking, Housing and Urban Affairs, U.S. Senate", 17 June.

Kwast, Myron L. and S. Wayne Passmore (1997),
"The Subsidy Provided by the Federal Safety Net: Theory, measurement and containment", Board of Governors of the Federal Reserve, FEDS Working Paper 1997-58, December.

Litan, Robert E. (1987),
What Should Banks Do? Washington DC: The Brookings Institution.

Rubin, Robert E. (1998),
"Testimony to the Senate Banking Committee", 17 June.

Santos, João Cabral (1996),
"Commercial Banks in the Securities Business: A review", The Federal Reserve Bank of Cleveland, Working Paper 96-10, November.

Tanoue, Donna (1999),
"Appendix A, Holding Company Affiliates and Operating Subsidiaries: Safety-and-Soundness Considerations" to Testimony on Financial Services Modernization Act of 1999 before the Committee on Banking, Housing and Urban Affairs United States Senate, 24 February.

Whalen, Gary (1997a),
"Bank Organizational Form and the Risks of Expanded Activities", Office of the Comptroller of the Currency, Economics Working Paper 97-1, January.

Whalen, Gary (1997*b*),

"The Competitive Implications of Safety Net-Related Subsidies", Office of the Comptroller of the Currency, Economics Working Paper 97-9, May.

Whalen, Gary (1998),

"The Securities Activities of the Foreign Subsidiaries of U.S. Banks: Evidence on Risks and Returns", Office of the Comptroller of the Currency, Economics Working Paper 98-2, February.

White, Eugene Nelson (1986),

"Before the Glass-Steagall Act: An analysis of the investment banking activities of national banks", *Explorations in Economic History*, 23, 33-55.

Annex III

Calendar of main economic events

1997

October

US and Japanese representatives reach an agreement over Japanese port practices.

The National Bankruptcy Review Commission releases its final report, recommending no major change to personal bankruptcy laws.

The Dow Jones Industrial average falls 7.2 per cent in one day, and trading halts come into effect for the first time. In subsequent months, markets rebound strongly.

November

The FOMC announces no change to policy, keeping its asymmetric directive towards tightening in the future.

December

US representatives meeting in Kyoto Japan agree to cut greenhouse gas emissions by 7 per cent of 1990 levels by 2008-12.

Negotiators reach an agreement on an international accord on financial services.

Representatives from twenty-nine OECD countries and five non-member countries sign the OECD convention on banning bribery of foreign officials.

The FOMC announces no change to interest rates, but removes its bias for future policy.

1998

February

A district court judge declares the line-item veto unconstitutional. The Supreme Court upholds his ruling in June.

The FOMC announces no change to policy.

March

The Department of Justice sues to block the Lockheed-Northrop Grumman merger.

California opens retail electricity sales to competition.

The FOMC announces no change to interest rates, but changes its bias towards tightening.

April

The Treasury Department announces its intentions to issue thirty-year inflation-backed securities.

A series of large financial deals are announced: Citibank and Travelers ($83 billion), Nations Bank and Bank of America ($67 billion), and Banc One and First Chicago-NBD ($30 billion). Two months later Wells Fargo and Norwest announce a $34 billion merger. Over the course of the year, regulators approve each deal, subject to some conditions; most importantly, the new Citigroup has to sell Travelers' insurance underwriting business.

May

The Department of Justice and state attorney generals file suit against Microsoft alleging a variety of illegal, anticompetitive practices.

The CFTC issues its concept release on derivatives regulation, provoking a significant controversy.

Daimler Benz takes over Chrysler in a $40 billion deal, creating the fifth largest auto company in world sales.

The FOMC announces no change to policy.

June

Congressional attempts to implement a far reaching deal with tobacco companies fails.

UAW workers strike a key GM parts plant, shutting down production at most of GM's North American facilities for over a month.

Wholesale spot electricity prices in the Midwest spike.

The President signs a six-year $218 billion highway bill that increases funding by 40 per cent.

FASB issues its final guidelines on derivatives accounting.

US and Japanese authorities intervene in the exchange market to support the yen.

The FOMC announces no change to policy.

August

Russia devalues the ruble and effectively defaults on some of its debt, eventually causing financial markets to seize up.

The FOMC announces no change to interest rates, but citing problems in financial markets, it removes its bias for future policy.

September

Attempts to win fast-track approval in Congress fail.

The Fifth Circuit Court overturns a lower court ruling allowing the FCC to deny long-distance licenses to local phone companies until they open up their markets to competition.

Thirteen banks agree to buy 90 per cent of Long-Term Capital Management, preventing the hedge fund from becoming bankrupt.

The FOMC cuts the federal funds rate by 25 basis points and moves its policy bias towards easing.

October

The Treasury Department reforms its auction practices for securities, moving all sales to a Dutch-auction format.

The Congress passes a FY 1999 budget, including $21 billion in emergency spending to get around the discretionary spending caps.

Between FOMC meetings, the Federal Reserve cuts rates 25 basis points; financial markets start to rebound.

November

A judge strikes down a Massachusetts law barring state business with companies that trade and invest in Burma.

Four tobacco companies reach a deal with 46 states ending various lawsuits.

The FOMC cuts the federal funds rate by 25 basis points, but changes its bias to neutral.

December

Exxon and Mobil announce their intention to merge in a deal valued at $77 billion that would create the largest company in terms of revenue.

The Trade Representative's Office releases its list of products that will be hit with 100 per cent tariffs if the dispute with the European Union over its banana regime is not satisfactorily settled.

The FOMC announces no change to policy.

1999

January

The United States warns Canada that it will impose up to $4 billion in trade sanctions if the WTO case involving magazines is not satisfactorily settled. It also threatens Japan over steel imports.

The President re-institutes Super 301 by an executive order.

The Supreme Court overturns a lower court decision, allowing the FCC to issue price guidelines in its attempt to open up the market in local phone service.

The President announces his plan for Social Security reform, which includes government investment in equities and supplementary private savings accounts.

February

The FOMC announces no change to policy.

March

The Medicare Commission fails to reach the necessary consensus to publish recommendations on reform. Congressional members vow to introduce legislation anyway.

The FOMC announced no change to interest rates.

BASIC STATISTICS

BASIC STATISTICS:

INTERNATIONAL COMPARISONS

	Units	Reference period [1]	Australia	Austria
Population				
Total	Thousands	1997	18 532	8 07
Inhabitants per sq. km	Number	1997	2	9
Net average annual increase over previous 10 years	%	1997	1.3	0.
Employment				
Total civilian employment (TCE)[2]	Thousands	1997	8 430	3 68.
of which:				
Agriculture	% of TCE	1997	5.2	6.
Industry	% of TCE	1997	22.1	30.
Services	% of TCE	1997	72.7	63.
Gross domestic product (GDP)				
At current prices and current exchange rates	Bill. US$	1997	392.9	206.
Per capita	US$	1997	21 202	25 54
At current prices using current PPPs[3]	Bill. US$	1997	406.8	186.
Per capita	US$	1997	21 949	23 07
Average annual volume growth over previous 5 years	%	1997	4.1	1.
Gross fixed capital formation (GFCF)	% of GDP	1997	21.5	24.
of which:				
Machinery and equipment	% of GDP	1997	10.3 (96)	8.8 (96
Residential construction	% of GDP	1997	4.4 (96)	6.2 (96
Average annual volume growth over previous 5 years	%	1997	7.3	2.8
Gross saving ratio[4]	% of GDP	1997	18.4	2
General government				
Current expenditure on goods and services	% of GDP	1997	16.7	19.4
Current disbursements[5]	% of GDP	1996	34.8	48
Current receipts	% of GDP	1996	35.4	47.9
Net official development assistance	% of GNP	1996	0.28	0.24
Indicators of living standards				
Private consumption per capita using current PPP's[3]	US$	1997	13 585	12 951
Passenger cars, per 1 000 inhabitants	Number	1995	477	447
Telephones, per 1 000 inhabitants	Number	1995	510	465
Television sets, per 1 000 inhabitants	Number	1994	489	480
Doctors, per 1 000 inhabitants	Number	1996	2.5	2.8
Infant mortality per 1 000 live births	Number	1996	5.8	5.1
Wages and prices (average annual increase over previous 5 years)				
Wages (earnings or rates according to availability)	%	1998	1.5	5.2
Consumer prices	%	1998	2.0	1.8
Foreign trade				
Exports of goods, fob*	Mill. US$	1998	55 882	61 754
As % of GDP	%	1997	15.6	28.4
Average annual increase over previous 5 years	%	1998	5.6	9
Imports of goods, cif*	Mill. US$	1998	60 821	68 014
As % of GDP	%	1997	15.3	31.4
Average annual increase over previous 5 years	%	1998	7.5	7
Total official reserves[6]	Mill. SDR's	1998	10 942	14 628 (97)
As ratio of average monthly imports of goods	Ratio	1998	2.2	2.7 (97)

* At current prices and exchange rates.
1. Unless otherwise stated.
2. According to the definitions used in OECD Labour Force Statistics.
3. PPPs = Purchasing Power Parities.
4. Gross saving = Gross national disposable income minus private and government consumption.

Belgium
10 181
334
0.3
3 719
2.3
26
71.4
242.5
23 820
236.6
23 242
1.5
17.8
8
4.5
1.2
22.4
14.4
51.2
49.4
0.34
14 703
420
457
453
3.4
7
2.2
1.7
76 309[7]
70.8
7
63 447[7]
64.8
7.4
12 977[7]
1

EMPLOYMENT OPPORTUNITIES

Economics Department, OECD

The Economics Department of the OECD offers challenging and rewarding opportunities to economists interested in applied policy analysis in an international environment. The Department's concerns extend across the entire field of economic policy analysis, both macroeconomic and microeconomic. Its main task is to provide, for discussion by committees of senior officials from Member countries, documents and papers dealing with current policy concerns. Within this programme of work, three major responsibilities are:

- to prepare regular surveys of the economies of individual Member countries;
- to issue full twice-yearly reviews of the economic situation and prospects of the OECD countries in the context of world economic trends;
- to analyse specific policy issues in a medium-term context for the OECD as a whole, and to a lesser extent for the non-OECD countries.

The documents prepared for these purposes, together with much of the Department's other economic work, appear in published form in the *OECD Economic Outlook, OECD Economic Surveys, OECD Economic Studies* and the Department's *Working Papers* series.

The Department maintains a world econometric model, INTERLINK, which plays an important role in the preparation of the policy analyses and twice-yearly projections. The availability of extensive cross-country data bases and good computer resources facilitates comparative empirical analysis, much of which is incorporated into the model.

The Department is made up of about 80 professional economists from a variety of backgrounds and Member countries. Most projects are carried out by small teams and last from four to eighteen months. Within the Department, ideas and points of view are widely discussed; there is a lively professional interchange, and all professional staff have the opportunity to contribute actively to the programme of work.

Skills the Economics Department is looking for:

a) Solid competence in using the tools of both microeconomic and macroeconomic theory to answer policy questions. Experience indicates that this normally requires the equivalent of a Ph.D. in economics or substantial relevant professional experience to compensate for a lower degree.

b) Solid knowledge of economic statistics and quantitative methods; this includes how to identify data, estimate structural relationships, apply basic techniques of time series analysis, and test hypotheses. It is essential to be able to interpret results sensibly in an economic policy context.

c) A keen interest in and extensive knowledge of policy issues, economic developments and their political/social contexts.

d) Interest and experience in analysing questions posed by policy-makers and presenting the results to them effectively and judiciously. Thus, work experience in government agencies or policy research institutions is an advantage.

e) The ability to write clearly, effectively, and to the point. The OECD is a bilingual organisation with French and English as the official languages. Candidates must have excellent knowledge of one of these languages, and some knowledge of the other. Knowledge of other languages might also be an advantage for certain posts.

f) For some posts, expertise in a particular area may be important, but a successful candidate is expected to be able to work on a broader range of topics relevant to the work of the Department. Thus, except in rare cases, the Department does not recruit narrow specialists.

g) The Department works on a tight time schedule with strict deadlines. Moreover, much of the work in the Department is carried out in small groups. Thus, the ability to work with other economists from a variety of cultural and professional backgrounds, to supervise junior staff, and to produce work on time is important.

General information

The salary for recruits depends on educational and professional background. Positions carry a basic salary from FF 318 660 or FF 393 192 for Administrators (economists) and from FF 456 924 for Principal Administrators (senior economists). This may be supplemented by expatriation and/or family allowances, depending on nationality, residence and family situation. Initial appointments are for a fixed term of two to three years.

Vacancies are open to candidates from OECD Member countries. The Organisation seeks to maintain an appropriate balance between female and male staff and among nationals from Member countries.

For further information on employment opportunities in the Economics Department, contact:

Management Support Unit
Economics Department
OECD
2, rue André-Pascal
75775 PARIS CEDEX 16
FRANCE

E-Mail: eco.contact@oecd.org

Applications citing "ECSUR", together with a detailed *curriculum vitae* in English or French, should be sent to the Head of Personnel at the above address.

The Electronic Advantage
Ask for our free Catalogue

The Fast and Easy way to work with statistics and graphs!

- Cut and paste capabilities
- Quick search & find functions
- Zoom for magnifying graphics
- Uses ACROBAT software
  (included free of charge)
- Works on Windows

OECD on the WEB: **www.oecd.org**

- ✂

Please **Fax** or **Mail** this page to the OECD Paris,
—— or to one of the four OECD Centres (*see overleaf*) ——

○ I wish to receive the OECD Electronic Publications Catalogue **Free of Charge**

Name _____   Profession _____

Address _____

City _____   E-mail _____

Country _____

Area of interest _____

Where to send your request:

In Austria, Germany and Switzerland

OECD CENTRE BONN
August-Bebel-Allee 6,
D-53175 Bonn
Tel.: (49-228) 959 1215
Fax: (49-228) 959 1218
E-mail: bonn.contact@oecd.org
Internet: www.oecd.org/bonn

In Latin America

OECD CENTRE MEXICO
Edificio INFOTEC
Av. San Fernando No. 37
Col. Toriello Guerra
Tlalpan C.P. 14050,
Mexico D.F.
Tel.: (52-5) 528 10 38
Fax: (52-5) 606 13 07
E-mail: mexico.contact@oecd.org
Internet: rtn.net.mx/ocde/

In the United States

OECD CENTER WASHINGTON
2001 L Street N.W., Suite 650
Washington, DC 20036-4922
Tel.: (202) 785 6323
Toll free: (1 800) 456-6323
Fax: (202) 785 0350
E-mail: washington.contact@oecd.org
Internet: www.oecdwash.org

In Asia

OECD CENTRE TOKYO
Landic Akasaka Bldg.
2-3-4 Akasaka, Minato-ku,
Tokyo 107-0052
Tel.: (81-3) 3586 2016
Fax: (81-3) 3584 7929
E-mail : center@oecdtokyo.org
Internet: www.oecdtokyo.org

In the rest of the world

OECD PARIS CENTRE
2 rue André-Pascal, 75775 Paris Cedex 16, France
Fax: 33 (0)1 49 10 42 76 **Tel:** 33 (0)1 49 10 42 35
E-mail : sales@oecd.org
Internet : www.oecd.org
ONLINE ORDERS: www.oecd.org/publications *(secure payment with credit card)*

OECD PUBLICATIONS, 2, rue André-Pascal, 75775 PARIS CEDEX 16
PRINTED IN FRANCE
(10 1999 02 1 P) ISBN 92-64-16982-2 – No. 50515 1999
ISSN 0376-6438